MARKET MOVERS

MARKET MOVERS

NANCY DUNNAN AND JAY J. PACK

WARNER BOOKS

A Time Warner Company

Copyright © 1993 by Nancy Dunnan and Jay J. Pack and Cloverdale Press Inc.

Warner Books, Inc., 1271 Avenue of the Americas, New York, NY 10020

 A Time Warner Company

Printed in the United States of America

First Printing: May 1993

10 9 8 7 6 5 4 3 2 1

Cover design by Julia Kushnirsky
Cover illustration by David Lui
Book design by Suzanne Reisel/Neuwirth & Associates

Library of Congress Cataloging-in-Publication Data

Dunnan, Nancy.
    Marker movers / Nancy Dunnan and Jay J. Pack.
        p.   cm.
    Includes index.
    ISBN 0-446-39340-1
    1. Capital market.   2. Finance.   3. Finance—United States.
4. Business cycles—United States.   I. Pack, Jay J.   II. Title.
HG4523.D86   1993
332'.041—dc20   92-34512
                                                              CIP

CONTENTS

■ ■ ■

PART V
GLOBAL MARKET MOVERS

PART VI
PEOPLE MARKET MOVERS

PART VII
EVENT-DRIVEN MARKET MOVERS

Introduction

■ ■ ■

"Money is a good thing to have. It frees you from doing things you dislike. Since I dislike doing nearly everything, money is handy."

—*Groucho Marx*

Money, as Groucho Marx told a reporter in his typically wry manner, enables us to do what we want—enjoy the good life, buy homes, educate our children. On a grander scale it helps us fund scientific research, help those who are less fortunate, and clean up the environment for future generations. In order to accomplish these and other goals, money—our own, our government's, and our institutions'—must be invested wisely and well. To do this requires a great deal of knowledge about our economy and, more specifically, our financial markets in order to forecast economic movements that can increase or decrease the value of our investments.

Whether you own a home or simply a credit card, manage money for others or invest your own, are an employee or run a business, you're directly affected by a number of "things" that shape your life and determine whether your assets are worth more or less today than they were yesterday. These things are market movers.

Some market movers, like retail sales, interest rates, and inflation,

1

are household words. You've heard these terms frequently, although you may not fully understand them or how they may affect you. Other market movers—unit labor cost, capacity utilization, yield curves—are more esoteric, but they also affect our lives and our assets. Highly respected people such as leading economic advisers can also be market movers, as can events such as war and trade agreements. These, too, move stock and bond markets.

Each month, economists, bank officials, stockbrokers, bond traders, and investors eagerly await an array of current statistics and information on our economy. This information, also called the "economic series," tells us whether our economy is expanding or contracting. It's crucial information to these professionals, but it's also information everyone can use. Store owners can predict Christmas sales; factory owners can set production quotas; individuals can decide whether it's the right time to buy a new car—simply by understanding market movers.

The economic overview provided by various market movers is your best defense against the increasingly complex, rapidly changing global economy. Even if you don't have an investment portfolio, you're still directly affected by market movers—*e.g.*, the amount of interest your savings earn, the rate on your mortgage, your chances of getting a better job or promotion.

By understanding market movers, you'll come to understand the business cycle, why it goes from expansion to contraction, and why inflation and recession is inevitable. You can use market movers to more accurately predict the current phase of the business cycle, and armed with this knowledge, you can prepare for and protect yourself from these boom-to-bust periods.

As our economy moves from prosperity to boom times, into and out of slow periods and recessions, Americans watch the descriptive patterns—the unemployment rate, housing starts, retail sales—which the economic series provides. The government, which is the principle source of this information, attempts to predict for itself and for others what is ahead and, meanwhile, what the best course of action is.

You may feel overwhelmed by this economic jargon, technical language, and financial statistics: the Dow Jones Industrial Average is at a new high; a severe credit crunch exists; short-term interest rates are rising; housing starts are slowing down; consumer confidence is at a low. The government spews out this data faster than Darryl Strawberry hits home runs. *Market Movers* explains the meaning of these technical phrases and how you can benefit from understanding them. It takes away the mystery and confusion surrounding the inexact science known as economics.

Anyone who reads the financial section of a newspaper or listens to the evening news is confronted by this bewildering array of economic facts and statistics. This book helps you interpret the financial news broadcast by the media. It will be a companion to programs such as "Wall Street Week," "Adam Smith's Money World," and CNN's "Moneyline," and to such publications as *The Wall Street Journal, Money,* and *Your Money.* When you read or hear that orders for durable goods are up or down or that the Federal Reserve has cut the discount rate, you'll know how these events affect your portfolio. Bulletins about foreign stock markets, the European Community Market, and the Group of Seven will suddenly make sense.

Market Movers not only enables you to recognize and understand the leading market movers, but it tells you where the information is reported, how to interpret that information, and most important, what to do with your assets based upon the direction in which these market movers move. For instance, you will learn when to take money out of CDs and buy stocks, or even more specifically, when to buy growth stocks and when to buy public-utility stocks, or when your money should be in corporate bonds or Treasury bills. You will learn the optimal times for starting a new business, borrowing or refinancing a mortgage, or taking a trip abroad.

Note: In late 1991 one of the single most important market movers, the gross national product, was renamed the gross domestic product, a measure of our nation's economic activity that does not include net exports. This change is addressed in part I. Throughout the book we will refer to the current measure, gross domestic product (GDP), except when discussing the rate prior to the third quarter of 1991.

The book is arranged into eight sections, seven of which are devoted to a specific type or category of market movers. The first, "Industrial and Business Market Movers," covers statistics and facts involved in the production of industrial goods—how much it costs to make and sell them, and how many people are involved in getting these goods to market. "Consumer Market Movers" describes the price trends of items we purchase, such as cars, houses, clothing, and even toothpaste, as well as how much debt we take on to buy these goods. The ups and downs of our economy—from bust to boom and the dips between—are explained in part III, "The Business Cycle." Truly financial market movers, such as interest rates, money supply, and the action of the Federal Reserve in controlling these factors, as well as the indexes of the stock and bond markets, are evaluated in part IV, "Monetary and Financial Market Movers." Part V, "Global Market Movers," describes a larger scene, which includes oil prices, foreign stock markets, Eurodollars, and the value of the U.S. dollar. People, too, are market movers as you will discover in part VI, "People Market Movers," where the importance of such dynamic leaders as the chairman of the Federal Reserve and TV personality Louis Ruckeyser, in addition to other well-known analysts and economists, are explained. Part VII, "Event-Driven Market Movers," examines the way in which events such as wars, trade agreements, and financial scandals impact on our economic lives. Finally, in part VIII, "Market Mover Investment Basics," you will learn the characteristics of basic investment options and get some tips on how to use them.

Throughout this book the relationships between the various market movers are explained. Some move in tandem. Others, like consumer credit, auto sales, retail sales, and housing starts, can be linked to predict consumer demand and, as a group, constitute an important indicator of the economy's direction. Some can be used to predict the future movement of other market movers. The monthly industrial production index, for example, allows you to predict the subsequent GDP, which is issued quarterly, and when Fed funds rise, you can be certain that interest rates will soon rise. Likewise, a sharp decrease in auto sales alone will affect the GDP. Many of the market movers are interrelated, and only with the broad economic overview provided in *Market Movers* can you get a good idea of the bigger picture from these single sources of information.

In the end you will have gained enough information to take whatever investments you have and become your own market mover.

PART I

...

INDUSTRIAL AND BUSINESS MARKET MOVERS

Among the many things that shape the economy and move our stock and bond markets is the nation's ability to produce goods and keep factories operating and people employed, with money to spend in their pockets. The market movers in this section measure this vital activity; they include the trends in the number of goods produced, how much it costs to produce those goods, how production affects unemployment, and since services as well as goods are a growing part of our economy, the rate of business starts and failures. First and foremost among these market movers is the gross domestic product (formerly the gross national product).

The industrial and business market movers are

Gross domestic product
Industrial production index
Durable goods
Capacity utilization
Unit labor cost
Producer price index
Unemployment rate
Business failures and business starts

Each can be used to ascertain our place in the business cycle. Gross domestic product, industrial production, and durable goods typically have the most immediate impact on the financial markets, although by definition every market mover has an effect on our stock and bond markets. It is important to note that individual market movers don't exist in a vacuum; these industrial and business market movers also influence other market movers covered in this book, particularly the consumer price index, which is included in the next section, and interest rates, inflation, and money supply, which are found in part IV. In general, the market movers in part I measure the United States' aggregate economic activity. They are a national income tally, gathering data on the nation's massive output of goods, and they lay the groundwork for an understanding of the market movers that follow in subsequent sections.

CHAPTER 1

Gross Domestic Product

■ ■ ■

The gross domestic product is the total dollar value of all final goods and services produced in the United States during a given time period; it is measured quarterly and annually. Note: *Until late 1991 the term* gross national product *(GNP) was used.*

Paul Samuelson, the Nobel Prize–winning economist, was fond of saying, "Man does not live by GNP alone." Although the gross domestic product (GDP) is not and should not be as important as marriage, family, and apple pie, it nonetheless influences all of these and other American institutions. A growing GDP makes it possible for Americans to live the good life, which explains why it's *the* most frequently monitored market mover and placed first in this book.

The GDP growth rate, the most important indicator of the nation's economy, shows whether the nation's income is expanding or contracting, and thus it is the broadest statistical indicator of our economic output and growth. Simply stated, the GDP is the sum of all final goods and services produced in a given time period, with each good or service assessed at its market value—at prices actually paid. For some goods and services, such as the national defense, there are no market prices available; therefore an estimated value is used.

In the definition provided above, note the qualifying word *final*. This term is best explained by example: if a farmer grows wheat and sells it to a miller, who in turn sells flour to a baker, who then sells bread to a customer, the contribution to the GDP is the value of the final product—the bread. If the dollar value of every sale in this example were added up, it would be double counting and would overstate the GDP. To avoid this error, only the value of the final goods or services is counted in the GDP.

The term *gross* refers to the fact that depreciation of structures and equipment is not subtracted from the value of output. *Domestic* refers to the output of a particular nation: production from the labor of U.S. residents and from the capital of U.S. residents' corporations within the geographical boundaries of the United States is included in the GDP. This means that the value added by overseas branches of American firms is not included in our GDP. The GDP does measure income payments to foreigners, although it excludes income receipts by U.S. residents from abroad.

WHAT IT COVERS

The GDP covers the goods and services produced and consumed in the private, public, domestic, and international sectors. These sectors are labeled

- personal consumption expenditure
- gross private domestic investment
- government purchases

(Gross *National* Product, the measure used until late 1991, also included net exports.)

Personal consumption expenditure is by far the largest category, accounting for over 65% of the total GDP. It includes household spending for DURABLE GOODS, such as automobiles, furniture, appliances, and other items that last three years or more; nondurable goods, such as food, fuel, cosmetics, drugs, and clothing, all of which have shorter lives; and services, which consist of rent, utilities, medical care, travel, and other intangible items. Nondurable goods account for about 40% of total personal consumption expenditures; services represent a slightly larger amount, and the remainder is made up of durable goods.

Gross private domestic investment consists of business spending for equipment and nonresidential structures by both profit and nonprofit organizations, as well as spending for residential construction. It includes items such as factories and office buildings, office computers and furniture.

Government purchases represents the services of federal, state, and local government workers (including public school teachers and police), as well as the purchases of civilian and defense goods and services. Transfer payments, such as pensions, welfare, Social Security, and interest are *not* included in our GDP.

Net exports (included in the GNP) reflected the foreign sector's contribution to the GNP. It measured the difference between what we sold abroad (exports) and purchased from abroad (imports). Net exports include both physical commodities and services—insurance, transportation, tourism, and corporate earnings from foreign operations. It was the total of U.S. income from investments in companies and securities abroad minus that of foreigners' income from investments in the United States.

Chart 1A, which documents the GNP between 1955 and 1990, shows how each of these sectors have fared.

WHAT'S NOT COVERED

Although the GDP is the broadest measure of economic activity, it does not cover every transaction. Purely financial transactions, such as trades in stocks and bonds and trading in secondhand items, are not included. Neither are capital gains nor nonmarket activities, such as housework, child care, etc. Informal barter deals, such as

Chart 1A ■ Real Gross National Product

Chart courtesy: Ned Davis Research Inc.

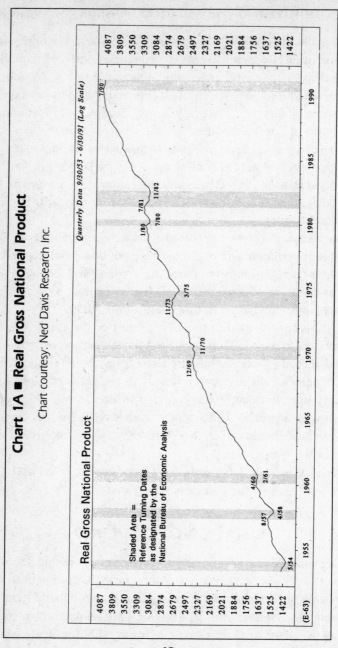

swapping one house for another, and the so-called underground economy, often conducted in cash to avoid taxes, are not factored in. These exclusions, especially the underground economy transactions, mean that the GDP significantly understates our nation's economic activity.

HOW IT'S REPORTED

When the GDP is reported in the newspaper it typically looks like chart 1B. Figures for the gross domestic product on an annual basis are reported every quarter by the U.S. Department of Commerce, although they are not actually available until about three weeks following the end of each quarter. The official compilation is shown in table 1A.

The Commerce Department's monthly release contains several key terms: real GDP, or GDP in constant dollars; nominal GDP, or GDP in current dollars; annual rate; and seasonally adjusted annual rate. To correctly interpret the GDP figures, it's important to understand these terms.

Real GDP, also known as *GDP in constant dollars,* removes inflation from the GDP. The impact of price changes on the value of the nation's output is factored out of real GDP, making it a more accurate measure of the increase in production. Each year's output is calculated in the prices of a base year. As of August 1992, the base year was 1983.

By eliminating the distortion of price changes, real GDP, or constant-dollar GDP, makes it possible to compare the level of output in one time period with that of another. If price changes were not taken into account, we could not gauge whether the differences in dollar value were because of changes in output or changes in prices.

Nominal GDP, or *GDP in current dollars,* unlike real GDP, does not adjust for INFLATION or other price increases and therefore is a higher figure than real GDP.

Table 1A ■ U.S. Commerce Dept. GDP Figures
(Billions of dollars.)

| | 1990 | 1991 | Seasonally adjusted at annual rates | | | | | |
| | | | 1991 | | | | 1992 | |
			I	II	III	IV	I	II
Gross domestic product	5,522.2	5,677.5	5,585.8	5,657.6	5,713.1	5,753.3	5,840.2	5,902.2
Personal consumption expenditures	3,748.4	3,887.7	3,821.7	3,871.9	3,914.2	3,942.9	4,022.8	4,057.1
Durable goods	464.3	446.1	439.5	441.4	453.0	450.4	469.4	470.6
Nondurable goods	1,224.5	1,251.5	1,245.0	1,254.2	1,255.3	1,251.4	1,274.1	1,277.5
Services	2,059.7	2,190.1	2,137.2	2,176.3	2,205.9	2,241.1	2,279.3	2,309.0
Gross private domestic investment	799.5	721.1	705.4	710.2	732.8	736.1	722.4	773.2
Fixed investment	793.2	731.3	733.9	732.0	732.6	726.9	738.2	765.1
Nonresidential	577.6	541.1	551.4	545.8	538.4	528.7	531.0	550.3
Structures	201.1	180.1	190.0	185.2	175.6	169.7	170.1	170.3
Producer's durable equipment	376.5	360.9	361.4	360.6	362.8	358.9	360.8	380.0
Residential	215.6	190.3	182.6	186.2	194.2	198.2	207.2	214.8
Change in business inventories	6.3	−10.2	−28.5	−21.8	.2	9.2	−15.8	8.1
Nonfarm	3.3	−10.3	−27.4	−27.0	−1.2	14.5	−13.3	6.4
Farm	3.1	0	−1.1	5.2	1.4	−5.3	−2.4	1.7
Net exports of goods and services	−68.9	−21.8	−28.7	−15.3	−27.1	−16.0	−8.1	−37.1
Exports	557.0	598.2	573.2	594.3	602.3	622.9	628.1	625.4
Imports	625.9	620.0	602.0	609.6	629.5	638.9	636.2	662.5
Government purchases	1,043.2	1,090.5	1,087.5	1,090.8	1,093.3	1,090.3	1,103.1	1,109.1
Federal	426.4	447.3	451.3	449.9	447.2	440.8	445.0	444.8
National defense	314.0	323.8	332.4	325.9	321.9	314.7	313.6	311.7
Nondefense	112.4	123.6	118.8	124.0	125.3	126.1	131.4	133.1
State and local	616.8	643.2	636.3	640.8	646.0	649.5	658.0	664.3

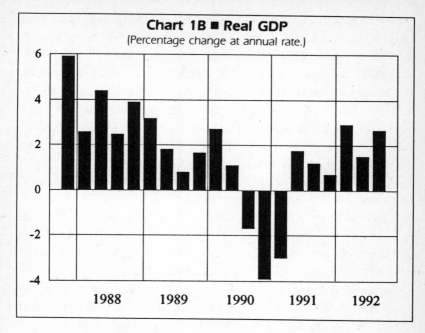

Chart 1B ■ Real GDP
(Percentage change at annual rate.)

Annual rate indicates that the data for the quarter, which covers only three months, has been multiplied by four to make it comparable to annual data.

Seasonally adjusted annual rate indicates that seasonal factors have been eliminated. This corrects the distortion in the figures that might occur when comparing one quarter to another. For example, during the final quarter (October, November, and December), RETAIL SALES are higher than during the rest of the year due to the Christmas season. When an entire year's data is measured, no seasonal adjustment is necessary, but when the year is divided into four parts, distortion due to seasons is inevitable.

WHY IT'S IMPORTANT

Why is gross domestic product such an important economic indicator and why does it move markets? GDP measures how we're doing as a nation in the same way that your gross income measures your financial state. Each of us may have a salary as well as other income. If the total figure declines or merely remains constant from year to year, we're not sanguine about buying a new car or a beach house. Moreover, even if we get a salary increase and the new salary allows us to purchase only the same amount as the previous year, we know that in constant, or real, dollars, our income is actually standing still. The same holds true with real GDP; from this indicator, we know if the country is moving ahead or standing still.

The GDP is used as a framework by the president and Congress to determine fiscal policies, federal spending, and taxes. The FEDERAL RESERVE uses the GDP to formulate monetary policies aimed at maximizing employment and minimizing inflation. The Fed does this primarily through controlling the MONEY SUPPLY and INTEREST RATES. (See chapter 19, "The Federal Reserve.")

The real GDP and its rate of change also affects our perceptions about the country's economic future, and this is why it is a market mover. A growth rate of less than 2% is regarded as slow; 2% to 5% is respectable; and above 5% is considered a boom. A boom, of course, is great—but only to a point. In fact, the economy cannot sustain a 5% growth rate for very long; it simply cannot continue to turn out more and more goods and services because the nation's production capacity at any one time is limited. On the other hand, a 1% to 1.5% growth in real GDP is barely more than our population growth and thus reflects a poor per capita gain.

Another important aspect of the GDP is that it foretells and defines an important economic event—a recession. Although Harry Truman described a recession as "when your neighbor loses his job," and a depression as "when you lose your job," economists delineate a recession by a decline in the GDP for two consecutive quarters. Chart 1C demonstrates how real GDP declines in recessions.

The impact of changes in the GDP on the stock and bond markets can be enormous. Increases and declines frequently move these markets long before we as individuals feel the impact. For instance,

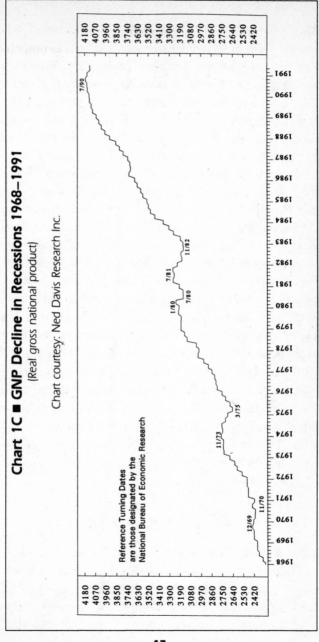

Chart 1C ■ GNP Decline in Recessions 1968–1991

(Real gross national product)

Chart courtesy: Ned Davis Research Inc.

Reference Turning Dates
are those designated by the
National Bureau of Economic Research

17

if the economy were slowing down at a rate that could result in a recession, the GDP need not actually decline two consecutive quarters before the stock market would begin to react. Stocks will start to tumble in advance of such an occurrence because of economists' predictions. If economists predict that the economy will slow down and they issue reports to the media, then portfolio managers, bankers, pension plan managers, stock brokers, and even individual investors react by buying or selling stocks.

Stocks and bonds are particularly affected when GDP figures come in *weaker than anticipated;* in this case the financial markets expect the Federal Reserve to keep pushing interest rates lower to prevent the economy from tumbling into a recession. A flat or lower GDP growth rate results in lower interest rates because a slower economy means corporations will not want to expand and consequently will not borrow as much money. It may mean that the economy will become truly sluggish, in which case the UNEMPLOYMENT RATE rises, inflation declines, and interest rates fall. The belief that interest rates will come down drives bond prices higher, and stock prices generally move up in their wake. However, when the GDP figures come in *stronger than predicted,* the markets, concerned that interest rates will rise, react in an opposite fashion.

(*Note:* As interest rates fall, prices of bonds rise because older, existing bonds paying higher rates are more prized.)

The real GDP, then, is a market mover with clout—not so much when it moves along the path that the GDP watchers expect it to, but when it does the unexpected.

MARKET MOVER TIPS

■ When real GDP expands at a healthy 3% to 5% annual rate, the economy's expansion is sustainable. Quality growth stocks are good investments at this time because they typically appreciate in price as the economy grows. This is also a good time to sell real estate and collectibles if they have appreciated in price.

■ If the GDP rate of growth is declining, review your stock portfolio and hold only those blue-chip issues that are solid, long-term investments.

DID YOU KNOW THAT?

After a severe recession in 1921–22, the GNP climbed 5% a year, and during the decade of the twenties, manufacturing output rose 64%. The leaders of this great boom were automobile sales and construction. Both the number of car sales and the value of construction more than tripled between 1915 and 1925.

CHAPTER 2

Industrial Production Index

■ ■ ■

This monthly index measures changes in the total physical output of factories, mines, and gas and electric utilities in the United States.

The industrial production index, or IP index, which dates back to 1919, is released by the FEDERAL RESERVE and is a component of the LEADING ECONOMIC INDICATORS. A significant distinction between the IP index and the GROSS DOMESTIC PRODUCT is that the IP index is based exclusively on physical output; it is not concerned with the dollar value of this output, but on the tons of steel, kilowatt hours of electricity, barrels of oil, tons of metal, numbers of cars, and so forth that are produced. Since the IP index reflects the rate of production, it is an economic indicator of goods, not services.

WHAT IT COVERS

The index is made up of about 250 individual components of durable and nondurable goods, mining, and utilities. Data on physical products is supplied by the Bureau of the Census, the Bureau of Mines, government agencies, and trade associations. Data on production

Table 2A ■ Industrial Production Figures		
	April 1991	May 1990
Total	**0.5**	**−3.3**
Consumer goods	0.8	−1.1
Business equipment	−0.3	−2.4
Defense and space	−1.0	−5.9
Manufacturing only	**0.2**	**−4.0**
Durable goods	0.2	−5.8
Nondurable goods	0.2	−1.6
Mining	**−0.1**	**−2.2**
Utilities	**3.9**	**3.3**

and worker hours are gathered by the Bureau of Labor Statistics. The amount of electrical power consumed comes from a survey of electrical companies by the twelve Federal Reserve banks.

As of November 1992, the index is calculated by using the base year, 1987, which is given a value of 100; data for all subsequent months and years is presented against this base. For example, if in a given month industrial production had an index value of 115.7, then production was 15.7% higher than the average rate in the base year 1987. (*Note:* In the spring of 1990, the index was updated and revised, with the year 1987 replacing 1977 as the base year. This revision more accurately reflected the current mix of industrial output. Certain industries, such as computers, were proportionally larger, and others, like clothing manufacturing, much of which has been lost to overseas manufacturers, declined in importance.)

HOW IT'S REPORTED

The Federal Reserve data is broken down into eight categories each month as shown in table 2A. The industrial production figures are actually announced about two weeks into each month, along with any revision for the prior three months. The total percentage change

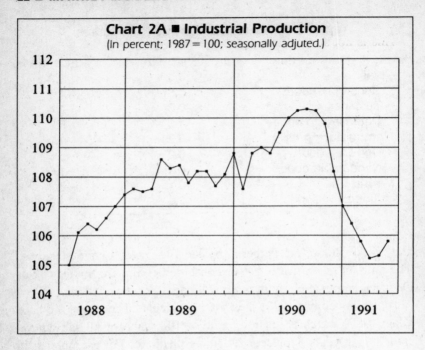

Chart 2A ■ Industrial Production
(In percent; 1987 = 100; seasonally adjuted.)

is also frequently presented in summary form as shown in chart 2A. From this chart you can see that industrial production hit a high in mid-1990 and fell sharply with the beginning of the 1990–91 recession.

WHY IT'S IMPORTANT

Industrial production and GDP are both important measures of our economy since their components are generally those that are most susceptible to BUSINESS CYCLE ups and downs. Industrial production, since it eliminates agriculture, services, finances, government, transportation, retail trade, construction, and communications, among others, is a much narrower index than the GDP. The GDP is so broad and all-encompassing that by the time it signals a change in the direction of the economy's growth rate, it's almost too late to do anything about it.

This is not so with the IP index. When overall production slows down, it shows up quickly on the index: mining will be cut back; electrical and gas utilities will provide less energy to their industrial customers; and factory assembly lines will slow down.

The IP index is announced monthly, not quarterly as is the case with the GDP, and this greater frequency of reporting enables economists and market watchers to get advance knowledge of forthcoming changes in the GDP. While GDP provides market watchers and consumers with a report card on the U.S. economy, telling us how we're doing, the IP index furnishes us with an early warning signal of any changes in the forthcoming GDP. A good example of this is found in the IP index as reported in *The Wall Street Journal* on March 18, 1991. The article noted that the IP index fell 0.8% in February, 0.5% in January, and 1.1% in December. "The slowing of the decline from December to January had raised hopes of a turnaround. But the February figure made it clear that the industrial sector's woes were continuing during the month. . . ."

This February decline is illustrated in chart 2A, covering July 1988 to May 1991. By February 1991 the IP index had fallen to 105.7 from its September 1990 high of 110.6, indicating a recession. This is an example of macroeconomic data describing and forecasting the direction of the nation's economy.

The IP index and GDP move together, but industrial production falls lower than the GDP during recessions and climbs higher during expansions. (See chart 2B.) IP is a far more volatile index and as such serves as a more definite and accurate forecaster of the economy's growth and decline.

MARKET MOVER TIPS

■ If the IP index drops sharply for two months in a row, you can expect the next reported GDP will also be lower, and vice versa.

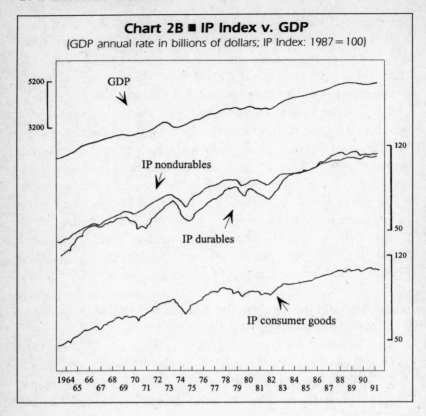

Chart 2B ■ IP Index v. GDP

(GDP annual rate in billions of dollars; IP Index: 1987 = 100)

- If the IP and the GDP both indicate we're in a recession, real estate prices are likely to fall; if so, buy property before a recovery.
- Your strongest use of the IP index is in identifying an economic recovery. If the IP rises three months in a row, it indicates the beginning of a recovery. Switch immediately into quality growth stocks.
- If the IP increases by 10% in five to seven months, INFLATION may follow.

DID YOU KNOW THAT?

Between the Civil War and 1900 the output of manufactured goods tripled. The key industrial product contributing to this boom was steel. Production leaped from 68,000 tons of finished steel in 1870 to 4.2 million tons in 1890.

CHAPTER 3

Durable Goods

■ ■ ■

Issued monthly, durable goods reports the total dollar value of all goods produced that have a useful life of three years or more.

In the last twenty years Americans have become a throwaway society. Every day we toss out millions of disposable coffee cups, diapers, paper towels, and napkins. Even paperback books end up in the trash can. When a small appliance breaks, it's easier and cheaper to buy a new one than find someone who knows how to repair it. Although we are surrounded by planned obsolescence, there are still many items that make it through more than a few years of use. Goods that have a useful life of more than three years are known as durable goods. The Commerce Department tracks orders for these durable goods on a monthly basis.

WHAT IT COVERS

The largest category of durable goods is nondefense capital goods. Capital goods are all goods not purchased directly by consumers. Instead, they are paid for by businesses in both the private and public sector. The category of nondefense capital goods includes engines; turbines; construction and mining equipment; materials-handling equipment; office and store machinery; electrical transmission and distribution equipment; electrical machinery; railroad, ship, and aircraft transportation equipment; and automotive equipment. It excludes military spending, household appliances, and electronic equipment.

HOW IT'S REPORTED

The Commerce Department issues a monthly report on the dollar amount of new orders given to U.S. factories. The full report contains figures for both durable and nondurable orders. However, a separate report, covering durable orders only, appears in the media, usually accompanied by a table, chart, or both. Data on orders for durables (and nondurables) is included with the INDUSTRIAL PRODUCTION INDEX.

Table 3A explains the Commerce Department's breakdown of durables: primary metals, nonelectrical machinery, electrical machinery, transportation equipment, capital goods, nondefense, and defense. (*Note:* Economists separate the defense figure and report it separately.) For June 1991 the largest component was capital goods, totaling $37.24 billion out of total durable good orders of $116.52 billion; capital goods were down 0.8% from the previous month.

Table 3A ■ Durable Goods Figures			
	June	May	% Chg.
Total	$116.52	$118.42	− 1.6%
Primary metals	10.74	10.36	+ 3.6
Nonelect. machinery	19.96	20.93	− 4.7
Electrical machinery	15.22	16.92	−10.1
Transportation equip.	29.85	28.78	+ 3.7
Capital goods	37.24	37.56	− 0.8
Nondefense	29.19	28.01	+ 4.2
Defense	8.06	9.54	−15.6

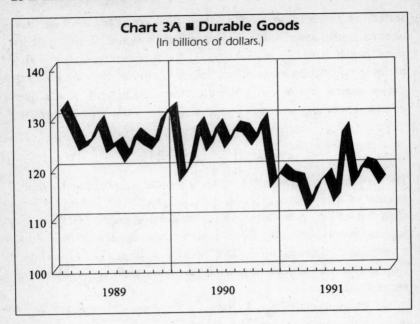

Chart 3A ■ Durable Goods
(In billions of dollars.)

A chart can show the trend in durable goods orders over several years. Chart 3A shows that durable goods orders fell to a low of about $112 billion in early 1991, reflecting the recession. The next months showed a fairly steady rise in orders, falling again in late 1991.

WHY IT'S IMPORTANT

Orders for durable goods quite accurately indicate the degree to which businesses and manufacturers are willing to invest capital for future needs. If businesses perceive that the economy is slowing down, they will cut back on spending, from typewriters to turbines. In turn, such knowledge affects the markets, which use durable goods orders as an indication of the health of the economy and future corporate earnings. When the economy is in a period of recession, and CAPACITY UTILIZATION is low, there's little incentive to invest in durable goods to increase capacity. Consequently, business managers delay or cancel spending earmarked for purchasing new equipment or building factories.

The relationship between durable goods orders, CONSUMER CONFIDENCE, and the state of the economy is often noted by the media. In *The New York Times* of June 26, 1991, it was reported that durable goods orders rose 3.8% in May. The most significant gain in over a year, it had been preceded by an increase in April as well. As the *Times* noted, "The rise, combined with other figures released today on home sales, consumer confidence and auto sales, added significantly to evidence that the economy is climbing out of recession." The *Times* report also gave information on nondefense orders, noting that outside of military orders, new durable goods orders rose 2.8%.

When looking at the durable goods orders it is important to note several individual components that can radically affect the total dollar amount and the monthly percentage change. The figure for *nondefense* capital goods is a particularly crucial one because defense spending is not directly related to the BUSINESS CYCLE. Economists typically subtract the defense components to arrive at a more accurate assessment of business conditions.

Nondefense capital goods orders are regarded by most economists as *the* key indicator of the durable goods series. It most clearly shows the intentions of the nation's manufacturers regarding investment in new plant and equipment, as well as in regard to increasing or decreasing production.

Total durable goods orders are also often affected by large swings in transportation equipment, especially aircraft orders. When it's reported, this figure is often broken out. If it shows a significant increase or decrease, you might factor it out to get a better indication of those durable goods orders that are truly a reaction to the business cycle.

Durable goods data can lift markets or cause them to drop almost immediately. For example, when orders for durables for June 1991 were reported as having dropped 1.6% instead of rising modestly as most economists expected, the DOW JONES INDUSTRIAL AVERAGE fell 17 points to 2966.23. The STANDARD & POOR'S 500 STOCK INDEX was off 0.78% to 378.64. Treasury bonds climbed more than 0.75 point, or more than $7.50 for each $1,000 face amount. The unexpected decline in durable orders caused investors to believe that instead of pulling out of the recession as was previously thought, corporate earnings would not be rising. The durable orders report was good news, however, for the bond markets, because a declining economy typically means lower INFLATION and lower INTEREST RATES, both of which push up bond prices.

MARKET MOVER TIPS

- When durable goods orders are up several months in a row, it's a strong indication that the economy is healthy. Buy stocks in durable goods producers, such as manufacturers of machine tools and transportation equipment.
- When durable goods orders level off or turn down after a substantial rise of one to three years, expect a recession to follow. Switch from cyclical common stocks (automobiles, chemicals) to defensive or recession-resistant stocks such as food and beverage companies. Also, buy bonds to lock in current yields, because a recession will bring about lower interest rates.

DID YOU KNOW THAT?

Orders for certain durable goods—railroad lines and cars—grew at an all-time high immediately after the Civil War. Between 1866 and 1876 railroad mileage in the United States increased by 111%. The growth spurt began in 1862, when Congress authorized the Union Pacific Railroad to build tracks from western Iowa to meet the Central Pacific, which was building tracks from California eastward. Up until that time there had been eleven different rail gauges used on the country's lines. President Lincoln chose the 4-foot–8½-inch gauge for the Union Pacific, which led to the standardization of all railroads at this width.

The Central Pacific, using Chinese laborers, laid 689 miles of track, and the Union Pacific, using mainly Irish workers and Civil War veterans, laid 1,085 miles of track. When the two roads met on May 10, 1869, at Promontory Point, Utah, a ceremonial golden spike was driven with great fanfare. Western Union dispatched the news, and across the country people celebrated by the ringing of bells. Lincoln's dream, to make it possible for Americans to travel from sea to shining sea, became a reality four years after his assassination.

CHAPTER 4

Capacity Utilization

■ ■ ■

*Also known as the factory operating rate, capacity utiliza-
tion measures the operation of the nation's factories as a
percentage of their theoretical full capacity, or maximum
rate.*

Anyone who works in a factory in America knows when times
are good and when they're bad. During boom times new workers
are being employed and production is moving along at a fast and
furious rate. At other times production slows down and workers are
laid off. For those of us who don't work in the nation's factories,
the capacity utilization rate is one of our best indicators of recessions
and expansions.

WHAT IT COVERS

Capacity utilization measures the rate at which U.S. manufacturers
are operating their factories; it's stated as a percentage of the maximum rate at which factories could operate under normal conditions.
For example, if a plant's maximum capacity is 1,000 automobiles
per week, but it's only producing 700, it's running at 70% capacity.
It's important to note that in most cases 100% capacity utilization

is unrealistic, since it cannot be maintained without incurring machinery breakdowns and accidents as well as inefficiency on the part of workers. In general, 80% to 85% of capacity utilization is the maximum that can be sustained on a realistic basis.

The formula used to find the capacity utilization rate (CU) is

$$CU = \frac{\text{industrial production index}}{\text{plant and equipment capacity}} \times 100$$

When production rises slower than capacity or declines, the rate decreases. When total production rises faster than total capacity, the capacity utilization rate increases.

HOW IT'S REPORTED

Released monthly by the FEDERAL RESERVE, the figures are actually available about the third week of every month. Chart 4A, covering 1988 to 1992, shows capacity utilization at a high of 85% in early 1989, falling to 77% in early 1991 and 1992. Throughout 1991 and early fall 1992 CU hovered between 77% and 79%. It also demonstrates an important relationship between capacity utilization and UNEMPLOYMENT. Chart 4B shows a much longer time span, from 1961 to 1991. From these charts you can see that CU hit a low of 70% at the beginning of 1975, and 68% to 69% at the beginning of 1983. The highest CU occurred in 1966, when it hit 90%.

WHY IT'S IMPORTANT

Capacity utilization is a useful indicator of recessionary and expansionary phases. The law of diminishing returns operates tellingly with this market mover. When the economy is in a phase of rapid expansion, with boom times in sight, manufacturers push their factory operations to the limit in order to fulfill customer orders and increase profits. Yet, at a certain level capacity is strained and the

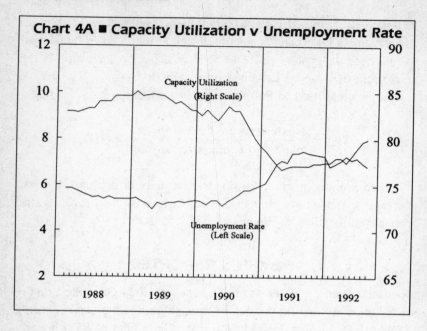

Chart 4A ■ Capacity Utilization v Unemployment Rate

manufacturers' costs begin to outpace profits, in part because they must hire new workers who may be inefficient and are sure to be expensive. They must also put old machinery back into production, and the old machinery is likely to break down under heavy use. Depending upon the industry, such diminishing returns may kick in between 87% and 90% of utilization; eventually the point is reached where the increases in output fail to produce increases in earnings.

When capacity utilization hits 85% or higher, the economy has reached the peak of its expansionary phase, and given the average business cycle, it's time to prepare for a possible recession. When demand is higher than the nation's capacity to produce, prices rise and INFLATION can occur. (See chapter 23, "Inflation.") The cost of goods rises but so do wages, limiting the factories' profitability. Conversely, when capacity utilization is in the 70% to 73% region, the bottom of the recession has been reached. At this point unem-

Chart 4B ■ Capacity Utilization

Chart courtesy: Ned Davis Research Inc.

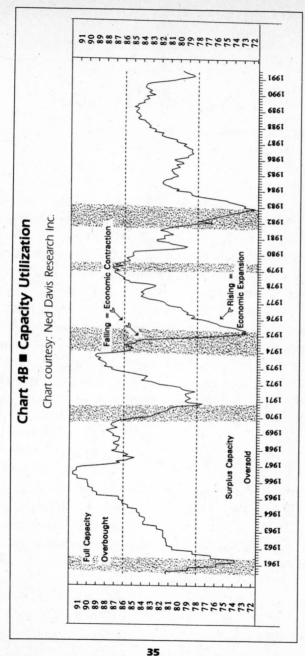

ployment is high, because employers have cut their labor costs as much as possible, as one can see in chart 4A.

MONEY MARKET TIPS

■ When capacity utilization falls below 80%, there is usually a higher unemployment rate. This is not an ideal time to change jobs or to be cavalier about the one you have.

■ Use the capacity utilization rate to time investments in a new business or common stocks. When the index is between 70% and 73%, the bottom of the recession has been reached and stocks are generally at lows, making it a favorable time to invest or start a new business and participate in the recovery.

■ Capacity utilization can also be used as an indicator of when to invest in companies that make plant equipment. The higher the CU, the more likely it is that plant and equipment shortages will develop, which then require more investment in machine tools, capital goods, and industrial equipment, as well as the factories and buildings to house them.

■ When the CU rises above 85%, it often forecasts a coming recession. The economy may be overheating, which can also bring higher inflation.

DID YOU KNOW THAT?

In 1851 at the British Crystal Palace Exhibition, American machinery astonished the Europeans, who regarded themselves as ahead of the United States in the burgeoning factory movement. Among the most awe-inspiring American machines was one that produced 180 ladies' hairpins every minute.

CHAPTER 5

Unit Labor Cost

■ ■ ■

The labor cost involved in assembling a product depends on the workers' wages and labor productivity. The cost per unit of product output is called unit labor cost.

Some workers are efficient; some are inefficient. Some are motivated; some are not. Some are like Jerome K. Jerome, who said, "I like work; it fascinates me. I can sit and watch it for hours." In some senses unit labor cost informs us of the degree of efficiency of our workers, whether they're looking at their work or doing it. However, in addition to the efficiency of our workers, their wages and the use of technology also play a part in determining unit labor cost.

WHAT IT COVERS

Unit labor cost is the ratio of compensation to productivity. Compensation includes wages, salaries, fringe benefits, and income from self-employment. The compensation figures used in the unit labor cost equation are based on employment payroll and household surveys, average weekly hours, and average hourly earnings. Productivity numbers are derived from figures gathered for the GROSS DOMESTIC PRODUCT, employment, and average weekly hours.

To state it another way, unit labor cost is a direct measure of the cost of labor per unit of output. Furthermore, it is an indication of how much more labor is required to produce each additional unit of output. Requiring more *labor time* to produce another product unit will, of course, raise labor cost per unit of output.

It is important to note the distinction between productivity and *labor* productivity. An increase in productivity need not include an increase in labor costs. The following is an example of this distinction as well as the method of calculating unit labor cost: A factory making watches needs one hour of labor to produce one watch. A new device is installed that enables four watches to be made in one hour. Labor productivity has quadrupled. Prior to the new device the unit labor cost was $20; this is based on the fact that the worker was being paid $20 an hour. With the new device, unit labor cost has been cut by three-quarters and dropped to $5 an hour. The rule to remember is that labor cost falls as labor productivity rises, and of course the opposite is also true.

Unit labor cost is frequently compared between one country and another. For example, if Japanese workers produce a car twice as fast as American auto workers and they both receive the same compensation, then unit labor cost is half as much in Japan as in America. If U.S. labor productivity rose to the same level as in Japan, then U.S. unit labor cost would fall to equal Japan's. In other words, a rise in labor productivity means a fall in unit labor costs.

HOW IT'S REPORTED

The measure of unit labor cost is issued on a quarterly basis by the U.S. Department of Labor. As of November 1992, the index is figured against the base year of 1977. The index, the percentage change from one quarter to the next, appears in the media about a month after the quarter it covers. Revisions and refinements appear within another month.

Chart 5A shows unit labor cost rising steadily until the back-to-back recessions of 1981 and 1982 squeezed out the high inflation rate, easing the rapid increase in wages. After this, unit labor cost leveled off.

WHY IT'S IMPORTANT

First of all, unit labor cost tells us how efficient we are as a nation. Second, it reports how much more labor productivity is necessary to produce additional output. Third, it discloses our position within the BUSINESS CYCLE. During a recession, for example, workers are laid off from manufacturing and factory jobs causing unit labor cost to decline. As cost declines, labor productivity rises. The reason is quite logical: During a recession, marginal workers who had been hired to increase production during boom times are let go. The factory then is left with its best and most productive workers. As the recession winds down and business picks up again, factories increase their production to meet new demand. Initially they do so by using their existing work force. But if business continues to grow and greater output is desired, extra—or marginal—workers are again hired to meet the increased demand. This may mean putting on an extra shift and cutting back on repair time for machines, which might impair productivity. Although output will rise with more workers on the job, eventually labor productivity will fall due to inexperienced workers or downtime, causing unit labor cost once again to rise.

Management usually decides that a drop in efficiency is worthwhile in order to push CAPACITY UTILIZATION, the rate at which factories operate, and meet the demand for more orders. Management's interest is in maximizing its profits in the long run, even if it temporarily drives up its unit labor cost. This management theory was pioneered by Henry Ford, who astounded the business world in

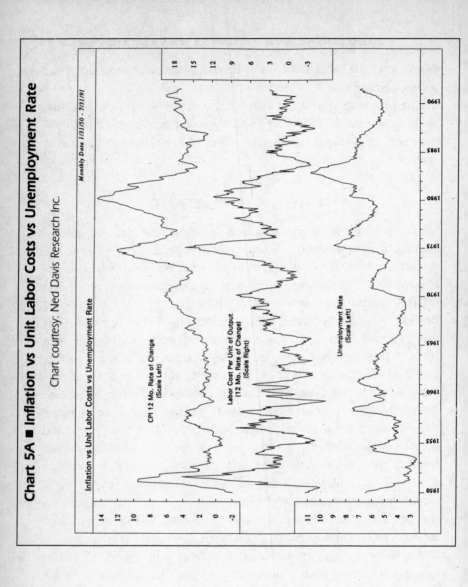

Chart 5A ■ Inflation vs Unit Labor Costs vs Unemployment Rate

Chart courtesy: Ned Davis Research Inc.

Inflation vs Unit Labor Costs vs Unemployment Rate

Monthly Data 1/31/50 - 7/31/91

CPI 12 Mo. Rate of Change
(Scale Left)

Labor Cost Per Unit of Output
(12 Mo. Rate of Change)
(Scale Right)

Unemployment Rate
(Scale Left)

40

1914 when he announced that he would give all his employees a minimum wage of $5 a day and would share with them $10 million of the previous year's profits. At the same time, Ford said that the Ford Motor Company would begin operating around the clock, with three shifts of eight hours each instead of the customary two nine-hour shifts. The official reason given for the raise in wages was that "social justice begins at home. We want those who have helped us to produce this great institution and are helping to maintain it to share our prosperity." But the automobile magnate had other ends in mind as well: he wanted his workers to be able to afford to buy a Ford car, and he recognized the value of loyalty. He saw this tactic as a means of making them work at maximum efficiency.

The effect of labor productivity and unit labor cost is especially crucial on the international front. If the unit labor cost inevitably rises in order to attain higher output in this country, whole industries may be moved to foreign shores where the unit labor cost is lower. This has been the case with clothing manufacturing. For years a large portion of garment manufacturing took place in New York City's garment district along Seventh Avenue. When the unit labor cost became too high, manufacturing was moved to Hong Kong, Korea, and Taiwan. Television sets, once made in America by Zenith, RCA, and Motorola, are now largely produced in Japan and other Pacific Rim countries.

The issue of competitiveness between nations, a topic frequently on the agendas of our political leaders, is essentially a discussion of unit labor cost. If wages are lower in Mexico or Taiwan and the workers can be taught the necessary skills to produce goods, their competitiveness, or labor productivity, will soar, taking the business away from the United States.

MARKET MOVER TIPS

■ Use unit labor cost to determine in which foreign countries to invest. Nations with the lowest unit labor costs will attract new business. In mid-1991 the Mexican stock market leaped ahead as worldwide investors anticipated the free trade agréement between Mexico and the United States. Mexico was appealing because of its low unit labor cost and high labor productivity. (See chapter 48, "North American Free Trade Agreement.") Instead of investing directly in foreign stocks, consider single-country mutual funds and closed-end stock funds.

■ The low unit labor costs of individual industries or companies can also be a basis for buying stocks of U.S. companies. For example, Boeing Airplane Company of Seattle is a world leader in commercial aircraft production and has very effective unit-labor-cost controls.

DID YOU KNOW THAT?

The first truly successful factory in this country was begun in 1790. In 1789 twenty-one-year-old Samuel Slater, who was in charge of machinery in an English cotton factory, sailed secretly to America. (At that time textile workers were not allowed to leave England.) Working from memory, he built several complicated carding machines and a water frame of twenty-one spindles for the Providence firm of Almy and Brown. Slater's name was added to the firm. This first cotton mill was replaced by another in 1793 at nearby Pawtucket. By the beginning of the nineteenth century, fifteen factories were in operation in New England.

CHAPTER 6

Producer Price Index

■ ■ ■

The producer price index measures the rate of change in wholesale prices of domestically produced goods.

The producer price index (PPI), formerly called the wholesale price index, measures the changes in prices charged by producers at various levels of processing.

WHAT IT COVERS

There are actually three PPIs: crude, intermediate, and finished goods. Crude goods are items that enter the market for the first time and have not been manufactured. They are not sold directly to consumers but rather to manufacturers, and they include items such as livestock, cotton, crude oil, grains, and scrap metal. Intermediate goods such as lumber, fertilizer, yarn, chemicals, electric power, internal combustion engines, and machine belts have been processed but typically require further processing to become finished. Finished goods require no additional processing and include both consumer goods and capital goods. Items used *as is* by households, businesses, the government, or foreign buyers are considered finished goods; they range from fresh vegetables and socks to cars, tractors, and machine tools.

Classifying products by end user (household, business, government, or foreigner) and by degree of completeness is called a "stage-of-processing" classification. Prices reflect the first sale of the goods by the producer so as to avoid double counting.

The index is primarily composed of manufacturing products (83.6%), but it also includes mining products (7.2%), agriculture (5.1%), and electric power (3.4%). The major groups included are farm products, processed food and feed, textiles and apparel, hides, skins and leather, fuels, chemicals, rubber and plastic products, lumber, wood products, pulp and paper products, metals, machinery and equipment, furniture and household durables, nonmetallic mineral products, and transportation equipment. The consumer equivalent of this index is the CONSUMER PRICE INDEX (CPI).

WHAT'S NOT COVERED

The service sector is not included in the PPI. This omission is unfortunate because the service sector has grown rapidly in the twentieth century.

HOW IT'S REPORTED

Compiled monthly by the Bureau of Labor Statistics, a division of the U.S. Department of Labor, the PPI is usually announced in the middle of the month. The bureau collects prices for thousands of individual goods. Like the CPI, the PPI uses a fixed-weight system, currently based on the year 1982. Figures are seasonally adjusted.

On January 12, 1991, the PPI, which decreased 0.6% in December 1990, was reported in *The New York Times* as a reflection of "a sharp decline in energy prices and the inflation-dampening effects of recession." The *Times* reported this decrease as the first decline

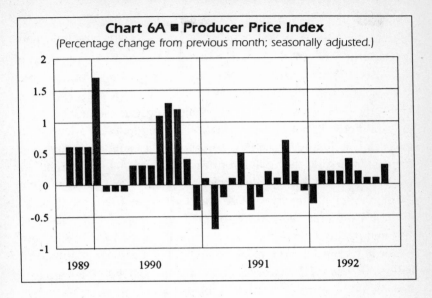

Chart 6A ■ Producer Price Index
(Percentage change from previous month; seasonally adjusted.)

since April 1990 and added, ''For all of 1990, the 5.6% increase in the finished goods index compared with 4.9% for 1989 and was the highest since 1981's 7.1% jump.''

Chart 6A demonstrates the rise in the PPI during the second half of 1990. This rise directly reflects the escalating price of crude oil during the Desert Shield Operation.

WHY IT'S IMPORTANT

As shown in the *Times* article above and two days later in *The Wall Street Journal*, the PPI can be used to interpret the real-life events within our economic system. The *Journal* reported: ''Producer prices . . . were heavily affected last year by the run-up in oil prices following Iraq's August invasion of Kuwait. Energy prices increased nearly 30% from 1989. Gasoline prices shot up 45.2%.'' In reporting the annual rates for 1990 and 1989, the *Journal* cited slightly different numbers from the *Times'*. This is because the *Journal* cited the "core rate": "Minus food and energy, producer prices rose 3.5%, trailing the 1989 core rate of 4.2%."

The term *core rate* refers to the cost of all finished goods excluding the costs of food and energy. In 1989, total producer prices were 4.9%, the core rate was 4.2%; in 1990, total producer prices were 5.6%, the core rate was 3.5%. Food and energy are subtracted from the total figure because their prices are so volatile: Food prices often make drastic jumps in response to bad weather conditions that ruin crops; conversely, they may drop when there are bumper crops. As we all know, oil and gasoline prices also experience violent price swings. After the invasion of Kuwait by Iraq in 1990, the price of oil rose from nineteen to forty-one dollars a barrel. Oil prices are also tied in closely with the actions of the Organization of Petroleum Exporting Countries (OPEC), composed primarily of third-world nations. When OPEC members cooperate and stick to their production quotas, the price of oil is stable in world markets, but when there's excess production among members, world oil prices fall. By factoring out the price changes in food and energy, the core rate PPI becomes a more accurate measurement of the economy.

The consumer price index is the most direct measurement of inflation as it affects the individual on a personal level. The PPI is a leading indicator of price changes at the wholesale level. Over long time periods the PPI and the CPI generally post about the same rate of price change. In the short run, however, the PPI typically increases or decreases before the CPI, due to the time it takes for producers' prices to be reflected in the prices paid at the consumer level.

The PPI also gives us a basis for determining whether inflation is caused by high demand or by bottlenecks in the production of goods, separate from costs and markups for getting the goods to the buyer.

MARKET MOVER TIPS

■ The PPI gives advance notice of the direction of consumer prices: if it moves up to 8%, prepare for high inflation and purchase big-ticket items before prices increase.

■ When the PPI moves up by several percentage points, expect interest rates to rise as the Fed tightens money in order to control inflation. Shorten the maturity of bonds and reinvest money as rates rise.

DID YOU KNOW THAT?

During the Civil War, J. B. Jones, a clerk in the Confederate War Department, wrote in his now-famous diary about the high prices of various producer goods. Beans were selling for $3 a quart, meal for $125 a bushel, and flour for $400 a barrel.

CHAPTER 7

Unemployment Rate

■ ■ ■

The number of unemployed in the United States expressed as a percentage of the total labor force gives the unemployment rate.

A major goal of our country's economic policy is to ensure reasonably full employment at all times. Noel Coward once said, "Work is more fun than fun," and it's certainly true that being employed is more fun than being unemployed.

The unemployment rate is so important to the nation's awareness of its own well-being that employment statistics of some sort have been published since 1820. In 1915 the Bureau of Labor, which was the predecessor of the Bureau of Labor Statistics (BLS), began surveying employers on a monthly basis to collect data on wages, employment, and earnings.

The lowest officially recorded unemployment rate since 1900 was 1.2% in 1944. At that time the economy was in full swing supporting World War II. Our highest level of unemployment occurred during the Great Depression, when millions of Americans—at one point nearly one-third of the labor force, or 13 million people—were unable to find any type of job at all for months, even for years. Such prolonged unemployment meant the loss of lifetime savings, homes, and health.

Of course, "full employment" does not mean that everyone has a job. Full employment occurs when there are jobs for all those who are ready and willing to work *and* who want and are seeking jobs. Congress gave us a definition of full employment in 1978 when it passed the Full Employment and Balanced Growth Act of 1978, also known as the Humphrey-Hawkins Act, which said that our national goal at that time was to attain a 4% rate of unemployment. Today, however, the most popular definition of full employment is a 5% rate of unemployment.

WHAT IT COVERS

The government reports the unemployment rate for the country on a monthly basis. It is based on a count of all the people who are without jobs and are actively looking for work. It covers everyone sixteen and older who lost or quit jobs they formerly held, as well as school graduates, students, and others without previous work experience. "Actively looking for work" means that someone has sought a job at least once in the previous four weeks by applying for work, answering a newspaper ad, visiting an employment agency, or seeking help from a friend or relative. Students are considered unemployed if they tried unsuccessfully to get work and if they are available to work at least part-time.

According to the government, employed persons are nonfarm and farm workers sixteen years and older who work full- or part-time (at least one hour a week), self-employed workers, and unpaid workers in family businesses who work at least fifteen hours a week. Those who are temporarily not working because of illness, vacation, strike, or a lockout are included among the employed even while absent from work.

WHAT'S NOT COVERED

"Discouraged" workers are not included in the unemployment figure. These are workers who say they want to work but are not looking for a job because they think nothing is available where they live or because they think they don't qualify for the jobs that are available.

HOW IT'S REPORTED

Around the second week of each month, the Bureau of Labor Statistics, a division of the Department of Labor, releases the number of unemployed during the previous month as a percentage of the total labor force. The figures are seasonally adjusted. To arrive at these figures, the Census Bureau surveys a sampling of approximately 60,000 households. Interviewers either visit or telephone the households.

Chart 7A demonstrates how unemployment began rising in the summer of 1990, just as the recession was about to get under way, going from about 5.2% and climbing steadily to a high of 7.8% in June 1992. By September 1990 the effect of the Iraqi invasion of Kuwait was being felt as OIL PRICES rose, the stock market fell, and there was general apprehension throughout the country. The steady rise in unemployment throughout the remainder of 1990 was a clear warning about the American economy.

WHY IT'S IMPORTANT

The unemployment rate is one of the most widely followed economic indicators of all the market movers. Its importance is easy to understand: it signifies the degree to which the economy is providing jobs for those who want them. Having a job and keeping it is the foundation of our economic, social, and psychological well-being.

The Congress and the FEDERAL RESERVE use the unemployment

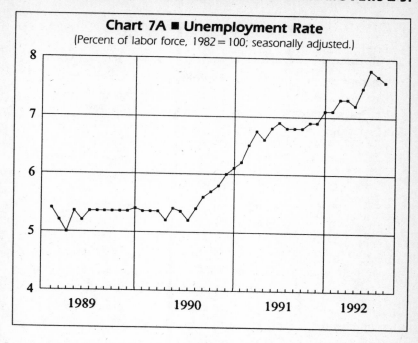

Chart 7A ■ Unemployment Rate
(Percent of labor force, 1982 = 100; seasonally adjusted.)

figure to decide whether to stimulate or restrain economic growth. When unemployment creeps above 6%, the Fed will intervene to lock in lower interest rates, which affects the stock and bond market, even CDs and Treasuries. (See chapter 19, "The Federal Reserve.")

Chart 7B shows the unemployment rate from November 1960 to June 1991. The peaks, representing high unemployment, during this post–World War II period look like a jagged mountain range. Each of these peaks represents a recession. The last one (1983) was the most severe; unemployment rose above 10%.

Most economists agree that 5% unemployment is within the acceptable range. Many consider it full employment. Yet a rate of 5.7% is often cause for concern. Why? The answer lies not in the actual figure, but in the direction of the rate: if it moves steadily upward and eventually reaches 6%, it spells trouble; 6% and higher indicates a recession.

Chart 7B ■ Unemployment Rate

Chart courtesy: Ned Davis Research Inc.

Keep in mind one final point when evaluating this market mover: the unemployment rate does not refer only to people down on their luck and out of a job because they were laid off or fired. In June 1989 approximately 42.5% of the unemployed were new entrants or reentrants to the job market, while another 15.5% were those who had *quit* their last jobs. The remaining 42% were indeed people who had lost their jobs.

MARKET MOVER TIPS

■ Use the unemployment rate to gauge your own work life. In an expanding economy, when unemployment is low (5% or below), it's easier to find a job. Begin a search in earnest at this point. It's also an opportune time for a job or career change.

■ If the unemployment rate is rising, hang on to your present job. Don't call in sick if you're not; be on time; suggest ways the company can save money. This is not the time to ask for a raise or extra perks.

■ When unemployment is above 6%, the Federal Reserve will begin to intercede and lower interest rates. Lock in yields on

CDs and bonds before rates fall further. When short-term interest rates fall to 1% or 2%, begin to add quality stocks to your portfolio in order to benefit from the forthcoming recovery.

DID YOU KNOW THAT?

When fifty-one-year-old Franklin D. Roosevelt was sworn in as president in 1933, one-third of the nation's labor force, or 13 million Americans, were unemployed. FDR assured the troubled country that "the only thing we have to fear is fear itself." To generate new jobs, he got Congress to appropriate $3.3 billion for the Works Project Administration (WPA). The Civilian Conservation Corps paid 2.5 million young men $30 a month to build roads, construct flood control systems, and replenish the nation's forests. Despite these and other work programs and the eventual economic recovery, in 1939 there were still 9 million Americans who could not find jobs.

CHAPTER 8

Business Failures
and Business Starts

■ ■ ■

Business failures represent the number of companies that go out of business because they owe money to creditors. Business starts tally the number of new businesses launched.

■ ■ ■ BUSINESS FAILURES ■ ■ ■

Not everyone who launches a new business succeeds. Some fail more quickly than others, often due to underfinancing and insufficient capital to get through the inevitable tough times, the downturns in the BUSINESS CYCLE. As Eddie Cantor cautioned a friend who was starting a business in the forties: "It takes years to make an overnight success." Those businesses that do not become a success become a statistic. Dun and Bradstreet Corporation (D&B) gathers data on business failures, and the results are reported in the financial media.

WHAT IT COVERS

Business failures include companies that are closed down because of bankruptcy, foreclosure, attachment, or receivership, as well as those whose owners shut the door voluntarily, leaving unpaid debts. The full report on business failures includes the dollar amount in liabilities (the amount of debt the day the business closed). Liabilities consist of all types of financial obligations, whether or not they were secured. The report also encompasses the age of the business and the cause of failure. Failures are broken down by state and type of business.

WHAT'S NOT COVERED

Business failures do not include businesses closed down simply because they did not have enough capital to continue on, did not make enough profit, or because the owner became ill, retired, or moved to a new location.

HOW IT'S REPORTED

The D&B reporters search through court records for bankruptcies, foreclosures, attachments, and so forth. Data on business failures that do not involve court listings are gathered from local credit management groups, sale notices in newspapers, sheriff and auction sales, and other sources.

The failure statistic is determined by dividing the number of failures by the number of businesses that D&B has in its data base of open businesses. This number is then multiplied by ten thousand to arrive at a rate of failures per ten thousand companies.

WHY IT'S IMPORTANT

The number of businesses that fail indicate the business world's ability to withstand financial difficulties. It is also a record of how much debt is left unpaid. A high proportion of bad loans hurts banks and other lending institutions and can cause the publicly traded bank stocks to fall. When business failures increase, others who have been contemplating starting a new business might hesitate to do so. On the other hand, when business failures decline or are low, entrepreneurs are likely to put their dream into action and start up a business.

To some extent the number of business failures relates to factors beyond the manager's or owner's skill. A decreasing GROSS DOMESTIC PRODUCT can adversely affect a business. High INTEREST RATES also have an onerous impact—particularly on businesses that are highly leveraged. Other factors that often cause business failures are inexperienced management, strong competition, unanticipated expenses, and of course, sizable debt.

■■■BUSINESS STARTS■■■

WHAT IT COVERS

This figure includes new corporate and unincorporated for-profit businesses that are either independently owned or are subsidiaries of existing firms and came into being to handle a new line of business.

WHAT'S NOT COVERED

Business starts do not take into account previously existing companies that were reorganized because of a change in ownership, a merger, or a change from corporate to noncorporate status. It does not count firms that change their name or location.

HOW IT'S REPORTED

The D&B figures cover the total number of employees, the state where located, and the type of industry. D&B records a business start when a potential creditor asks D&B for a credit rating on the firm. If a credit rating is never requested for a business from D&B, it will *not* be included as a business start. And if a credit rating is requested three years after the business was started, it is not included as a business start but is added to D&B's data base of existing firms.

This system means that many small new businesses, moonlighting entrepreneurs, and other businesses that for one reason or another never had anyone ask about their creditworthiness are excluded from coverage.

WHY IT'S IMPORTANT

An upturn in business starts translates into an increase in the number of people employed as well as increases in expenditures for plants and equipment. It also indicates an optimism about the economy and a willingness to take on the various burdens and responsibilities associated with a new business endeavor.

MARKET MOVER TIPS

■ When business failures are on the rise, it often indicates that interest rates are high: the business cycle is most likely at its peak or near to it, and the economy will soon take a turn for the worse. Lock in high yields on Treasuries, A-rated corporate bonds, and long-term CDs. Move some of your funds into stocks of recession-resistant industries such as food, beverage, drugs, and utilities.

■ When business starts are on the rise or at a high point, it typically indicates that the economy is either recovering or robust. If so, move out of money funds and CDs and into growth stocks, which should appreciate along with the overall economy.

■ An increase in the number of new businesses means an increase in the number of loans being made. As new businesses borrow and spend, new money is created, which in turn gives a boost to the stock market.

■ Use the trends in business starts or business failures as a general business indicator, confirming what you sense is happening in the business cycle. A high number of failures is cause for concern.

DID YOU KNOW THAT

The Italians gave us our word *bankruptcy:* when a medieval money merchant ran into financial trouble, his *banco,* or bench, in the market place where he met his customers was broken to indicate that his business had failed.

Bankruptcy has happened to some of the best of people. One of the first was Edward II, king of England in the fourteenth century. His passion to rule led to the invasions of France in 1339 and again in 1340; the expenditure left him £30,000 in debt and bankrupt.

Charles Goodyear, who discovered a way to vulcanize rubber, left $200,000 worth of debts when he died.

Mark Twain backed the Paige typesetting machine, rather than Alexander Graham Bell's telephone company, to the tune of $250,000. He lost his investment and declared bankruptcy in 1894.

In 1921 Walt Disney founded the Laugh-O-Gram Corporation in Kansas City. When his backers pulled out, he declared bankruptcy and took off for Hollywood with a small suitcase containing several changes of clothing. In this case Disney had the last laugh.

PART II

...

CONSUMER MARKET MOVERS

Whereas part I dealt with major industrial factors, part II focuses on things the consumer—you and I—are intimately involved with. These market movers measure the prices of hundreds of items we purchase, how much income we have to purchase them with, and whether we feel confident about our ability to pay for these items. Consumer market movers specifically cover the cost of items, the direction of sales, and the amount of disposable income and credit Americans have to make purchases. These measures include:

Consumer price index
Personal income
Consumer confidence index
Consumer installment credit
Auto sales
Retail sales
Housing starts

The consumer price index (CPI) is the most direct measure of the cost of living and is closely watched by the government, institutions, and individuals. Auto sales, retail sales, and housing starts have a tremendous impact on the gross domestic product, since consumer spending is its single largest component, and these are watched closely by the Federal Reserve (see chapter 19), which raises or lowers short-term interest rates to stimulate or restrict economic growth and consumer spending. Consumer market movers are affected by interest rates and inflation, which are included in part IV, and the unemployment rate. Some, like housing starts and the consumer confidence index, are particularly susceptible to event-driven market movers (part VI) such as war. Consumer market movers are probably the most easily understood by the layperson; their effects are also among the most far-reaching.

CHAPTER 9

Consumer Price Index

■ ■ ■

The consumer price index measures the change in consumer prices for a fixed basket of goods and services bought by households. Because it prices the same items each month, it is also a measure of inflation or deflation.

Many people do their grocery shopping once a week, filling up their carts with approximately the same amount of food. The total bill may fluctuate somewhat based on the time of year—fresh vegetables cost less in summertime, for instance, and entertaining during the holidays may add to the bill. If the grocery bill is steeper every week, however, it's a sign of INFLATION, a general rise in the price of goods and services. The rate of inflation, or the percentage change in your grocery bill and other items over a period of time, is measured by the consumer price index (CPI).

The concept of measuring the cost of consumer items is not new. During World War I the predecessor of this index, known as the cost-of-living index, was regularly published, and by the twenties it was the basis for about half of the nation's wage settlements. A price index was used as far back as the Revolutionary War to adjust the pay of Massachusetts soldiers hard hit by war-induced inflation. To calculate their index, officials used a "market basket" consisting of such items as five bushels of corn, sixty-eight pounds of beef, ten pounds of wool, and sixteen pounds of leather. Canny Americans have always been interested not only in how much they're paid, but also how much their money will buy.

WHAT IT COVERS

Each month, the U.S. Department of Labor gauges the prices in a "basket" of goods and services. Included among the approximately 100,000 items in this basket are such things as groceries, clothing, gasoline, medical care, entertainment, education, personal care, tobacco products, housing, and transportation.

The CPI compares average prices paid by consumers during the current month (or year) to the average prices paid during a base or reference period. As of November 1992 the base period is 1982–84. In 1988 the value of the CPI was 118.3, which means the market basket cost was 18.3% above the price levels of the 1982–84 base period. The CPI for November 1992 stood at 133.8 or 33.8% above the price levels of 1982–84.

The first step in calculating this index is to weight its components so that each is given its proper percentage of the whole. Because most people spend more on housing than on handkerchiefs or sugar, the price of housing is given more weight than handkerchiefs or sugar in the index.

Each month, the Bureau of Labor Statistics (BLS) sends agents to the same retail stores and service establishments throughout the country to obtain the prices of about 100,000 items. The result is a comparison of the current price of a fixed market basket of consumer goods and services of constant quality to the price of that market basket in a specific base period. BLS statisticians then break down the numbers into figures for local, regional, and national levels.

WHAT'S NOT COVERED

The CPI does not measure the cost of goods purchased by rural households, military personnel, or individuals living in institutions, such as prisons, old-age homes, and long-term hospital-care facilities.

HOW IT'S REPORTED

The CPI is published in the third or fourth week following the month for which the prices have been gathered. The press announces the inflation rate as the percentage change in the CPI from the prior month: "Inflation rose 0.5% in April or 5.4% at an annual rate."

On January 17, 1991, the day after the start of the war in the Persian Gulf, *The New York Times* reported that "consumer prices rose three-tenths of a percent in December . . . putting the year's inflation rate at a nine-year high and signaling that the recession has so far failed to control rising costs." The *Times* noted that the 1990 CPI increase of 6.1% (1989 was up 4.6%) "was the sharpest advance since an 8.9 percent jump in 1981."

The *Times* article explained that the rise in oil prices since the August 2 invasion of Kuwait by Iraq accounted for most of the 1990 inflation. "But even if the often volatile food and energy prices are excluded," the *Times* said, "inflation remained robust—climbing four-tenths of a percent in December and 5.2 percent for the year."

The movement of the CPI is shown in chart 8A. Note the rise in costs toward the end of 1990, when the United States became involved in Operation Desert Shield.

WHY IT'S IMPORTANT

Not surprisingly, the consumer price index is the most widely followed indicator of the cost of living. Everyone wants to know if it will cost more or less to live, and the CPI is closely watched by

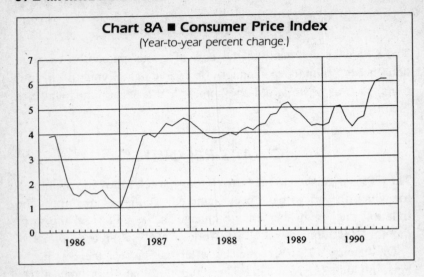

Chart 8A ■ Consumer Price Index
(Year-to-year percent change.)

economists and journalists, Wall Street and Main Street. Thomas Riley Marshall, vice president of the United States, isn't remembered for much except his remark to the chief clerk of the Senate in 1917: "What this country needs is a good five-cent cigar." The CPI shows how close we are to Marshall's wish for the American consumer.

Today, factory workers, government and service employees, corporate executives, and owners of small family businesses all make key decisions based on this index. The CPI is used as a guide by the FEDERAL RESERVE to determine whether economic growth should be stimulated or restrained. The index is built into wage increases, benefit and retirement packages, collective bargaining agreements, Social Security benefits, and many other aspects of our lives. Inflation adjustments to salaries, wages, pensions, and Social Security benefits are often keyed to the change in the CPI. The CPI is even used in the indexing of federal income tax returns in order to limit inflation-induced tax-bracket creep.

If the CPI rises by only 2% a year, inflation is regarded as low, 2% to 4% is moderate; above 5% is relatively high and worrisome. Many experts feel that when the CPI is above 6% to 8%, inflation is so strong that the Federal Reserve will take action to curb it.

When the CPI rises, it has a negative impact on stocks, bonds, and even CDs. For example, if you purchase a four-year $1,000 Treasury note or CD yielding 8% annually, you would receive $80 a year in interest. But if consumer prices are leaping ahead at the rate of 5% a year, the real purchasing power of your $80 in interest is falling by 5% a year.

A surge in the CPI often pushes the Federal Reserve to adopt a tight monetary policy, which means higher INTEREST RATES. In turn, higher rates hurt stocks as investors leave the market for high-yielding CDs, Treasuries, and money market funds.

MARKET MOVER TIPS

- When the CPI falls by 1% or more for two or more consecutive months, buy interest-sensitive stocks, such as utility stocks. To lock in yields before they fall, add quality corporate bonds and Treasuries.

- When the CPI rises by 1% or more for four or more consecutive months, expect interest rates to rise. Purchase short-term CDs and Treasury bills, and as rates rise, reinvest.

- When the CPI (and inflation) rise, ask your broker to look into real-estate investment trusts (REITs), especially health-care REITs. These trusts own properties, and their payouts to shareholders are often based on the base rents plus a percentage of total revenues. These revenues will rise along with inflation.

DID YOU KNOW THAT?

In 1782 it took $100 in paper money to buy $1 in silver. That year inflation was documented for the first time in this country. The cost, in paper currency, for essential items was high:

- A pair of shoes cost $100.
- A bushel of corn cost $40.
- A pound of tea cost $90.
- A barrel of flour cost $1,575.

CHAPTER 10

Personal Income

■ ■ ■

Personal income measures the money earned by those who are at work, whether employed by others or self-employed, plus interest and dividend income, as well as Social Security and other benefits.

Comedian Henny Youngman once said, "I've got all the money I'll ever need if I die by four o'clock." Many of us feel that way: no matter how much income we have, it's never enough.

It's the responsibility of the U.S. Department of Commerce to track the annual income of every American. Within the category of personal income, several important subcategories are studied by economists: disposable personal income (DPI), personal outlays, and personal savings.

WHAT IT COVERS

Personal income measures all household income, which is composed of wages, fringe benefits, self-employment income, rental income, interest, dividends, Social Security and unemployment benefits, food stamps, and other income maintenance assistance. A category that often appears in the media is *disposable personal income*, which is the amount households receive *after* payment of taxes—income, estate, gift, and personal property taxes, as well as fees, fines, and penalties to federal, state, and local governments.

Personal savings is the difference between disposable personal income and personal outlays, the total of consumer spending for goods and services and interest payments on consumer loans. Personal savings is given as a percentage of DPI. When consumers finance spending from their savings or by selling real estate and investments to businesses, governments, or foreigners, the savings rate falls. Personal savings is an indication of the consumer's willingness—or lack of it—to spend. Therefore the personal savings rate is quite an accurate predictor of future spending trends.

The U.S. Department of Commerce presents the numbers as follows:

Personal income
   Wages and salaries
   Factory payrolls
   Transfer payments*
Disposable personal income
Personal outlays
   Consumption expenditures
   Other outlays
Personal savings

Transfer payments refers to Social Security, veteran's benefits, unemployment compensation, and welfare.

HOW IT'S REPORTED

The figures are available in the third week of the month following the month for which they are gathered. *The Wall Street Journal* of May 31, 1991, carried the figures for April as follows: "Personal income edged up 0.1% in April while consumer spending dropped by 0.1% . . . further indicating the economy remains weak but doesn't seem to be worsening.''

In May 1991, *Economic Trends*, the Federal Reserve Bank of Cleveland's publication, stated the matter with a wider perspective: ''Over the past several months, the trend of consumer spending has strengthened, although disposable income continues to decline. . . . The continued expansion of consumer spending growth is a key ingredient of economic recovery.''

Both the *Journal* and *Economic Trends* are describing a situation in which personal income is falling, a troublesome fact *if* it is paired with lower consumer spending. However, consumer spending actually grew modestly during the spring of 1991. This makes sense if you take into account that Americans are loath to reduce their standard of living and will keep on spending at least at a modest rate until credit is no longer available, savings are diminished, or rising UNEMPLOYMENT starts to pinch. Over a sustained period lower personal income will slow down consumer spending, as shown in chart 9A. For the most part, as disposable income rises or falls, so does consumer spending.

Personal income can be presented as a percent change from the corresponding month of the previous year as it is in chart 9A or in total trillions of dollars as in chart 9B. Often the numbers are seasonally adjusted.

WHY IT'S IMPORTANT

Personal income is significant because it has an enormous influence on consumer spending, which, as the largest single component of the GROSS DOMESTIC PRODUCT, accounts for about two-thirds of our GDP. Likewise, the personal savings rate, which reflects the consumer's willingness to spend, is an important indication of future spending patterns.

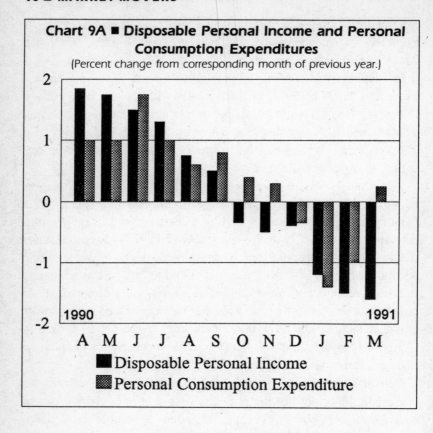

Chart 9A ■ Disposable Personal Income and Personal Consumption Expenditures
(Percent change from corresponding month of previous year.)

- ■ Disposable Personal Income
- ▨ Personal Consumption Expenditure

MARKET MOVER TIPS

■ Because consumer spending is so important to our economic growth, any sharp and prolonged decline in personal income will force the FEDERAL RESERVE to lower short-term INTEREST RATES in order to encourage banks to make loans and consumers to borrow. If personal income falls several months in a row, check the FEDERAL FUNDS rate. If it, too, is dropping, lock in the prevailing high rates with bonds and CDs, because chances are the Fed may continue to lower rates.

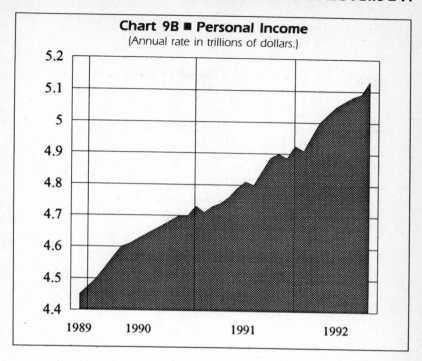

Chart 9B ■ Personal Income
(Annual rate in trillions of dollars.)

- Given the aforementioned situation, buy interest-sensitive stocks (public utility companies and banks), provided they are well managed and have strong balance sheets. Stocks of these two industries thrive during periods of low interest rates.

DID YOU KNOW THAT?

The rich don't always indulge in consumer spending. Hetty (Henrietta) Howland Green (1835–1916) kept a balance of over $31,400,000 in one bank alone and is said to be the greatest miser of all time. She was so stingy that she lived off cold oatmeal in order to save on fuel for her stove. When Hetty died in 1916, she left a $95 million fortune.

On the other hand, Malcolm Forbes, the owner of *Forbes* magazine, took great joy in spending money—on himself and his friends. When he died in 1990 at the age of seventy, his fortune was said to be somewhere between $400 million and $1 billion. On his seventieth birthday, he flew eight hundred of his favorite pals to his Morocco mansion to help him celebrate the occasion. Forbes was not shy about consumer spending. In addition to his mansion in Morocco, he owned a ranch in Colorado, an island in the Pacific, a chateau in France, an estate in New Jersey, and an apartment in New York. When not traveling by limousine, aboard his famous yacht, or in a balloon, Forbes could be found going to work astride a motorcycle.

The public can still enjoy some of Forbes's consumer spending: his personal museum, on the ground floor of the *Forbes* magazine office building in Manhattan, contains his collection of toy soldiers, toy boats, and Fabergé eggs.

CHAPTER 11

Consumer Confidence Index

■ ■ ■

The consumer confidence index reflects consumers' attitudes toward the economy, the job market, and their own financial situation.

Americans' sentiments regarding the strength or weakness of the country's economy are often expressed in popular songs: "Happy Days Are Here Again" in the late twenties, for example, and "Brother, Can You Spare a Dime?" during the Great Depression. The ups and downs of our "national moods" are more officially registered by the consumer confidence index, published by the Conference Board.

WHAT IT COVERS

The survey is based on consumer responses to questions about their personal financial circumstances, their outlook for the country's economy, and their feelings about buying or delaying major purchases. Responses are keyed against consumers' feelings on these same matters the previous year: are conditions better or worse? Naturally, there are no absolute levels to measure optimism or pessimism, but a comparison of the levels of confidence between one period and another can be made.

HOW IT'S REPORTED

Results are generally made available within the first week or ten days into the month after the survey was taken. As of November 1992, the base year for the consumer confidence index is 1985, whose index is given as 100; subsequent periods are reported as a percentage change.

WHY IT'S IMPORTANT

Chart 10A shows that in the first part of 1990, the index was in the 105 to 112 region, below the all-time highs of 115 to 121 reached in 1989. Starting with the invasion of Kuwait by Iraq in August 1990, however, the index began to fall, plunging to 61 in December and to 54 in January 1991. In January 1992 confidence fell even lower to 50. In 1991 and 1992 confidence remained low, a reflection of rising unemployment rates and a very mild, slow paced recovery.

The war and the recession were the main reasons given for this sharp collapse of confidence, along with the nationwide drop in housing prices. Homes have long been the mainstay of value for Americans, and as long as the prices sellers receive are substantially above their cost, the American consumer continues to feel both rich and confident. In 1990 and 1991, when home prices dropped, to the accompaniment of war and recession, consumer confidence made a dramatic downward adjustment.

In a *Wall Street Journal* article on January 30, 1991, Edward Yardini, senior vice president at Prudential-Bache Securities, was quoted as saying that consumer confidence—reported at 54—"can't get much worse." Yardini then referred to the so-called "misery index," which is the sum of UNEMPLOYMENT and INFLATION rates.

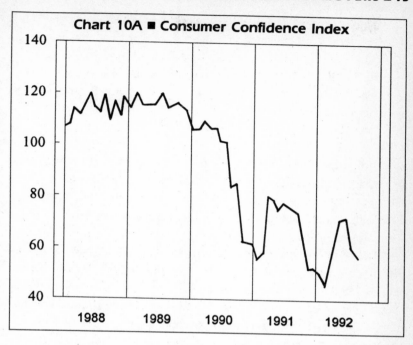

Chart 10A ■ Consumer Confidence Index

It tends to move in the opposite direction from the consumer confidence index. When the twin negatives of higher unemployment and higher inflation cause the misery index to rise, consumer confidence almost invariably drops.

Like most things in the world of economics, the numbers can change with breathtaking swiftness, a fact that prompted George Bernard Shaw to say, "If all economists were laid end to end, they would not reach a conclusion." In any case, on March 27, 1991, under the headlines "Consumer Confidence Soared Following End of Gulf War; Jump Was Biggest Ever," the *Journal* reported:

Confirming other recent tentative indications, the Conference Board's Consumer Confidence Index rose to 81 in March from 59.4 in February, the largest month-to-month increase in the survey's 22-year history.

The Conference Board figures indicate that, while consumers feel better, they aren't delighted with all aspects of the economy, analysts say. "The notion that the recent abrupt improvement in confidence will catapult us out of recession is excessively optimistic," declared Fabian Linden, executive director of the Conference Board's Consumer Research Center.

At this time, the consumer confidence index was flashing a very optimistic signal, primarily because the seemingly successful end to the Persian Gulf War made Americans feel optimistic. However, both inflation and unemployment, ingredients of the misery index, were not registering such a quick recovery. Thus, the consumer confidence index was not by itself the most accurate gauge of recovery. After the sudden burst of confidence in March 1991, confidence fell steadily throughout the remainder of 1991, a reminder that a sudden swing of a single market mover is a signal to look at other market movers before jumping to a conclusion.

Consumer sentiment frequently foretells economic swings, for when consumers are pessimistic they reduce spending, try to pay off some of their debts, and boost the amount in savings accounts and money market funds. The decision to purchase a home or other expensive item is heavily influenced by the consumer's feeling about future economic conditions.

Low inflation makes consumers optimistic and keeps consumer confidence high, thus further boosting borrowing and spending. On the other hand, a high rate of inflation generally means unfavorable consumer sentiment and, in turn, low consumer spending and borrowing. This, of course, is why inflation brings about recessions: it suppresses consumer sentiment. A low rate of inflation propels an economic recovery and expansion and then boosts consumer confidence. The key factor to keep in mind is that inflation and consumer confidence usually move in opposite directions.

MARKET MOVER TIPS

■ If inflation is high and consumer confidence falls below 80, prepare for a recession.

■ See Market Mover Tips in chapter 7, "Unemployment Rate," and chapter 23, "Inflation," which cover the components of the misery index.

DID YOU KNOW THAT?

Americans were so confident in the mid-twenties that two out of three households put in electricity and promptly bought lamps, refrigerators, washing machines, and toasters by the truckload. Cautious middle-class Americans abandoned their time-honored fear of debt and became proud consumers of these and other newfangled inventions, especially the radio. In November 1920 there was one radio station; by 1923 more than 500 broadcasting systems were in operation.

CHAPTER 12

Consumer Installment Credit

■ ■ ■

The total of all loans to consumers for financing the purchase of goods and services and for refinancing existing loans is reported as consumer installment credit.

J. P. Morgan once told someone who inquired about the expense of maintaining his yacht, "If you have to ask how much it costs, you can't afford it." Credit cards have allowed millions of Americans to imitate the likes of J. P. Morgan and make purchases without asking the price—or at least without paying too much attention to the cost until thirty, sixty, or ninety days after the purchases are made. Charge now and pay later has become the American way. With everyone from students to grandparents buying into the future, we have become a nation run on plastic.

Consumer and mortgage lending accounts for approximately one-third of all American bank debt. The damage started in the eighties: between 1982 and 1986 credit card debt grew at an annual rate of 9.5% per year—nearly twice the rate during the seventies. Why such a wild spending spree? Americans felt rich: they had bigger paychecks, the value of their real estate doubled and tripled, and at the same time INFLATION was low.

The debt wagon barely paused at all until two things occurred: first, the government, through the 1986 Tax Reform Act, phased out tax deductions for interest paid on consumer loans; and second, the stock market crash in 1987 knocked CONSUMER CONFIDENCE down a peg or two, as did the recession of 1990–91. As the nineties got underway, we were still borrowing, albeit at a less frenetic pace.

WHAT IT COVERS

Consumer credit represents loans to consumers for buying items and for refinancing existing consumer loans. A financial transaction is considered a loan if it is repaid in two or more monthly payments. This means that credit card purchases are considered a loan if they are not paid in full within the grace period. Consumer credit loans are made by commercial banks, finance companies, credit unions, retailers, savings institutions, and gasoline companies.

The key categories of consumer credit are automobile loans; revolving credit card loans used to purchase items or for cash advances; home improvement loans; loans to buy recreational vehicles, vans, and pickup trucks; and student loans. Both secured and unsecured loans are included.

WHAT'S NOT COVERED

Mortgages are not counted as consumer credit loans, neither are loans secured with real estate, including home equity loans. The omission of home equity loans is a large one since more and more consumers are taking out such loans to purchase big-ticket items, to remodel homes, and to pay off outstanding debt on high-interest credit cards. Therefore, the consumer credit figures do not fully reflect the amount of outstanding consumer loans. (The advantage of a home equity loan is that the interest is tax deductible; interest on consumer loans is not.)

HOW IT'S REPORTED

The FEDERAL RESERVE releases monthly figures about six weeks after they are gathered. The numbers represent a total dollar amount and are broken down by lending institution and credit type. The figures that make up consumer credit are gathered from monthly surveys taken by the Federal Reserve, the Federal Home Loan Bank Board, the National Credit Union Administration, the Credit Union National Association, and the Bureau of the Census.

Chart 11A, covering 1990 through 1992, shows how consumer credit is reported. Note the decline in the total outstanding debt, seasonally adjusted, since late 1990. The high was reached in November 1990 ($736.411 billion) and was followed by a monthly decline to the $731.83 billion reported in April 1991. Ideally, this is not what should happen. Consumer credit is supposed to expand in order to keep the economy expanding. These declining consumer credit numbers reflect the recession of 1990–91.

For a longer perspective on consumer credit, chart 11B, covering the years 1950 through 1990, is helpful. It reflects a dramatic and accurate picture of how sensitive consumer credit can be. The net change in consumer credit rose substantially in the late seventies, and it really took off after the back-to-back recessions of 1980 and 1981–82. This splurge in consumer spending was the result of lower inflation, lower taxes, and prosperity stimulated by Reaganomics. After the heyday of the eighties, consumer credit again dropped into negative territory, as it had during the recessions of 1974 and 1980 and in 1987 when the stock market crashed.

WHY IT'S IMPORTANT

Consumer credit helps chart the course of the economy. When consumers are confident about their jobs and optimistic about the future, they are willing to go into debt or to increase their existing

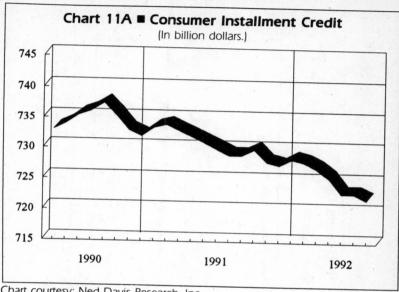

Chart 11A ■ Consumer Installment Credit
(In billion dollars.)

Chart courtesy: Ned Davis Research Inc.

debt to support their buying habits or wishes. Naturally, this helps businesses and the economy grow. Conversely, when they feel cautious about the future or when their level of debt becomes so high that monthly carrying charges become worrisome and slow them down, consumer credit declines.

Consumer credit along with PERSONAL INCOME is a sound source of data about consumer purchasing. Although consumer credit typically rises over time, the rate of the rise is faster during expansions than during recessions. You can use consumer credit as an indication of where we are within the BUSINESS CYCLE, to determine if we are entering a recession, coming out of one, or in an expansionary phase. If consumer credit is rising, we are in a recovery phase; if it's dropping, we're heading into a recession.

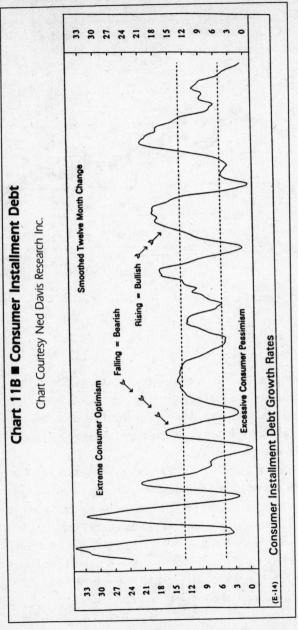

Chart 11B ■ Consumer Installment Debt

Chart Courtesy Ned Davis Research Inc.

Smoothed Twelve Month Change

Extreme Consumer Optimism

Falling = Bearish

Rising = Bullish

Excessive Consumer Pessimism

Consumer Installment Debt Growth Rates

(E-14)

MARKET MOVER TIPS

■ When consumer credit is rising, it's a good time to take a look at your own level of debt and reduce it by at least 10%.

■ It's best to have no consumer debt at all, especially since there's no tax write-off on the interest. If you must borrow, use a home equity loan; the interest is tax deductible.

DID YOU KNOW THAT?

The first multiuse charge card was created by a New York business-man who was entertaining guests at a restaurant and didn't have enough cash to pay the bill. The man, Frank McNamara, vowed he would never again be so embarrassed. He and an attorney came up with the idea of a charge card, and on February 28, 1950, the Diners Club Card was launched. It was accepted in only twenty-seven dining establishments, and during the first year only two hundred people, mainly Mr. McNamara's friends, carried the card at an annual fee of five dollars.

CHAPTER 13

Auto Sales

■ ■ ■

The total number of domestically made cars and trucks sold during a given period defines auto sales.

America's love affair with the automobile has been a long and faithful romance, dating back to the early twenties, when Henry Ford reduced the price of his Model T to three hundred dollars in order to boost sales. (The story goes that Henry would give you any color you wanted as long as it was black.) The country responded enthusiastically. By producing the most serviceable product at the lowest price, Ford captured the market.

Later in the twenties, General Motors began offering frills in order to compete with Ford's no-frill approach. GM's bigger, faster, and heavier automobiles offered the consumer choices in colors, fabrics, attachments, and models. The company was able to charge more and soon took the lead away from Ford. Since then the American automobile industry has offered new models at higher prices every year. During prosperous times, like the final years of the "Roaring Twenties" and the late years of the eighties, cars are an outward symbol of the nation's wealth. In the prosperous fifties we were introduced to more exotic models each year as the major car makers designed cars to look like airplanes, rolling living rooms, and statements of the buyer's prosperous station in life.

The heyday of the American automobile continued until the arrival of the German and Japanese imports. Volkswagens and, later, Toyotas symbolized a new era of efficiency and economy. The imports were overwhelmingly approved by a public anxious to save money and conserve fuel, and American gas guzzlers began to lose market share, a situation from which they're still trying to recover.

WHAT IT COVERS

Three times each month, around the fifth, fifteenth, and twenty-fifth, figures on the unit sales of domestically made cars and trucks (including foreign cars and trucks made in the United States) are released by the Commerce Department. The data is seasonally adjusted to reflect an annual rate of sales.

HOW IT'S REPORTED

On March 6, 1991, *The Wall Street Journal* reported that auto sales decreased 4.5% (to a seasonally adjusted rate of 5.9 million vehicles) in late February, noting, "Dealers said they haven't yet seen the sales rebound that they hope will follow the victory in the Persian Gulf." Furthermore, the *Journal* reported, "Overall sales of domestic and imported cars and trucks for all of February . . . dropped a hefty 21% from a year earlier." As is often the case when reporting economic indicators, the *Journal* also noted an unusual element: "One striking aspect of the late-February results was the 37% decline at Honda Motor Co., which had once seemed nearly immune to market declines."

In February 1991 the economy was still in a recession and although there were some signs of an early end to it, no one was taking any comfort from the U.S. auto sales figures. Adding to the

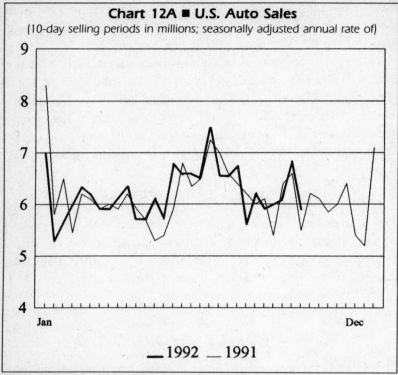

Chart 12A ■ U.S. Auto Sales
(10-day selling periods in millions; seasonally adjusted annual rate of)

___1992 ___1991

Source: Commerce Department

fairly bleak picture was the fact that RETAIL SALES and CONSUMER CONFIDENCE had also fallen.

By October 1992, as shown in chart 12A, car sales fell once again, selling at a seasonally adjusted annual rate of 5.8 million vehicles, far below the 7 million high reached in 1991.

WHY IT'S IMPORTANT

There are four key indicators of consumer demand and the direction of the American economy, and automobile sales is one of them.

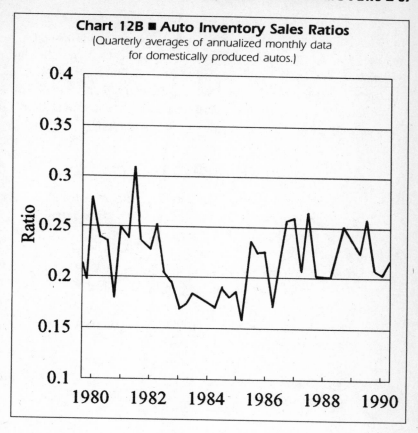

Chart 12B ■ Auto Inventory Sales Ratios
(Quarterly averages of annualized monthly data
for domestically produced autos.)

(The others are CONSUMER INSTALLMENT CREDIT, RETAIL SALES, and HOUSING STARTS.) Tracking auto sales helps economists predict recessions and prosperity. In 1952 Charles E. Wilson, secretary of defense under President Dwight D. Eisenhower, said, "What's good for the country is good for General Motors, and vice versa." Although this was a high mark of corporate arrogance at the time, as Mr. Wilson knew, time and time again, domestic auto sales have led the BUSINESS CYCLE into both recovery and recession.

Another related statistic that's useful for predicting the future of the economy, if not the country, is shown in chart 12B, the inventory/sales ratio. Auto inventories—unsold cars as a percentage of cars sold—rises noticeably during recessions. In this example the recessionary periods are indicated by the shaded areas.

It's important to note that auto sales alone can affect the GDP. In 1974 and 1979 auto sales fell sharply due to fears of gasoline shortages; in both cases this fall in sales impacted the GDP.

MARKET MOVER TIPS

■ If retail sales pick up after a recession, wait for a strong rebound in automobile sales to confirm the improvement in consumer demand.

■ If auto sales rise, expect an improving economy, greater consumer confidence, and eventually, lower interest rates. Buy stocks in the best-performing companies in the automobile and related industries, including glass, tire and rubber, steel, and upholstery, provided the companies are well managed and have strong balance sheets.

■ If auto sales drop two months in a row, sell domestic auto stocks and anticipate trouble in the economy.

■ If auto sales surge and go through the 8 million mark, expect inflation.

DID YOU KNOW THAT?

Americans didn't always like cars. Robert and Helen Lynd, sociologists, studied how the automobile changed American values in the twenties. Writing about Muncie, Indiana (aka Middletown, USA), they noted that the first car appeared there in 1900. By 1906 there were 200 cars, and by 1923, 6,221. Parents were unhappy as young couples took to driving off on their own, gaining privacy for the first time. One Muncie housewife complained that her teenage children "never go out when the family motors. They always have something else on." The town's leading minister denounced "automobilitis, the thing those people have who go off motoring on Sunday instead of going to church." Their protests were in vain; Muncie and every other American community soon took to the road in a big way.

CHAPTER 14

Retail Sales

■ ■ ■

Retail sales are the total dollar amount of all U.S. sales in retail stores.

England may be a nation of shopkeepers, but America is a nation of shoppers, so much so that the U.S. Commerce Department prepares a report every month on the total dollar amount of goods sold by retailers.

Since consumer sales are the most important and largest single component of our GDP, the various components of consumer buying are studied and broken down individually into AUTO SALES, HOUSING STARTS, and so forth. The key component of consumer buying is retail sales: sales made from purchases in stores of everything from dolls to dishwashers.

Another figure often reported in connection with retail sales—and a key determinant of these sales—is disposable income. Disposable income is the after-tax income of consumers or, to put it another way, personal income less personal taxes. The amount of disposable income consumers have is, of course, directly related to consumer spending. Taxes lower the amount of consumer spending, and at

Table 4A ■ Retail Sales
(Five-week September period)

	'92 sales millions	'91 sales millions	% change
Wal-Mart Stores	4,162	3,253	+ 28.0
Kmart	3,223	2,874	+ 12.2
Sears	2,130	2,000	+ 6.2
Dayton Hudson	1,520	1,340	+ 14.0
J.C. Penney	1,168	1,012	+ 15.4
Melville Corp.	967.6	892.9	+ 8.4
May Dept. Stores	1,019	919.5	+ 10.8
Federated	688.2	651.0	+ 5.7
Limited Inc.	601.3	532.5	+ 13.0
Woolworth	504.0	496.0	+ 1.5
TJX Cos.	319.0	265.0	+ 20.0
Gap Inc.	315.0	255.0	+ 24.0
Mercantile Stores	237.9	218.3	+ 9.0
Caldor	173.0	156.0	+ 10.7
Charming Shoppes	112.0	92.8	+ 22.0
Jamesway	79.4	75.4	+ 5.3

various times in the past, most notably in 1981, major tax cuts stimulated consumer spending and retail sales. In fact, in 1981 President Reagan persuaded Congress to cut personal taxes by $250 billion over a three-year period. This led to a substantial increase in disposable income.

WHAT IT COVERS

Retail sales figures are prepared by the U.S. Department of Commerce. In addition, Alex. Brown and Sons prepares a weighted sales index of thirteen major retail chains. As of October 1992 the chains included in the index were Wal-Mart, Kmart, Sears, J. C. Penney, Dayton Hudson, May Department Stores, Melville Corporation, Woolworth, Limited Inc., TJX Companies, Mercantile Stores, Gap, Federated, Caldor, Jamesway, and Charming Shoppes. (See table 4A.)

HOW IT'S REPORTED

The figure for total sales includes both store and catalog sales. The percentage change from the same time period a year ago is also given. The figures are gathered on a monthly basis and released during the second week of the month. They are *not* seasonally adjusted.

WHY IT'S IMPORTANT

Unless retail sales grow from year to year, the economy is heading for trouble; therefore, economists, market watchers, and the FEDERAL RESERVE focus closely on the annual percentage change in retail sales. *Value Line*, a weekly publication considered by many analysts and investors to be the best tool for stock selection, noted in its February 22, 1991, issue:

> Consumers remain wary. Their reluctance to spend is reflected in recent retail sales and consumer credit data. In January, for example, retail sales fell 0.9% from December's level . . . and is another indication that consumers are in no mood to commit to long-term payments.
>
> The Federal Reserve is moving to counter buyers' reluctance . . . in hopes of breathing life into a weak economy.

How does the Fed counter consumers' reluctance to buy? In this country's economy the consumer is king. The government, retailers, and manufacturers want each of us to have sufficient disposable income as well as an optimistic outlook so we will spend this disposable income. Consequently, if retail sales are not growing on an annual basis, the Fed will very likely lower interest rates to stimulate the economy. (See chapter 19, ''The Federal Reserve,'' and chapter 17, ''Interest Rates.'')

Consumer spending, as expressed in retail sales, is the heartbeat of our economy. The Federal Reserve, whose job it is to keep our economy growing, is not likely to allow retail sales to suffer any serious and long-term setback.

MARKET MOVER TIPS

■ If retail sales do not grow year to year, lower INTEREST RATES will follow.

■ If and when the Fed lowers interest rates to boost retail sales and other aspects of the economy, remember to lock in yields and extend bond maturities before rates fall even further. This is also a good time to purchase blue-chip stocks, which will benefit from an economic recovery.

■ When retail sales are reported, check *The Wall Street Journal*'s list of major retailers. Note the most successful ones—those posting the largest positive percentage changes in sales. Most of these retailers are publicly traded companies. Consider including their shares in your portfolio provided they are well managed and have strong balance sheets.

DID YOU KNOW THAT?

New Yorkers have always liked to shop, but not in their neighborhood. At the end of the nineteenth century, the city's best retail shops were located in a nine-block, nonresidential stretch from Fourteenth Street to Madison Square along Broadway and Sixth Avenue, known as the Ladies' Mile. In 1906 Benjamin Altman infuriated the city's well-to-do citizens who lived in elegant Fifth Avenue mansions when he opened his store at the corner of Thirty-fourth Street and Fifth. He was so sensitive to their fury that he disguised his store by putting it behind a Florentine facade and instructing the architect not even to put his name on the outside. Nonetheless, B. Altman's thrived and became famous for its housewares and furniture until it closed on December 30, 1989.

CHAPTER 15

Housing Starts

■ ■ ■

Housing starts tracks the total number of new single-family homes, townhouses, co-ops, condos, and multifamily apartment buildings on which work has begun.

Ever since the first saltbox made its appearance on the rugged coast of New England, we have been totaling up the value of our homes. The government, through the U.S. Department of Commerce, does it officially on a monthly basis.

WHAT IT COVERS

Each house and each unit within a building, whether it's privately owned or is public housing, is counted as one housing start. The figures are based on the number of permits issued and is determined by a mail survey as well as a survey of approximately 840 areas by on-site investigators. The data on housing starts in localities that do not require permits is estimated by monthly on-site surveys. Public housing starts are obtained from the U.S. Department of Housing and Urban Development.

WHAT'S NOT COVERED

The housing starts indicator does not include mobile homes, additions and renovations to existing buildings, and any conversions of nonresidential buildings into residential buildings.

HOW IT'S REPORTED

The figures on housing starts are provided by the Bureau of the Census, which is part of the U.S. Department of Commerce. The figures, released the third week of the month, are seasonally adjusted. Chart 13A shows that in September 1992 housing starts reached 1,256,000 units, compared to a high of nearly 1.6 million in February 1990. Housing starts fell fairly steadily throughout 1990, and rose fairly steadily in 1991 and early 1992. Housing by type— single or multifamily—is also available, as shown in chart 13B.

WHY IT'S IMPORTANT

Because of the extreme sensitivity of this statistic, it can be used to predict the future trend of the economy. Housing starts are very sensitive to mortgage rates as well as the CONSUMER CONFIDENCE INDEX. After the stock market crash of October 1987, housing starts suffered a sharp drop as Americans became more fearful of spending money. Chart 13B shows the number of starts over the period from January 1987 through January 1991. Chart 13A, covering the period from October 1989 through September 1992, shows quite clearly how housing starts hit a high in January 1990 and then began a long descent through the year. This was a forerunner of the recession that began in July 1990.

Typically, housing starts begin to fall six months in advance of a decline in the rest of the economy. This relationship between housing starts and the economy was noted in *The Wall Street Journal* of June

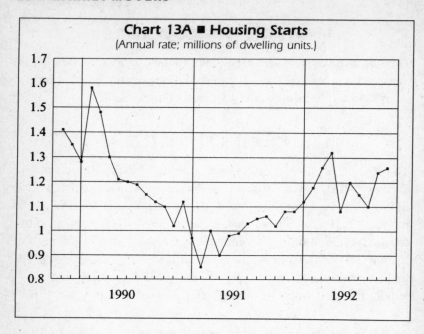

Chart 13A ■ Housing Starts
(Annual rate; millions of dwelling units.)

19, 1991: "Housing starts have been moving up haltingly since hitting a low annual rate of 847,000 in January. Economists said the housing starts data are consistent with the broadly held view that the recovery will be tepid compared with past rebounds. Michael Carliner, economist for the National Association of Home Builders, noted that so far, 'the recovery in housing is less than robust.' "

With a longer time span, from 1970 to 1991, chart 13C (on page 98) demonstrates how housing starts fall during recessions and climb during periods of recovery and expansion.

Housing starts not only predict the future direction of our economy; they also react violently to *unforeseen* shocks that shake consumer confidence, as was the case in the period immediately following the stock market crash of October 1987.

Because housing is so expensive, most people purchase new housing only when their incomes are high enough and mortgage rates

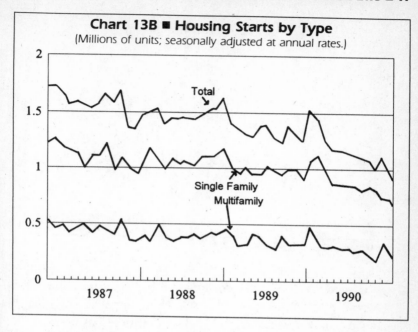

Chart 13B ■ Housing Starts by Type
(Millions of units; seasonally adjusted at annual rates.)

low enough to make it affordable. Thus, housing starts rise when interest rates are low and/or disposable personal income is rising. For the same reasons, housing starts and existing home sales tend to move together as shown in chart 13D.

Many industries, especially cement, glass, lumber, electrical and plumbing supplies, and other construction materials, depend on the level of housing activity. New home owners also benefit the producers of large household appliances, such as refrigerators, stoves, and dishwashers, and of furniture, carpeting, drapes, and kitchen supplies.

MARKET MOVER TIP

■ When the housing industry starts to recover, you can expect improved earnings for many of the industries that supply

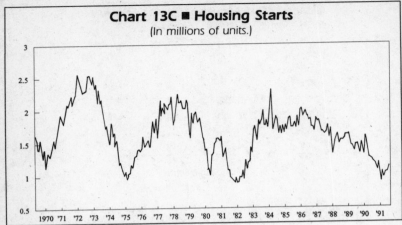

Chart 13C ■ Housing Starts
(In millions of units.)

Chart courtesy: Ned Davis Research Inc.

goods and services to the construction business; these include cement, glass, lumber, and household appliances. When the housing market weakens, avoid stocks in these businesses.

DID YOU KNOW THAT?

During the Great Depression and World War II, the number of new houses averaged about 300,000 per year. In the fifties the number was about four times higher. By 1960 more than one in three Americans lived in suburbs—as many as lived in the cities.

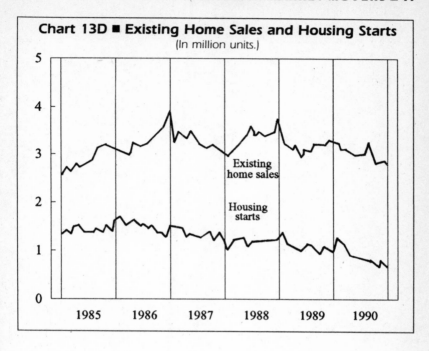

Chart 13D ■ Existing Home Sales and Housing Starts
(In million units.)

PART III

...

THE BUSINESS CYCLE

The American business cycle, the up and down trend of economic activity, is gauged by market movers. Our position in the business cycle is a market mover in and of itself since it affects consumer confidence, the actions of the Federal Reserve (part IV), and the financial markets. The cycle typically lasts from three to four years and goes through four distinct phases. As we move through these phases, key market movers such as interest rates, unemployment, gross domestic product, durable goods, and so on, change. In this section the characteristics of each phase, as well as the impact that each phase has on our personal financial holdings, are explained.

CHAPTER 16

The Business Cycle

■■■

After examining a number of the major market movers, it should be clear that the GROSS DOMESTIC PRODUCT and INDUSTRIAL PRODUCTION don't stand still. Likewise, DURABLE GOODS and the PRODUCER PRICE INDEX (PPI) rise and fall. These and the other economic series covered in parts I and II move up and down in imperfect unison. Their continual rise and fall—or if you like, the expansion and contraction of the economy—describe what economists call the business cycle.

Why does our economy expand until it booms, eventually run out of steam, then contract and fall into a recession? The answer is quite simple: our economy runs on credit. When consumers go to the bank to borrow money to buy big-ticket items or take out a mortgage, money is "created." When the bank makes a loan to consumers (or businesses), it extends a credit to their account, which expands the total MONEY SUPPLY. On the corporate side, businesses borrow in order to expand their productive capacity and meet rising consumer demand. All peacetime economic expansions are fueled by consumers and corporations borrowing money. When the money runs out, or more precisely, when the debt level becomes too heavy for banks to carry, the economy peaks and begins to contract.

During a contraction consumers and businesses decide to stop spending and start reducing their debt levels. Business watches carefully for signs of consumers curtailing credit and spending; when they see it beginning to occur, they start to cut back any plans to expand. In this fashion the business cycle generally runs three to four years from beginning to end and has four distinct phases. An examination of the cycle in detail demonstrates how market movers can be used to both describe and predict each of the four phases.

THE FIRST PHASE: FROM TROUGH TO RECOVERY

The trough, or the bottom, of the business cycle is as good a place as any to begin. The trough follows a contraction of the economy brought on by too much consumer debt, houses priced too high to move, and high INTEREST RATES, which have discouraged consumers and businesses from borrowing. During the contraction period, prior to the trough, high interest rates also caused stock prices to fall. At some point in every expansion, this inevitable slowdown occurs: consumers realize they can no longer handle additional debt. Businesses then see that demand for their products and services is no longer increasing, and so they, too, cut back, reducing production and lowering prices on goods and services. As soon as both consumer and business borrowing and spending fall, production and income also fall, and economic contraction begins. People are laid off and the UNEMPLOYMENT RATE rises. If this situation is severe enough and lasts long enough, it's called a recession. (Economists label a contraction a recession when GDP drops over two consecutive quarters.)

During the trough phase of the business cycle, the gross domestic product, which is the final output of goods and services produced in the American economy for a given quarter, falls about as far as it will in the cycle as a whole.

While the changes in GDP describe the big picture, the changes in industrial production and CAPACITY UTILIZATION, provide a sharper image with greater detail. Industrial production, which measures the changes in output of the basic industries of mining, manufacturing, and gas and electric utilities, may still be falling at the trough of the business cycle. Capacity utilization, the rate at which factories operate, drops to its lowest point—around 70%—at the trough. Chart 14A shows dramatically what happens to the IP index and CU rate during the trough phase of the business cycle.

During this first phase factories typically operate with fewer shifts, workers may be laid off, with only the most efficient remaining on their jobs while corporate America devotes its efforts to repairing and refurbishing its productive capacities. At this time, labor productivity is high, and the UNIT LABOR COST declines. Unit labor cost needs to be low if our economy is to expand and if we are to raise our standard of living.

In the trough of the business cycle, labor productivity *is* high and unit cost *is* a bargain, providing incentive for the cycle to begin moving toward a recovery. Business finds that the trough's lower unit labor cost enables them to offer price incentives to consumers to get them buying again. Consumers, who have been resting from their shopping binges during the previous expansion and paying off debt, are ready to come out and spend again.

The producer price index shows the changes in prices that are charged by producers of finished goods. It is reflected in the eventual prices that consumers will pay. The PPI tends to move in unison with unit labor cost. In other words, in the trough of the cycle, when costs of labor and producer prices are low, factory production is a bargain, and goods are produced that will begin to attract rejuvenated consumers.

Chart 14A ■ Industrial Production

Chart courtesy: Ned Davis Research Inc.

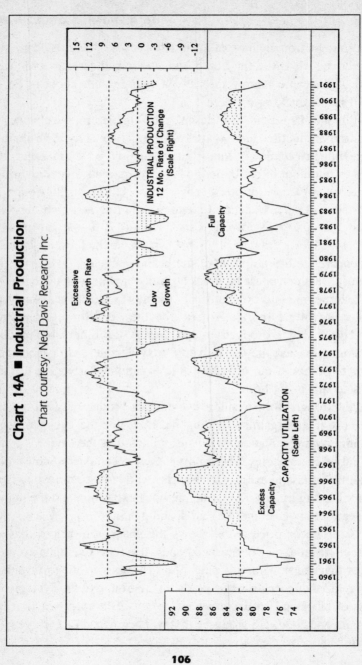

To summarize: in the trough-to-recovery phase of the business cycle

- gross domestic product is down.
- industrial production is down.
- capacity utilization is down.
- unit labor cost is down.
- producer price index is down.

THE SECOND PHASE: FROM RECOVERY TO EXPANSION

During the trough phase of the business cycle, interest rates and inflation were low, making it fairly easy for consumers to consider borrowing money again—and spend. In the second phase, moving from recovery to expansion, consumers actually begin to do so. Corporations, aware that consumers are on the move again, borrow in order to increase production to meet the new demand for products. During this recovery phase investors anticipate higher corporate profits and buy stocks, sending up the DOW JONES INDUSTRIAL AVERAGE. Jobs become more plentiful and unemployment is lower than it has been for some time. Prices have flattened. These price moves are tracked by the CONSUMER PRICE INDEX (CPI), which measures the prices of food and beverages, housing, apparel, transportation, medical care, and entertainment.

During this recovery to expansion phase, the CONSUMER CONFIDENCE INDEX and PERSONAL INCOME also rise. With a low inflation rate, a higher level of employment, and low interest rates, consumers feel confident about spending money and going into debt to do so. They start borrowing and buying—cars, homes, and other big-ticket items. Money is then created to fuel the move of the business cycle from recovery to expansion.

To summarize: in the trough-to-recovery phase of the business cycle

- Dow Jones Industrial Average is up.
- consumer price index is down.
- consumer confidence is up.
- personal income is up.
- AUTO SALES, RETAIL SALES, and HOUSING STARTS are up.

THE THIRD PHASE: FROM EXPANSION TO PEAK

As the expansion rolls along, all of the economic series are strong. Houses and autos are selling well. Employment in both the construction and automobile industries is up. Consumer credit is growing, and retail sales are improving. Corporations, quick to respond to consumer demand and plan for future increases, continue to expand plant usage and increase capacity to meet the elevating demands of the boom conditions. Capacity utilization approaches its maximum—the 86%-to-90% range. In this phase of the cycle, capacity starts to be strained, and efficiency as well as labor productivity suffers because extra workers are hired to meet increased demand. These extra workers are often inefficient, and this results in a rising unit labor cost. The gross domestic product shows strong growth quarter to quarter. Also on the rise are industrial production and the producer price index.

Whether or not the consumer price index will also rise during this phase is uncertain. During the expansion of the late eighties, there was no great inflationary surge as had been the case in the expansions that occurred before the Volcker Fed put the damper on INFLATION in the recession of 1981–82. Even though the CPI did not rise in the eighties, the cost of individual items certainly did. Housing prices skyrocketed, and the prices of real estate hit all-time highs in the late eighties. Antiques, collectibles, and fine art brought breathtaking prices at auctions across the country, creating another specialized type of inflation. Common stock prices also soared to new highs as the junk-bond-induced frenzy of corporate takeovers reached a fever pitch. This, too, created a new type of inflation, in this case, financial inflation. Whether or not inflation gets out of hand and causes the CPI to rise, the fundamental economic series that characterized Phase I of the cycle are now reversed.

To summarize: in the expansion-to-peak phase of the business cycle

■ capacity utilization is up.
■ unit labor cost is up.
■ gross domestic product is up.
■ industrial production is up.
■ producer price index is up.

THE FOURTH PHASE: FROM PEAK TO CONTRACTION

As surely as what goes up must come down, all economic expansions end in a recession. Even after the long and comparatively noninflationary expansion that began in 1983 and didn't end until mid-1990, this law of the business cycle asserted itself.

Recessions are typically begun by inflation and brought on by the FEDERAL RESERVE tightening credit (see chapter 19, "The Federal Reserve"). The Fed's efforts to curtail high inflation never eliminated it entirely from our economic system until Paul Volcker, the chairman of the Federal Reserve, took action. After the 1980 recession Volcker decided that the Fed would make a major effort to squeeze inflation out of the system once and for all—regardless of the cost in unemployment and economic slowdown. The result was the severe Fed-induced recession of 1981–82. During this long recession the reactions of the economic series were severe, as shown in chart 14A. Industrial production dropped to below 70%, as did capacity utilization, plunging lower than the 1974–75 recession low.

The Fed-induced recession of 1981–82 successfully curbed inflation; it was followed by the longest period of economic expansion in our post–World War II history. This expansion was accompanied by a very modest and acceptable rate of inflation, and the typical four-year business cycle, ending in recession, was extended to seven years.

In the second phase of the cycle (recovery to expansion), the consumer price index declined, and this raised personal income. Consumer confidence also rose as consumer demand increased, expressing itself in increased demand for autos, consumer credit, retail purchasing, and new housing.

In phase four all of these economic series reverse. The CPI rises, cutting into personal income. This was less true as the eighties came to a close, but certainly housing became much more expensive and expanded real-estate speculations and junk-bond financing piled up a mountain of debt, which eventually contributed to the savings and loan bailouts. Consumers, who had discovered the magic of using home equity loans to fuel their buying, found themselves pinched and frightened as unemployment rose and the prices of their homes collapsed. As did all the prior expansions, the free-spending eighties ended in recession.

Before the expansion of the eighties, it was inflation that reduced labor productivity, increased unit labor cost, and caused personal income to fall. The pre-eighties expansions always ended in recessions after inflation seemed to get out of hand. The rate of inflation grew to 15% in the 1979 expansion.

Although the eighties were an exception to the norm—the rate of inflation only climbed to 5%—there were many other economic consequences. By the end of 1992 we're still feeling the impact of the corrosive excesses of the eighties. Among the trouble spots are

■ far-reaching damage to our banking system and damage to the insurance industry and pension funds, caused by poor real-estate loans and excessive financing of corporate takeovers

■ the crisis in the savings and loan industry, with future bailout costs estimated to be in the neighborhood of $500 billion

- the crisis in junk bonds and the widespread losses they have brought
- the rising U.S. government deficit and the necessity of keeping long-term Treasury-bond interest rates at high levels to support the debt, which threatens the recovery from the current 1990–91 recession

These are just the most prominent problems that America must face in 1993 and beyond.

To summarize: in the peak-to-contraction phase of the business cycle

- consumer price index is up.
- personal income is down.
- consumer confidence is down.
- auto sales, retail sales, and housing starts are down.

DID YOU KNOW THAT?

The various phases of the business cycle have given birth to a number of popular songs. "Happy Days Are Here Again," written in the late twenties, told a weary public that the sad times were gone at last.

George Gershwin's "I've Got Plenty o' Nothin'" from *Porgy and Bess* tells of a man's plight—he has no car, no mule, and no lock on the door, but he does have his gal.

During the Great Depression, one of the country's most popular songs was "Brother, Can You Spare a Dime?" By 1933 the country was singing happier tunes—"We're in the Money" also called "The Gold Diggers' Song," which celebrated the return of the times when people had a silver dollar or two to turn their "dreams into gold."

PART IV

...

MONETARY AND FINANCIAL MARKET MOVERS

Many of us are aware of the importance of interest rates. We see the effect of changing rates on our money market account, CDs, and on our home or business mortgages. Likewise, inflation which determines the cost of living pervades many aspects of our lives. Interest rates and inflation are just two of the many key monetary market movers introduced in this section. These also include indexes and averages, such as the Dow Jones Industrial Average, that measure the movement of the stock market and, as they are scrutinized, influence small and large investors. The market movers covered here are:

Interest rates
Yield curves
Federal Reserve
Open market operations
Fed funds
Money supply
Inflation
U.S. debt and deflation

Credit crunch
Leading economic indicators
Dow Jones Industrial
 Average
Standard & Poor's 500
 Stock Index
Wilshire 5000

Interest rates are introduced first, since the subsequent monetary market movers largely determine the direction of short-term interest rates. Like all market movers these monetary measures affect others, including the value of the dollar (part VI) and the GDP. Inflation is another key market mover determined by the action of others, specifically a high capacity utilization rate and unit labor cost and low unemployment. Inflation can also be used to foretell recessions or economic recovery. Understanding monetary market movers is central to understanding monetary policy and the underpinnings of our economic system.

CHAPTER 17

Interest Rates

■ ■ ■

Interest rates represent the cost of borrowing money, expressed as a percentage rate, for a given period of time.

Interest rates represent the cost of our most valuable commodity, namely, money. The price of money—*i.e.*, its interest rate—varies according to supply and demand and, to a lesser extent, in response to the FEDERAL RESERVE's monetary policy. Interest rate levels are also related to the length of the loan and the degree of risk involved. Generally, the shorter the loan, the less the risk, and therefore the lower the interest rate; short-term loans with low interest rates are easier for borrowers to pay and more likely to be paid back on time. Interest rates fluctuate daily as borrowers (consumers, corporations, and the U.S. Treasury) and lenders (banks, consumers, and corporations) negotiate the interest rate at which they will make loans and deposits.

Interest rates for various types of loans are tracked on a regular basis by the Federal Reserve, the U.S. Treasury, and other investment services. These interest rates, available shortly after the time period they cover, are published in *The Wall Street Journal, Bar-*

ron's, and other newspapers. Typically, rates will be given for the previous day and the corresponding day a year ago.

The most frequently quoted interest rate measures are those relating to Treasury bills and Treasury notes.

Treasury bills. Often simply referred to as T-bills, these government securities, sold by the U.S. Treasury to finance our national debt, are default free and considered the highest-quality loan. Treasury bills are sold to investors in minimum denominations of ten thousand dollars. Their interest is free from state and local taxes—as are T-notes and T-bonds. T-bills are short-term issues that mature (or come due) in three months, six months, or one year. They are sold at a discount from face value. (The interest due on maturity is computed and deducted from the face value.) The yields on T-bills are watched closely for signs of interest rate trends. The interest rates on many floating-rate loans and variable-rate mortgages and other investments are tied to these bills.

T-bills are the primary instrument used by the Federal Reserve in its regulation of the MONEY SUPPLY through its OPEN MARKET OPERATIONS. The three- and six-month bills are the most frequently quoted. When T-bill rates are high, they attract buyers who are seeking safety. Fear of a stock market crash, war, or other international turmoil also creates a demand for these securities.

Treasury notes. Also issued by the U.S. Treasury, these default-free, low-risk securities have maturities ranging from two to ten years. The three- and seven-year notes are the most often quoted. T-notes are sold in denominations of one thousand or five thousand dollars, depending upon their maturity. When initially offered they are not sold at a discount, as are T-bills, but instead sold with a stated interest rate. In the secondary market, T-notes are traded below or above face value, depending upon the current level of interest rates. When rates rise, the value of the note falls since newer notes with higher interest rates will be more prized by investors.

Treasury bonds. These long-term debt instruments are sold by the government in maturities ranging from ten to about thirty years. The thirty year bond is most often quoted. The minimum investment is $1,000 and in every other way they are like T-notes.

Prime rate: the interest rate commercial banks charge their most credit worthy customers. Prime rate is determined by a bank's cost of funds—the discount rate they must pay to borrow from the Federal Reserve—as well as the rates that borrowers are willing to pay. Prime rate tends to be standard across the banking industry and when a major bank moves its prime up or down, others follow. The prime rate is a key rate since loans to less credit worthy customers are often tied to the prime rate. For example, a blue chip company such as Exxon or General Electric may borrow huge amounts of money at prime, but a smaller, less well established company might be forced to borrow from the same bank at prime plus 2%. Occasionally, large companies may be able to borrow at a rate below prime.

Discount rate: the interest rate that the Federal Reserve charges member banks for loans, using government securities as collateral. The discount rate provides a floor on all other interest rates since commercial banks must set their loan rates above the discount rate.

Federal funds rate: the interest rate charged by banks with excess reserves on deposit at a Federal Reserve district bank to those banks which need overnight loans in order to meet reserve requirements. The fed funds rate is the most sensitive indicator of the direction of interest rates since it is set daily by the market, unlike the prime rate and the discount rate which are changed by banks and by the Federal Reserve Board, respectively, from time to time. (See chapter 21, "Federal Funds".)

Telephone bonds. Yields on these bonds, offered by the seven regional "baby bell" companies, are higher than on Treasury issues because they are not backed by the full faith and credit of the government.

Municipal bonds. The Municipal Bond Index, published by *The Bond Buyer*, tracks the rates on securities issued by state and local governments and their agencies. Interest on municipals is exempt from federal and state taxes in the issuing state. The newspaper generally publishes the average weekly yields for twenty general obligation bonds and twenty-five revenue bonds. General obligation bonds are municipal bonds backed by the full faith and credit of a state or municipality. A GO bond, as it is known, is repaid from general revenue and borrowings. Revenue bonds are paid off with revenue from the specific project built by the money raised by the sale of these bonds. These include such enterprises as toll bridges, highways, hospitals, and stadiums; the tolls, rents, or other charges collected by the facility go directly to paying off the borrowers.

Note: When studying interest rates of bonds you will come across the term *coupon*. The coupon is the interest rate—expressed as an annual percentage of the face value—the issuer of the bond promises to pay the bond holder. For example, a bond with an 8% coupon will pay $80 per year per $1,000 of face value. Payment usually is made at six-month intervals.

WHY RATES ARE IMPORTANT

Interest rates affect all of us, whether we're borrowing, spending, or saving. When rates are low, businesses as well as individuals tend to borrow, and when rates are viewed as high, they borrow less and save more, taking advantage of the higher interest rates on money market funds, CDs, etc. Corporations decide whether or not to expand or hold a higher inventory not only on the basis of business conditions but also according to the cost of the money—its interest rate—needed for expansion. When rates are high, businesses must feel confident that demand will continue in order to offset the higher cost of expansion.

Most Americans buy automobiles on credit, finance real estate with mortgages, and make many retail purchases with credit cards. For consumers, therefore, interest rates determine the amount of their monthly payments and how much debt they can comfortably assume. Cars, appliances, homes, and other items sell more rapidly when interest rates are low, thus boosting our GDP, and sales slow down when rates rise.

The U.S. Treasury is the biggest borrower of money: our Treasury debt, now over $3 trillion, grows at the rate of $1 billion a day. Each quarter, the Treasury comes to the bond market to sell more than $30 billion in Treasury notes and bonds to finance this debt. This is in addition to weekly and monthly sales of T-bills and T-notes. When rates are high, these treasuries are more attractive, thus the government has a vested interest in the rise and fall of interest rates.

In general, interest rates both react to and influence the direction of our economy, our money supply, INFLATION, the GDP, and even the strength and VALUE OF THE DOLLAR.

HOW INTEREST RATES MOVE

In times of economic expansion, when consumers are borrowing heavily in order to buy and when corporations are borrowing to expand so they can increase production in order to keep up with consumer demand, *interest rates will rise*. More people want money; thus it's a more prized commodity.

Conversely, during recessions, when consumers are repaying debt and spending less, the demand for money drops. This reduced consumer demand for goods means businesses borrow less. At the trough, or low point, of the BUSINESS CYCLE, *interest rates fall* to their lowest level.

It is the job of the Federal Reserve, as mandated by Congress, to keep the economy on an even keel—that is, to avoid high inflation on the one hand and depression on the other. It is the Fed's mandate to promote long-term, noninflationary growth and to promote as full a rate of employment as possible without triggering inflation. The Fed does this in part by manipulating interest rates, restraining the use of credit and borrowing during times of expansion, and encouraging borrowing when the business cycle has contracted, is at its low point, and as it begins to recover. This is accomplished largely through the Fed's open market operations.

MARKET MOVER TIPS

- If you sense interest rates are about to rise, take out a loan before any big move upward. If interest rates are about to fall or starting to fall, wait as long as possible to borrow in order to get the lowest rate.
- Buy long-term Treasury bonds when rates are high. A-rated corporate bonds are also sound investments at high rates.
- Lower interest rates are typically a boon for stocks because lower rates promote improving business conditions and higher earnings for corporations. High-quality utilities, however, are a good addition to a portfolio. Utilities behave like bonds: they rise in price when interest rates fall, and vice versa. Utilities also have higher yields than most other stocks.
- Consider refinancing an existing mortgage if the new rate is at least 2% lower than your current mortgage rate and you plan to remain in your house for several more years.
- Study the yield curve charts (15A, 15B, and 15C on pages 123–125.) The point where the line bends like an elbow marks the year of maturity at which you will receive the highest possible rate without taking the risk of the longest maturity.

DID YOU KNOW THAT?

Bertrand Russell understood man's passion for high interest rates better than most. In *The Conquest of Happiness* he wrote: "Almost every American would sooner get eight percent from a risky investment than four percent from a safe one. The consequence is that there are frequent losses of money and continual worry and fret. . . . what the typical modern man desires to get with [money] is more money, with a view to ostentation, splendor, and the outshining of those who have hitherto been his equals."

CHAPTER 18

Yield Curve

■ ■ ■

A yield curve is a graph that illustrates the relation between bond yields and maturities.

Yield curves, or bond yield/maturity graphs, can be used to "predict" a recession, although their principal use is in deciding which bond to buy at what time and at what maturity. Yield curves act as a market mover because over time the changes in the yield curve indicate the rise or fall of rates in the future—*i.e.*, whether the FEDERAL RESERVE is tightening or loosening the MONEY SUPPLY—which affect contractions and expansions.

WHAT IT COVERS

A yield curve is a plotted line on a graph showing the yields of bonds of the same quality for a range of maturities. It can be used to show the yields for any type of fixed-income security, such as municipal or corporate bonds, but it is most often used on Treasuries. The bonds presented on any one graph are always of the same quality or credit rating. In other words, a yield curve cannot compare junk bonds with Treasury bonds.

Chart 15A is one type of yield curve; this one is for Treasuries. The horizontal line shows the range of maturities: three months, six months, one year, two years, five, seven, ten, up to thirty years. The vertical axis gives the yields in percentages. In this example the yields range from 5% to 9%. The curve shows the yields for the maturities, from the shortest to the longest, on two different dates: January 1, 1990, and May 31, 1991. For instance, on January 1, 1990, six-month Treasuries yielded 8% while thirty-year Treasuries yielded approximately 7.8%. The line for May 31, 1991, shows yields on six-month Treasuries at about 5.6% and thirty-year maturities at nearly 8.5%.

Note that the yields given on the yield curve are always the *yield to maturity* and not the coupon rate on the security. The coupon rate remains fixed; it is set when a security is issued. The yield to maturity changes as this fixed-coupon security moves in price either to a premium (above face value) or a discount (below face value).

The yield curve chart (chart 15A) demonstrates that over an eighteen-month period, from January 1, 1990, to May 31, 1991, short-term interest rates fell (from 8% to 5.6%) while long-term rates rose (from 7.8% to 8.5%). An investor can use this information to understand the direction of future rates and to confirm the movement of the economy. Essentially, chart 15A shows that the yield curve moved from an inverted, or negative, curve in January 1990 to a normal, or positive, curve in May 1991.

To better understand this, it is important to understand the meaning and the forces behind the three basic types of yield curves. The three basic yield curves—normal, inverted, and flat—are largely a result of the actions of the Federal Reserve trying to stimulate or dampen the economy. The most typical situation, labeled normal, or positive, occurs when short-term rates are lower than long-term rates. When a normal yield curve exists, investors who are willing to tie up their money over a long period of time are rewarded for

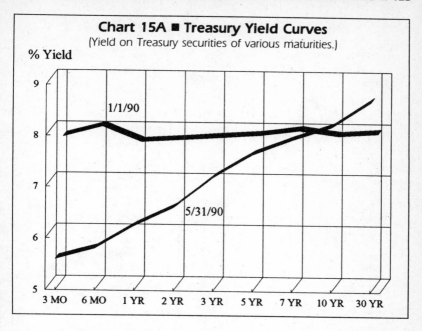

Chart 15A ■ Treasury Yield Curves
(Yield on Treasury securities of various maturities.)

this risk by getting a higher yield than they would on shorter-term bonds. As shown by chart 15A, this is the case for the May 31, 1991, yield curve.

An inverted, or negative, curve exists when securities with the shortest maturities have yields a percentage point higher than those with longer maturities. An inverted yield curve occurs when the Federal Reserve is trying to keep money tight by selling securities through its OPEN MARKET OPERATIONS or by raising bank reserve requirements. (See chapter 19, ''The Federal Reserve,'' for details.) When this happens, money is expensive to borrow, therefore investors receive higher INTEREST RATES. (The Fed tightens the money supply in order to curb inflation and prevent an expansion from booming out of control.) Chart 15A depicts an inverted yield curve for January 1, 1990. Chart 15B shows an even more dramatic inverted yield curve for 1981. Yields on three- and six-month Treasuries were between 16.5% and 17.2%, while longer-term issues had

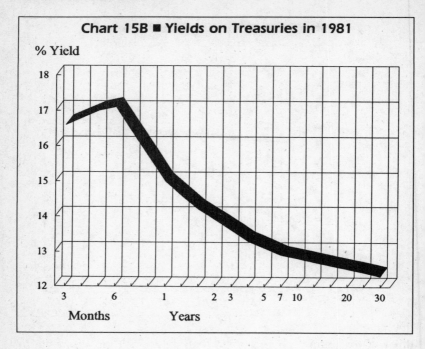

Chart 15B ■ Yields on Treasuries in 1981

% Yield

Months   Years

far lower yields. In fact, thirty-year bonds were yielding only between 12% and 13%. This inverted yield curve foreshadowed the Fed-induced 1982 recession.

A yield curve is called flat when all maturities, long and short, have approximately the same yields. A flat curve generally exists during the transition time between a normal curve changing to an inverted curve or vice versa. Chart 15C shows a fairly flat yield curve for June 29, 1990, especially for the shorter maturities.

In the nineties rates have been low, especially in comparison with the double-digit rates of the early eighties. These lower rates are a boon to a sluggish economy because they encourage borrowing and increased economic activity. But for investors with money in money market funds, CDs, and savings accounts, they present a dilemma.

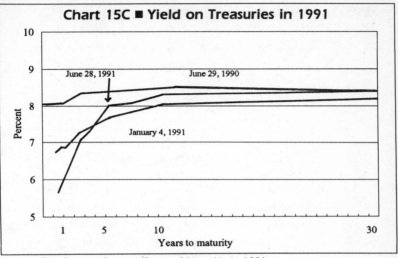

Chart 15C ■ Yield on Treasuries in 1991

Source: The Federal Reserve Bank of New York, 1991

It's tempting to move out of these investments in order to capture higher yields with longer-term bonds. But before seeking out the highest yields, it's important to understand the "market risk" involved. *Market risk* refers to the possibility that the general level of interest rates will rise after you have purchased a fixed-income security. This will cause your bond to fall in price as newly issued bonds offer higher rates and are more prized.

Table 5A shows the percentage change in principal value for bonds of various maturities (assuming an 8% coupon for each) when interest rates rise or fall by one percentage point. The potential price change increases with maturity, so longer-term bonds are more volatile than shorter-term ones.

If rates rise 1%, a $1,000 bond with a one-year maturity and an 8% coupon would decrease in principal value to $990.60; a thirty-year bond would decrease to $896.20. If rates fell 1% on these same bonds, the one-year bond would be worth $1009.50, and the thirty-year bond, $1,124.70.

Table 5A ■ 8% Coupon Rate Bonds		
Maturity in Years	Rates Fall 1% and Bond Prices Rise by . . .	Rates Rise 1% and Bond Prices Fall by . . .
1	0.95%	−0.94%
5	4.16%	−3.96%
10	7.11%	−6.5%
30	12.47%	−10.32%

WHY IT'S IMPORTANT

The basic purpose of a yield curve is to determine if short-term interest rates are higher or lower than long-term interest rates. The yield curve has also proven a fairly reliable predictor of recessions. Very often when short-term interest rates have been more than a percentage point above long-term rates—causing an inverted yield curve—a recession has followed. The inverted yield curves of 1967 and 1968 were exceptions; the economy slowed down but there was no official recession. Studies indicate that recessions are always preceded by a yield curve inversion, but recessions do not necessarily follow every yield curve inversion.

A flat yield curve indicates a change—or transition period—between a positive and inverted curve. This flat yield curve frequently occurs when the Fed is in the process of tightening or loosening money: If the previous curve was normal, the Fed is tightening money; if it was inverted, the Fed is loosening money.

MARKET MOVER TIPS

■ When the yield curve is flat and there's very little difference between yields on short- and long-term Treasuries, you have little to gain by taking on the risk of price fluctuations that accompany longer maturities.

■ When short-term rates are low and long-term rates are high (above 8%), the risk/reward relationship is altered, and it's worthwhile to buy longer-term notes or bonds to lock in the high yields.

- If the yield curve is normal and then starts to flatten out, the Fed is tightening money and short-term rates will continue to rise. Sell all but long-term stock holdings, especially those whose businesses will suffer in a recession, such as paper, chemicals, and machinery. The stock market generally suffers when rates are high because investors will sell their stocks and put their money where yields are high—in bonds, CDs, even money market funds.

- If the yield curve has been inverted and starts to flatten out, the Fed is loosening the money supply and all interest rates will soon come down. Lock in the highest and longest yields you can to profit from the current high rates. Also buy good-quality growth stocks because their businesses will thrive and their stock prices will be more attractive in a lower-interest-rate environment.

DID YOU KNOW THAT?

The Union sold government bonds to finance the Civil War. Treasury Secretary Salmon P. Chase appointed the brilliant Philadelphia banker, Jay Cooke, to raise much needed funds for the North. Cooke's aggressive campaign to sell "five-twenties"—bonds that bore 6% interest, could be paid off after five years, and had to be redeemed in twenty—was so successful that nearly a million Americans invested and the entire loan of half a billion dollars was oversubscribed.

CHAPTER 19

The Federal Reserve

■ ■ ■

System established by Federal Reserve Act of 1913 whose main function is to regulate the national money supply, set reserve requirements for member banks, supervise the printing of currency, and act as a clearinghouse for the transfer of funds throughout the banking system.

In 1920 Will Rogers, the cowboy philosopher, noted, "There have been three great inventions since the beginning of time: fire, the wheel, and central banking." The United States, however, was slow in coming to appreciate the last of these groundbreaking developments, being the last major industrialized nation to establish a central bank. Perhaps one of the reasons was that after the Revolutionary War, Americans remained suspicious of centralized control of almost any kind.

As late as the beginning of the twentieth century, most banks had relatively small amounts of cash at hand on a regular basis. Small country banks deposited their cash reserves in larger banks, which in turn deposited them in city banks. Such pyramiding of funds frequently led to severe problems: Poor business conditions or crop failures caused frequent panics, during which depositors lined up outside their banks, waiting in long lines for their money. Quite often the local banks were unable to meet such a sudden and widespread demand for cash; they turned to larger banks. The larger banks were sometimes able to meet the smaller banks' requests, but not always. Sometimes banks simply closed their doors and unfortunate depositors lost all of their money.

Instead of a central bank to regulate the supply of money, thousands of individual banks, each operating in a local area, had the power to determine how much money there was in the country. This meant the money supply was subject to abrupt changes, causing the country to go through rapid boom and bust periods. In the nineteenth century, financial panics occurred with comparative frequency, and some of them brought on severe depressions. The famous bank panic of 1907, which occurred during a time of general prosperity, caused millions of depositors to lose their savings and left the American public anxious: it seemed there was no way of knowing when—or how severe—the next depression might be. To most Americans it also brought home the fact that the U.S. banking system was in need of reform. The idea of a central bank had been explored before, but it was not until the panic of 1907 that Americans became convinced that their banking system was out of date.

In 1908 the National Monetary Commission was established. It recommended the creation of an institution that would establish an elastic currency and supervise the banking system so that financial panics like those of 1883 and 1907 could be avoided. The resulting legislation, the Federal Reserve Act, was passed by Congress and signed by Woodrow Wilson in 1913. The act established the Federal Reserve System and required all national banks to become members. State banks could, but were not required, to join.

From the beginning it was clear that the Federal Reserve System could do much more than simply counter financial panics. It did not take long for other objectives to be added to their agenda, and today the Fed, as it's known, has several assignments: assisting economic growth and stability, ensuring a high level of employment, and fighting INFLATION. The Fed is also involved in stabilizing the dollar in foreign exchange transactions.

The actions taken by the Fed are significant market movers. By understanding the Fed's policies and intentions, which are covered by the press, you can more accurately predict the rise and fall of INTEREST RATES, the rate of inflation, the VALUE OF THE DOLLAR, and recession and recovery.

HOW THE FEDERAL RESERVE SYSTEM IS ORGANIZED

The Fed is run by its board of governors in Washington, D.C. The board consists of seven members, appointed by the president of the United States and confirmed by the Senate for a term of fourteen years; members cannot be reappointed. The terms of the chairman and vice chairman of the board, also appointed by the president and confirmed by the Senate, run for four years; in this case, reappointment is possible as long as the member's fourteen-year term has not expired. All seven board members sit on the Federal Open Market Committee (FOMC) along with five regional Reserve bank presidents. The FOMC meets regularly throughout the year and is responsible for Federal Reserve transactions in the money market. This body controls short-term interest rates. (See chapter 20, "Open Market Operations.")

There are twelve Federal Reserve banks, located in Boston, New York, Philadelphia, Cleveland, Richmond, Atlanta, Chicago, St. Louis, Minneapolis, Kansas City, Dallas, and San Francisco. Branches of these banks are located in twenty-five cities across the nation. These banks act as a central banker for the commercial banks in their region.

HOW MONEY MOVES AROUND THE COUNTRY

Each Federal Reserve bank issues its own paper money, called Federal Reserve Notes. We tend to call them bills: $1, $5, $10, $20, $50, and $100 bills are in circulation today. The Federal Reserve banks issue these notes in accordance with the needs of their areas.

When a bank needs more coins and bills to meet customer demand, it can order this cash from its Federal Reserve bank or branch. Public demand for money varies: during the Christmas season more people want cash for shopping, for example. Banks also require extra cash when a customer wants to withdraw a large amount. The Fed will loan banks money to meet such fluctuating demand. However, the bank must pay the Fed interest, called the discount rate.

THE FED'S MONETARY POLICY

The Federal Reserve has an enormous impact on consumers, investors, and businesses; by managing the nation's MONEY SUPPLY, it attempts to make certain that the total amount of money in circulation is neither too much nor too little. Too much money in circulation results in inflation; too little may create a period of declining production and unemployment, resulting in a recession. To prevent the evils of inflation or recession, the Fed tries to keep spending in balance with the production of goods and services. Since it has no direct control over production, the Fed turns its efforts toward regulating the amount of money consumers, investors, businesses, and even the government have to spend. It controls our money supply in three different ways:

1. It changes the reserve requirement.
2. It changes the discount rate.
3. It buys and sells government securities (Treasuries) through its open market operations.

The Reserve Requirement

Years ago, a bank's reserves consisted of the gold and silver held in its vaults, but today's reserves are currency. This is termed a fractional reserve system. The Fed requires member banks to keep a percentage of their own cash deposits on reserve at a regional Federal Reserve bank. The reserve rate varies from 8% to 18% on demand deposits, the banks' term for checking accounts, and from 1% to 6% for time deposits (savings accounts). The reserve rate is not universal: it fluctuates depending on the size of the bank as well as the type of deposit; larger banks typically have a higher reserve rate than smaller banks, and time deposits are given a rate according to the ease of withdrawal.

By changing the reserve requirement or percentage, the Fed directly affects the ability of member banks to make loans to customers. For example, if the Fed raises the reserve requirement, local banks have less money available to loan customers. Banks respond by charging borrowers higher interest rates, consequently people and businesses borrow and spend less. Raising the reserve requirement is called "tightening" the money supply. When the Fed decreases the reserve requirement, known as "loosening" the money supply, interest rates on bonds, CDs, other fixed-income securities, and mortgages will fall.

The Discount Rate

The Federal Reserve can also control the flow of money by changing the discount rate, the interest rate it charges member banks when it loans them money. When the discount rate is low and borrowing is less expensive for member banks, this ultimately results in lower interest rates on loans for bank clients, thus encouraging borrowing. When borrowing is easier and cheaper, people and businesses spend more and the economy expands. A low discount rate also means low interest rates on CDs, money market funds, and bonds. People are encouraged to borrow and spend, not save.

Open Market Operations

The Fed uses its open market operations to control money supply and short-term interest rates. (See chapter 20, "Open Market Operations," for a more in-depth description of this market mover; also see chapter 17, "Interest Rates.") In this case the Fed alters commercial bank reserves through the purchase or sale of government securities. Through the Federal Reserve Bank of New York, the Fed buys and sell such securities in the secondary market to and from major securities dealers.

If the Fed believes the economy is growing too fast and inflation is rising too much, it will take steps to raise short-term rates and tighten the money supply. By selling large quantities of Treasury securities, such as T-bills and T-notes, it ensures that buyers write checks drawn against their commercial bank accounts and made out to the Fed. The Fed then presents these checks to the commercial bank for payment, reducing that bank's reserves and slowing down the bank's ability to make loans. This tightening of the money supply causes interest rates on loans and savings to rise.

On the other hand, if the Fed wants to help revive the economy it will take steps to increase, or loosen, the money supply by providing member banks with more reserves. In this case, the Fed *buys* government securities. The sellers of these Treasuries deposit the checks they receive from the Fed into their banks, increasing the banks' money reserves. With this influx of money, banks can increase their loans. If consumers and businesses then borrow and spend the money, output and employment are stimulated.

Through the reserve requirement, the discount rate, and open market operations, the Fed can control the money supply to help end inflation. When the prices of goods and services begin to rise and it looks like inflation is rising, the Fed usually tightens lending and credit. Consumers and businesses cut back on spending and borrowing money. This, in turn, helps put total spending in balance with the production of goods and services; prices then start to stabilize.

When the country is headed toward (or is in) a recession and the number of unemployed rises, the Fed typically makes it easier for banks to increase their lending by loosening the money supply. This tends to reduce interest rates and stimulates spending with borrowed money, increases total spending, and boosts the level of production in the country. As production rises, unemployed workers return to the work force.

THE FED'S SEVEN KEY ROLES

1. **A bank for bankers.** If a local bank wants to lend money to its customers, it may have to borrow from its own bank, the Fed. The interest rate the Fed charges its member banks is called the discount rate.

2. **An auditor.** The Fed regularly examines every member bank's records to make certain all regulations are being followed.

3. **Controller of the money supply.** The Fed buys and sells Treasuries through its open market operations in order to maintain a balance between money and goods.

4. **Currency comptroller.** When coins and paper money become worn or damaged, the Fed removes them from circulation and orders the Treasury to replace them with new currency.

5. **The government's bank.** The U.S. Treasury has its account with the Fed. The Federal Reserve issues saving bonds and Treasury bills, notes, and bonds for the government. It also releases money so the government can pay its bills, such as Social Security and interest on Treasury securities.

6. **A clearinghouse.** The Fed serves as the nation's check-clearing system.

7. **Storer of gold.** The gold vault at the Federal Reserve Bank of New York contains the largest accumulation of gold in the world. The gold belongs to many noncommunist countries, including the United States.

MARKET MOVER TIPS

- The appointment and reappointment of the Fed's chairman and vice chairman are as important to future monetary policy as the election of the president of the United States. Economists watch these events carefully to decide if any new policy directions may result. When you read of a new appointment or reappointment, be sure to read the commentary by economists and analysts. For example, if Alan Greenspan had not been reappointed in July 1991, the market would have fallen. Greenspan is known as a strong proponent of fighting inflation, and failure to reappoint him would have sent a negative signal to the financial community. (See chapter 37, "Chairman of the Federal Reserve.")

- Even without any alterations in the Fed's board, economists often write about the Fed's shifts in philosophy in response to changing economic conditions such as recessions or lower inflation. Keep abreast of these discussions and focus on the main concerns of the Fed's board members. Their concerns are your concerns.

- If you read in the "currency markets" section of the financial press, that the DOLLAR is falling and the Fed is intervening to slow its fall, this means the Fed wants the dollar to stabilize. A lower dollar makes the cost of American exports cheaper to foreigners. U.S. corporations that rely heavily on exports will thrive with a lower dollar. It's a good time to invest in multinational corporations.

DID YOU KNOW THAT?

In 1914 a great controversy raged over the prospective locations of the twelve Federal Reserve banks. In January the secretary of the treasury and the secretary of agriculture traveled back and forth across the country, listening to local leaders testify in favor of their cities. Sioux City, Iowa; Springfield, Massachusetts; and other small towns did not really expect to be selected. But when Baltimore was passed over in favor of Richmond, a mass protest was held. On April 15 thousands of financial, business, and civic leaders crowded into the Lyric Theater to hear Baltimore's mayor and the governor of Maryland vigorously denounce the board's decision. Their words fell on deaf ears in Washington.

CHAPTER 20

Open Market Operations

■ ■ ■

Federal Reserve purchases and sales of government securities—Treasuries—in order to raise and lower short-term interest rates are open market operations.

It is the responsibility of the Federal Reserve to respond to stresses in our money system and to keep the economy stable. If the prices of goods and services rise and the nation faces a high rate of INFLATION, the Fed tackles this problem by trying to reduce the amount of money banks have available for loans. When there's less money in the system, INTEREST RATES rise, causing inflation to decline.

During a recession, when business slows down, the Fed wants to revive the economy by making more money available to the banks. Interest rates will then fall, corporations will be encouraged to borrow and expand their operations, and the economy will pick up. Equally important in this particular scenario is the role of the average American: consumers are more likely to borrow to purchase a new car, a major appliance, or a home when interest rates are low. Encouraging consumer purchases then is a significant means to reviving the economy.

Both these scenarios—inflation and recession—have something in common: they depend on the rise or fall of interest rates. The Fed has several tools at its disposal to raise or lower interest rates. One of these is its open market operations. (The other tools are the reserve requirement and the discount rate, covered in chapter 19, "The Federal Reserve.") The open market operations, however, are the Fed's principal mechanism for directly altering the amount of money in the banking system and, ultimately, the direction of interest rates. This operation involves the purchase and sale of government securities (Treasuries) in the open market in order to increase or decrease the reserves in the banking system.

The open market operations are run by the Federal Open Market Committee (FOMC), which is made up of the seven governors of the Federal Reserve (appointed by the president) and the five Reserve bank presidents, one of whom, the president of the Federal Reserve Bank of New York, is a permanent member. Under the Humphrey-Hawkins Act of 1978, FOMC members must set annual goals for the growth of money and credit that are consistent with the nation's healthy growth. (See chapter 22, "Money Supply.") To do this, the committee meets on a regular basis in Washington, D.C. At these formal meetings the FOMC must vote on a course of action for monetary policy—specifically to tighten or ease the money supply or to stay with the status quo until the next meeting. Their decision is given as a directive to the Federal Reserve Bank of New York for implementation through the bank's open market trading desk; the New York bank buys and sells government securities on behalf of the entire system.

These buy-and-sell transactions are executed with a number of Treasury securities dealers. For example, if the Fed wants to dampen economic growth and inflation, it will tell the New York desk to sell government securities. The securities dealers then draw down their bank accounts to pay the Fed for these securities. This means the dealers are taking huge amounts of money out of commercial banks, reducing the banks' ability to make loans.

When the Fed wants to encourage economic growth, the trading desk in New York will buy securities. The dealers then deposit the funds they receive from the Fed into their bank accounts; the commercial banks gain reserves and their ability to lend is expanded.

The size of transactions involved helps to appreciate the significance of open market operations. On a daily basis, trading in U.S. Treasury securities exceeds $80 billion. The open market operations has a profound impact on the money supply—and our lives.

HOW THE FED PUMPS MONEY INTO THE ECONOMY

To loosen the money supply, the Fed will order an open market purchase, which sets the following sequence of events in motion:

1. The FOMC orders the Federal Reserve Bank of New York to purchase government securities. The Fed buys $12 million in Treasury bills from a securities dealer. It pays for them with a Federal Reserve check.
2. The securities dealer deposits the Fed's $12 million check in his commercial bank. The deposit is added to the dealer's account.
3. The dealer's bank puts 12% of the $12 million (or $1.44 million), the reserve amount required by the Fed, into its Federal Reserve account. The bank loans the rest of the funds—$10.56 million—to the ABC Corporation.
4. The ABC Corporation now has $10.56 million in its account at Bank B. In essence, $10.56 million has been added to the money supply.
5. The ABC Corporation buys $10.56 million worth of equipment from the XYZ Corporation. The XYZ Corporation deposits the $10.56 million in Bank C, where it has its account.
6. Bank C deposits 12% of $10.56 million (or $1.27 million) in

its Federal Reserve bank, as required, and lends the rest to other customers, increasing the money supply by an additional $9.29 million. At this point the total money supply has been increased by $19.85 million ($10.56 + 9.29).

7. This process of lending money and depositing 12% in the Federal Reserve banks continues until all of the Fed's original $12 million has been put into bank reserves. At that point the money supply has been expanded by approximately $100 million.

It's necessary to add a precautionary note: The above-mentioned scenario assumes that all banks will loan their excess funds. This is not always the case, which is one of the reasons why the Fed can not always achieve its goals with absolute accuracy. During bad times banks may choose to hold on to excess reserves rather than enter a risky loan market. Therefore, it is easier for the Fed to tighten the money supply than loosen it.

Although open market operations do change the money supply, the most immediate effect is felt in the FEDERAL FUNDS rate, the rate commercial banks charge one another for temporary—usually overnight—loans. This basic rate affects all other short-term rates, such as the prime rate, CDs, and Treasury bills. (See chapter 21, "Federal Funds," and chapter 17, "Interest Rates.") Although the Fed funds rate is set by individual banks, it is responsive to the market—and the Fed influences the market. Through its open market operations, the Fed essentially controls the Fed funds rate. When the Fed loosens the money supply, large amounts of money are injected into the banking system, and the Fed funds rate is lowered since there's less need for commercial banks to borrow from each other.

The Fed funds rate affects *all short-term* interest rates. Long-term rates are to a great extent beyond the Fed's control. The long-term market is influenced by considerations other than the Fed funds rate. Investors in this long-term market focus instead on the assumed inflation rate; intermediate- and long-term interest rates in overseas markets, especially Britain, Germany, and Japan; and the outlook for the U.S. economy. (The difference between short-term and long-term interest rates can be graphically seen in chapter 18, "Yield Curve.")

MARKET MOVER TIPS

■ The most visible sign of the Fed's open market operations is in the Fed funds rate. (See chapter 21, "Federal Funds," for additional market mover tips.) The initial results of a change in open market operations will be a higher or lower Fed funds rate and, subsequently, higher or lower short-term rates.

■ During a BUSINESS CYCLE contraction or recession, open market operations will lower short-term rates as much as possible without fueling inflation. At this time purchase solid growth stocks and lock in yields on CDs, bonds, and Treasury notes and bonds before rates fall further.

■ During a business cycle expansion or peak, open market operations will raise short-term rates to restrain the expansion and reduce the severity of any ensuing contraction. Sell cyclical stocks and switch to short-term Treasury bills and notes, and CDs. Or park cash in a money market fund. Interest rates will be going higher, and you want liquidity to purchase fixed-term securities as rates climb.

DID YOU KNOW THAT?

Some historians have blamed the Federal Reserve for the stock market crash of 1929. The market began its roller-coaster ride leading up to the crash after August 1927, when the Fed cut the discount rate to 3½%. It did this to assist Britain, Germany, and France, which were in dire financial straits. The lowered rate also made money available for stock purchases. Investment bankers then floated huge numbers of securities, many of which remained unsold to the public despite the lower rates. There were those who blamed Winston Churchill, who, as Britain's chancellor of the exchequer, held gold at the inflated price of $4.86 a pound, which led to the British general strike. This in turn prompted the Fed to drop U.S. rates. President Calvin Coolidge comes in for his share of blame, too. In January 1928, with brokers' loans at $4½ billion and Wall Street running scared, he seemed to encourage the bull market when he said: "The business of America is business. This is only a natural expansion of business . . . nothing to worry about."

CHAPTER 21

Federal Funds

■ ■ ■

Federal funds (or Fed funds) are the funds Federal Reserve System member banks keep on deposit at the Fed to meet their reserve requirements.

The FEDERAL RESERVE requires member banks to keep cash reserves on deposit at their district Federal Reserve bank. These funds are known as Federal funds. A bank's reserve account is similar to an individual's checking account: the bank makes deposits to it and transfers funds out of it. But unlike an individual the commercial bank cannot allow the balance to fall to zero. Instead, it must maintain a minimum average balance: a percentage of the total it has on hand and has committed as loans. The exact amount depends on the size of the bank's deposits and the Federal Reserve's requirements at the time. (See chapter 19, "The Federal Reserve.") The Fed can and does change these requirements.

Banks do not earn interest on these reserve deposits. Therefore, there's an incentive for commercial banks to try to loan any excess monies to banks that have a temporary need for additional currency to meet the reserves. This need for additional reserves on the part of individual banks may arise when a large borrower is slow in repaying a bank loan or when the rate of deposit withdrawals and transfers turns out to be greater than anticipated. Most Fed funds loans are short term—usually overnight, although longer loans, known as term loans, do exist. The interest rate the lending bank earns is called the Fed funds rate.

The Fed funds rate fluctuates daily depending upon business and market conditions. When business is booming and individual banks are scrambling for additional money to lend to customers, the Fed funds rate will rise. Conversely, during a recession the rate will fall, and the Fed will try to stimulate the economy by lowering rates to encourage borrowing. (See chapter 20, "Open Market Operations.")

HOW IT'S REPORTED

The Federal funds rate is reported in the financial newspapers on a regular basis. Unless it has changed substantially, it is usually listed along with other INTEREST RATES, such as the T-bill rate, the discount rate, and the prime rate. However, significant changes in the Fed funds rate are reported in greater depth.

Barron's regularly reports the Fed funds rate on overnight loans as a "benchmark for other money market rates." On March 1, 1991, *Barron's* reported the week's closing Fed funds rate at 6.26%, down from 8.25% a year before. In lockstep with Fed funds, other rates had also fallen:

Thirteen-week Treasury bills	6.19%	vs.	7.72%
Jumbo bank CDs ($100,000+)	6.35%	vs.	7.74%
Prime rate	8.88%	vs.	10.00%

The Wall Street Journal and other papers also report the Fed funds rate.

In March 1991 the Federal Reserve began a serious effort to lower interest rates and encourage banks to lend and consumers to borrow in an effort to stimulate the American economy and end the recession that had begun in mid-1990. Although lower rates should ultimately be good for the economy and the stock market, they nevertheless hurt investors who rely on income from high-yielding CDs and money market funds. The actions of the Federal Reserve at this time were reported in all of the major newspapers.

MARKET MOVER TIPS

■ Investors should check the Fed funds rate each week. Those who invest in CDs, bank money market accounts, and other short-term investments are most affected since the Fed funds rate is the basic rate from which other money rates are determined. Banks generally set their CD rates based on their perception of what the Fed funds rate will be in the future. For example, a bank will sell a three-month CD at 8.25% when it can borrow in the Fed fund market at 7.5%. The bank has calculated that the Fed funds rate will not rise above 8.25% in the next three months. When the Fed funds rate rises or falls, you can expect rates on CDs, bank money market accounts, and other short-term loans to do the same.

■ When the Fed funds rate rises by a quarter percentage point, delay rolling over your CDs. Rates are on their way up and you will get a higher rate by waiting.

■ When Fed funds are rising, you can expect all other interest rates to follow. Stagger CD maturity dates to capture rising rates.

■ When rates even out, lock in high yields.

■ When Fed funds are dropping, begin paperwork to buy real estate or refinance an existing mortgage, because mortgage rates will be coming down.

■ When Fed funds are falling, the Fed is earning money, and this will help both the prices of growth stocks and older, high-coupon investment-grade bonds.

DID YOU KNOW THAT?

In the nineteenth century, before the Federal Reserve was put into place, "wildcat" banks fudged about their cash reserves. At that time banks were required to keep precious metals on hand to redeem notes held by customers. Honest bankers often placed their gold and silver reserves in vaults in plain view, but others threw a layer of coins on top of a pile of nails, fooling the public and bank examiners into thinking they had more reserves than was the case. These dishonest banks were called wildcats because they were located in the woods, miles from civilization, where wildcats would feel safe sitting on their doorstep!

CHAPTER 22

Money Supply

■ ■ ■

The total stock of money in the economy, primarily currency in circulation and deposits in savings and checking accounts, makes up the money supply.

Money and where it comes from is a bewildering topic for many people. Perhaps the most common belief is that money is created by the Treasury using its printing presses to produce as much currency as the country needs and uses. This is a mistaken impression; paper currency and coins make up only about one-quarter of the total money supply. The U.S. Treasury prints only enough paper money to accommodate the public's need for everyday cash. The balance—about three-quarters of the total—is not backed by paper currency and is "created" when banks make loans.

Every time a bank makes a loan to a business so it can meet a payroll or buy new equipment, the money supply is increased. Consumer loans contribute an even larger portion of the total money supply. In each case, when a business or a consumer takes out a loan, the Treasury does *not* print an equivalent amount of hard cash. The bank, however, does extend a credit to the borrower in the form of an account against which the borrower can make payments. Thus the creation of money is really the creation of bank loans that go into checking accounts; the banking industry calls these checking accounts "demand deposits."

In essence the banks and the FEDERAL RESERVE operate on a good-faith system, requiring the banks to keep in the Federal Reserve a percentage of their total deposits, and the Federal Reserve to keep on hand the amount of currency that is needed for everyday transactions. When commercial banks find that they have more cash than they need to meet reserve requirements and everyday demand, they are free to use this money to make loans, extend credit, and further increase the money supply.

Before America gained its independence, the British did not allow the colonists to issue money. The colonists were forced to operate their economy on a barter system. In 1652 Massachusetts defied the crown's rule against minting money in the New World and began striking the pine tree shilling. Although the British closed down the Boston Mint in 1686, the colonists didn't give in, and over the next decades they continued to mint a variety of coins.

Once America was free of British rule, state-chartered banks began issuing notes (paper money). Most banks designed their own notes, and by the 1860s an estimated eight thousand banks were circulating a variety of notes. However, not all state bank notes were accepted in all parts of the country, causing people to generally distrust paper money unless it was backed by precious metals. Addressing this distrust, the U.S. Treasury issued greenbacks, redeemable in gold or silver, to finance the Civil War. In 1900 the United States officially went on the gold standard, and until 1933 the American dollar was redeemable in gold at the U.S. Treasury. A limited gold standard remained in effect until 1971 when President Nixon ended the convertibility of dollars into gold. By that time our gold reserves were not sufficient to meet the legal requirement of backing up currency at 25%. Since this limited backup did not allow people to exchange their dollars for a 100% value in gold, it meant that gold reserves truly had little significance anyway. The gold reserve was dropped entirely.

WHAT IT COVERS

Money supply refers to the total amount of money in the economy, made up primarily of currency in circulation and deposits in savings and checking accounts. Ann-Marie Meulendyke, manager and senior economist with the Federal Reserve Bank of New York, contrasts the textbook definition of money as "a medium of exchange, a standard of value, a standard of deferred payments, and a store of wealth" with her own: "The actual financial instruments that exist in the United States." Meulendyke noted that the second definition "omits items that have most of the characteristics of money and are often better stores of value."

Our money supply falls into three official categories: M-1, M-2, and M-3.

M-1 consists of the following:

Currency in circulation
Commercial bank demand deposits
NOW and ATS (automatic transfer from savings) accounts
Credit union share drafts
Savings bank demand deposits
Nonbank traveler's checks (*e.g.*, American Express)

M-2 consists of M-1 plus these:

Overnight repurchase agreements issued by commercial
 banks
Overnight Eurodollars
Savings account deposits
Money market deposit accounts

Money market mutual fund shares
Time deposits under $100,000 (*e.g.*, smaller CDs)

M-3 consists of M-2 and these items:

Large time-deposits or jumbo CDs of $100,000 and more
Term repurchase agreements (longer than overnight)
Term Eurodollars (longer than overnight)
Money market mutual funds held by institutions and not by
  individuals

(*Note:* The definition of money supply is occasionally altered to reflect new financial instruments.)

WHAT'S NOT COVERED

Money supply does not include stocks, corporate and municipal bonds, life insurance, real estate, collectibles, and other tangible goods.

HOW IT'S REPORTED

Total money supply figures are issued weekly by the Federal Reserve. They are based on data from a number of sources, including commercial banks, money market mutual funds, the U.S. Department of the Treasury, and Federal Reserve surveys. These figures are reported in newspapers, providing the total in billions of dollars and in percentage amounts as the annual growth rate. For example, in July 1991 the money supply was reported in *The New York Times:*

Table 6A ■ Money Supply					
	One Week Ended		Annual Growth Rate		
	July 1	June 24	3 mos.	6 mos.	12 mos.
M-1	862.1	858.6	7.4%	6.7%	5.2%
M-2	3396.5	3396.5	4.6	4.1	3.3
M-3	4152.3	4161.4	1.8	2.9	2.1

WHY IT'S IMPORTANT

The Federal Reserve uses money supply figures to decide whether to stimulate or limit the economy's growth. Under the Humphrey-Hawkins Act (aka the Full Employment and Balanced Growth Act of 1978), the Federal Reserve reports its annual MONEY SUPPLY targets to Congress twice a year. The targets are given as a percentage—for example, 4% to 7% annual growth. It is the responsibility of the Federal Reserve to set a targeted growth rate that keeps the balance between goods and services and the money supply.

Our money supply, then, has little to do with the Treasury cranking out dollar bills. Instead, it's expanded through an official monetary policy that limits or increases deposits in commercial banks. The Fed manages the money supply by raising or lowering the reserves that banks are required to maintain; changing the discount rate, the rate at which banks can borrow money from the Fed; and using its open market operations, trading government securities, either to take money out of the banking system or put it in. (These three actions are described in detail in chapter 19, under "The Federal Reserve"; chapter 17, "Interest Rates"; and chapter 20, "Open Market Operations.")

When the Federal Reserve fails to meet its money supply targets, it will take steps to redress the situation. These actions—to lower or raise short-term INTEREST RATES—are directed against an imbalance in the money supply, which causes INFLATION, recession, and unhealthy economic growth. These tangible actions are market movers whose roots are embedded in the rise or fall of money supply.

MARKET MOVER TIPS

■ If the growth of money supply falls below the range the Fed has targeted for the year, expect the Fed to lower short-term interest rates in order to encourage borrowing—and increase the money supply. (See chapter 17, "Interest Rates," for specific investment choices.)

■ Conversely, if the money supply growth rate is higher than the Fed's annual target, the Fed will raise short-term interest rates to curb excessive growth.

DID YOU KNOW THAT?

Theatrical people have unique ways of managing their personal money supply. Billy Rose's approach: "Never invest your money in anything that eats or needs repairing." The actor George Raft, who had an estimated $10 million, summarized his method: "Part of the loot went for gambling, part for horses and part for women. The rest I spent foolishly."

CHAPTER 23

Inflation

■ ■ ■

Inflation is a sustained rise in the prices of most goods and services.

The cost of goods and services has been a major concern of Americans since the founding of the country. In 1791 food and other staples more than tripled in price as both the states and the Continental Congress issued bills of credit that quickly became worthless. Many honest people were unable to pay their debts. Speculators tried to control the market by purchasing available goods before they reached the sellers. In some states these monopolizers, as they were called, were fined and imprisoned. In a desperate effort to control inflation and help its citizens, Congress resorted to fixing both the price of labor and goods as well as requisitioning commodities, including corn, flour, beef, pork, and hay.

The Continental Congress succeeded in checking inflation, but only temporarily. Inflation has continued to be a major part of our economic fiber, troubling the rich as well as the poor. The billionaire Howard Hughes, who could well afford the price of just about anything, was fond of saying, ''A million dollars is not what it used to be." Nelson Baker Hunt, who, along with his brother, almost cornered the market in silver in 1980, updated Hughes's impression of inflation by noting that "a *billion* dollars isn't what it used to be." W. C. Fields, known for enjoying a martini or two, kept track of inflation in a more personal way: "The cost of living has gone up another dollar a quart." As we go to press, inflation is running at an annual rate of approximately 4%, and economists are now referring to inflation as "too much money chasing too few goods."

Since the mid-1960s inflation has pushed up prices over 300%. It has been a steady upward spiral, although in 1986 the consumer cost-of-living index actually fell, primarily due to a drop in oil prices. One of the reasons for high inflation in modern times is the growth of the service sector in the twentieth century. Productivity gains, which dampen inflation, are less substantial in the service sector than in the production of goods.

WHAT IT COVERS

Inflation comes in two flavors: *demand-pull inflation,* in which the demand for goods and services pushes up prices; and *cost-push inflation,* in which the cost of producing goods and services forces manufacturers and others to increase their prices in order to make a profit. In both cases, *the cause is the availability of too much money*.

There are several official measurements of inflation, which you can read about in separate entries: chapter 9, "Consumer Price Index"; chapter 1, "Gross Domestic Product"; and chapter 6, "Producer Price Index."

The general level of prices that is mentioned in the press as inflation covers a combination of different goods and services. At the top of the list for most people are food prices, which are affected by weather conditions that reduce crop production and raise prices— you've probably noticed this happening with orange juice. But even after the adverse weather conditions return to normal, orange juice is often sold at the new, higher prices—that's inflation. Specifically, this principle is called the "ratchet tendency," which means that prices (and wages) go up, but rarely come down.

Other prices remain steady for long periods of time and then move up all at once, also creating inflation. This tends to be the case with telephone and electric utility costs. Rates remain fixed for years until the companies providing these services apply to their regulatory authorities for a rate increase. If the rate increase is granted, rates for these services will rise and stay at the new levels.

Energy is also a critical element of inflation. If oil is supplied to the American market at fifteen dollars per barrel and then moves up to eighteen dollars per barrel, the additional three dollars works its way out of our pocketbooks, showing up in what we pay for gasoline at the pump and for heating oil. These increases will also be reflected in the CONSUMER PRICE INDEX.

SOURCES OF MONEY

The money fueling inflation comes from two sources: the government and commercial banks. When consumers can easily borrow money, they will increase their spending on automobiles, furniture, clothing, travel, entertainment—just about everything. Businesses borrow to keep up with consumer demand, building new factories and plants and buying new equipment. All this spending, which originated with bank loans, causes inflation.

Consumers aren't the only ones pushing up prices. One of the major spenders in this country is the government. State and local governments provide education and roads as well as administration of courts, police, waste collection, and so forth. The federal government provides national defense, foreign aid, educational and mortgage loan programs—not to mention the costly guarantees of deposits at banks and savings and loan associations if these become insolvent.

DEMAND VERSUS CAPACITY

It's easy to see how credit-happy consumers, businesses anxious to meet demand, and bureaucratic governments spend and take on more debt, pushing our economy's capacity to its limit and causing inflation. *Inflation occurs when demand or spending exceeds the capacity of the economy to produce*. This lack of capacity to produce enough to meet demand is intensified when a strike or walkout takes place, when crops fail, or when war and energy shortages infiltrate the system.

Two factors that contribute to sustained price increases are a too rapidly growing MONEY SUPPLY and low INTEREST RATES. New money, which supports higher prices, is created when banks make loans and investments. As noted earlier, contrary to popular belief, it is not created by the U.S. Treasury printing money, but by the FEDERAL RESERVE's control over the money supply. Briefly, the Fed controls short-term interest rates and the amount of excess cash reserves banks hold. Low interest rates, of course, encourage borrowing, and a bank with excess funds on hand will try to loan out these funds in order to earn interest. When a borrower takes out a loan and the money is credited to his account at the bank, new money is created. (The ability or willingness on the part of our banks to create new money by making loans is explained in chapter 19, "The Federal Reserve," and chapter 20, "Open Market Operations.")

When the state, local, or federal government spends more than they collect in taxes, they make up the difference by selling securities—primarily municipal bonds (for state and local governments) and U.S. Treasury bills, notes, and bonds (on the part of the federal government). These bonds are in effect loans to the government, just like consumer or corporate loans, and they, too, create money. These loans and their subsequent creation of money for the government stimulate demand, increase production, and boost employment. When employment and production levels are high, demand for goods and services grows even more. The result? Inflation.

Armed with borrowed money, consumers, corporations, and governments compete in the marketplace for available resources. These resources include such diverse basic goods and services as steel to make automobiles, labor to build houses, and energy to light and fuel the society. As the supply of final goods and services is eroded by demand, these basic resources go up in price, CAPACITY UTILIZATION is strained, and factories on overtime further raise costs. Less-skilled workers are pressed into service and the UNIT LABOR COST rises. In this vicious circle workers find that their wages buy less, and to the extent that they are able, they press for higher wages. Many labor contracts have cost of living clauses that automatically raise wages as price levels increase. This, too, adds to the pressure for higher prices.

Another factor that enters into the inflationary process is called "inflationary expectation." If it is perceived that, for example, 5% is the best-guess projection of the future inflation rate, then this rate tends to become part of everyone's expectations. Consumers will buy homes, cars, or antiques now rather than invest their money in long-term thirty-year Treasury bonds. Businesses may follow the policy of expanding capacity at current prices rather than waiting for future demand to give them incentives to expand. In effect, inflation becomes a self-fulfilling prophecy.

HOW IT'S REPORTED

The inflationary numbers reported in the media are derived from the consumer price index's percentage change at an annual rate. See chart 16A.

WHY IT'S IMPORTANT

Inflation affects our personal purchasing power, our ability to compete in world markets, to enjoy life, to take care of the less fortunate, to keep our towns and cities clean and safe. Inflation, in fact, is like

Chart 16A ■ Consumer Price Index (Inflation)
(Year-to-year percent change.)

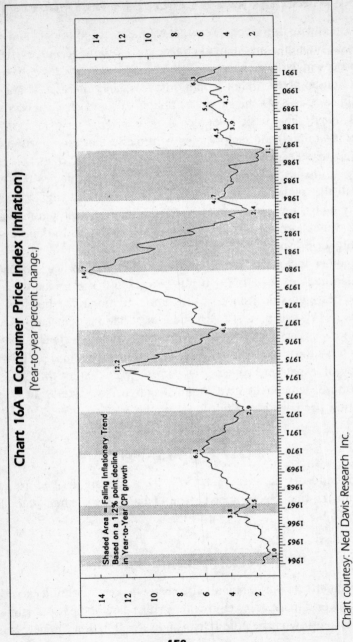

Shaded Area = Falling Inflationary Trend
Based on a 1.2% point decline
in Year-to-Year CPI growth

Chart courtesy: Ned Davis Research Inc.

a tax. Unlike other taxes, which are supposed to be equitable, inflation taxes those least able to pay. If both the family with $10,000 and the family with $100,000 have suffered a 5% loss of buying power because of inflation, the family with $10,000 has suffered a much more serious loss than the one with $100,000. This is why inflation is called "the cruelest of taxes."

A family which earned $15,000 in 1970 would be left with real disposable income of $12,772 at the end of that year. In order for the same family to have that same disposable income in 1980 dollars, they would have had to have earned $30,000 in 1980. (This increase would be due to inflation *and* taxes.)

Inflation impacts business by artificially inflating profits. Business must then pay taxes on these profits and meet labor's demands for higher wages. Inflation also makes it difficult for business to accurately plan for the future or to determine the cost of new or expanded facilities. Sometimes an inflationary environment leads to a break in prices and a recession, which of course makes future projections even more difficult. If business decides not to invest in new facilities, the expansion of the economy may be curtailed, limiting increases in productivity, which are essential for our growing economy.

If government borrowing, due to inflation, becomes large enough, private borrowers such as consumers and corporations may be crowded out of the bond markets, or interest rates charged to the private sector may be driven so high that borrowing becomes difficult or impossible.

WHAT CAN BE DONE?

Inflation, if left unchecked, is a merry-go-round propelled by too much money. It is our government's policy to maintain relatively stable prices, reasonably full employment, and stable, long-term economic growth. There are two principal policy options for achieving these three goals: *monetary policy* and *fiscal policy*.

Monetary policy is mostly carried out by the Federal Reserve, which curbs the excessive growth of credit and dampens private demand for goods and services. It does this, first, by raising the discount rate, the rate of interest paid by lending banks and institutions who are members of the Federal Reserve system, which discourages the banks from borrowing.

The Fed's second tool of monetary policy is the control of the reserve requirements that banks must keep on deposit with the Fed. Lowering reserve requirements enables banks to loan more funds to their customers; raising the reserve requirements restrains their lending capacity.

The third and most important monetary tool of the Fed is its OPEN MARKET OPERATION. Through this, the Fed can tighten the excess funds of banks and other financial institutions.

Fiscal policy—the government's budgetary and taxing controls—is another major weapon the government employs to restrain inflation. The government can raise taxes to reduce disposable income, and lower government spending for public projects to dampen business activity. Yet as we all know, it is pretty difficult to get Congress and the president to agree to cuts in government spending. Nevertheless, changing the tax rates and reducing government spending are ways that Congress and the administration can alter inflation.

MARKET MOVER TIPS

- Will Rogers had perhaps the best market mover tip of all: "Invest in inflation. It's the only thing going up."
- Watch for the classic signs of inflation: a rise in the CPI, a low UNEMPLOYMENT RATE, high capacity utilization, and rising raw material prices. Turn to inflation fighters: hard assets such as precious metals, real estate, and collectibles traditionally keep pace with inflation.
- When inflation rises, the Fed raises interest rates to keep a lid on the cost of living. Most stocks suffer, but not all. Aspirin,

toothpaste, soaps, and medicine continue to be in demand regardless of the status of the economy. Stocks in well-run drug and pharmaceutical companies and food and beverage companies are inflation fighters, as are public utilities and health-care companies.

- In the case of rising inflation, look for stocks in the companies most able to raise prices. A good gauge: how close to capacity an industry is operating. Companies can raise prices more when they can turn out more products.
- As the Fed raises interest rates to control inflation, shift to shorter-term CDs and Treasuries and reinvest in new issues as rates rise.

DID YOU KNOW THAT?

Inflation is often at its worst in wartime. During the Civil War wages fell far behind prices. In real income a worker in the North between 1861 and 1865 lost 35% of his wages. In 1861, at the Philadelphia armory, the government paid a seamstress seventeen cents for making a shirt. Three years later, when prices were at their peak, her wages were cut to fifteen cents.

CHAPTER 24

U.S. Debt and Deflation

■ ■ ■

In every business cycle expansion and peak periods are followed by a period of recession, when consumers and businesses have too much debt. As the recession deepens, prices of many goods and services fall because of lower demand. A severe recession may produce a downward spiral of prices called "deflation."

The United States entered the nineties burdened with debt. We were paying more in interest and dividends to foreigners who owned our Treasuries and corporate stocks and bonds than we were earning from exports and other U.S. investments abroad. In addition, the Treasury was using the bulk of the proceeds from its quarterly sales of T-notes and T-bonds to pay the interest on our government's debt.

By 1992 our total Treasury debt had exceeded $4 trillion and was growing at a rate of over $460 billion per year (or $1.27 billion *per day*). Such numbers seem astronomical to the average person, but economists say this debt level is not worrisome as long as our GROSS DOMESTIC PRODUCT continues to grow. If a deep recession were to occur, however, this debt level could threaten to turn a recession into a depression.

Many economists believe that the amount of our national debt is not serious because we largely owe this debt to ourselves. Herbert Hoover had a similar viewpoint. He said, "Blessed are the young for they shall inherit the national debt." It's true; the debt is largely owed to us: in 1990 our foreign debt equaled only 7.5% of our GDP of $5.465 trillion. The growing burden of interest payments, however, has been forcing Congress to raise taxes, and if taxes are raised during a deep recession, a collapse in prices, resulting in deflation, can follow. Deflation is in many ways as difficult for the Fed, business, and consumers to cope with as inflation. (See chapter 23, "Inflation.")

REAL ESTATE AND THE BANKING SYSTEM

In 1991 the nation's debt woes had not resulted in deflation, but they were mirrored in two specific areas: real estate and banking. As 1991 began, real estate prices in most parts of the country had been dropping for at least a year. Commercial real estate had been particularly hard hit, and many recently constructed shopping malls and office buildings stood empty. Rents on older commercial buildings were held low in order to hang on to tenants.

The owners of individual homes, condominiums, and cooperative apartments who had been enamored with their real estate purchases for decades, suddenly found that their "investments" were difficult if not impossible to sell at anything near the prices reached at the top of the market.

As a result, defaults and late payments on mortgages became everyday events, and major banks throughout the nation were in trouble because of defaults on their loans on commercial real estate and home-owner mortgages. Many banks had also financed risky corporate takeovers by giving highly leveraged loans. These loans, too, turned sour and added to the banking system's woes. These poor loans were a key factor in the savings and loan disaster.

FEDERAL POLICY

In any previous era—right up to the end of World War II—the state of affairs that existed in 1991 might have set the stage for a full-scale recession and/or depression accompanied by massive unemployment and a general financial collapse. Throughout 1991 and 1992, however, the FEDERAL RESERVE lowered the discount rate, lowered the FED FUNDS rate, and generally encouraged banks to make loans. Although the recession continued, a full-scale disaster was prevented.

WHY IT'S IMPORTANT

The Federal Reserve's position of lowering INTEREST RATES and thus encouraging banks to extend credit averted the 1990–91 recession from turning into deflation. Under these circumstances, if the Fed had not taken such steps and if the high debt levels triggered deflation, several disastrous events would have followed:

- a total collapse of commercial real estate prices
- the end of all nonessential purchases of goods and services, followed by a severe drop in prices
- the selling of stocks, bonds, and mutual funds by frightened investors to raise cash, resulting in chaos and a declining market
- widespread unemployment, reaching 10% and climbing higher

Recognizing when America's debt is too high, when deflation has crept into the economy, is critical in making personal and business financial decisions. Debt can eat away at earnings, soak up savings, and generally be unproductive. Heavy debt as well as deflation manages to destroy wealth. We have seen such destruction in the real estate market, in banks and their stocks, in insurance companies and their stocks. Deflation and debt also create a general feeling of fear that the nation is not on a sound economic footing. To gauge whether our national debt level is too high, the individual must pay attention to reports in the press regarding economists' and the government's concerns about this issue.

We also feel debt in our communities. In 1992 many states and cities throughout the nation continued to suffer from high debt levels and lower tax revenues. Many were forced to cut back employment and restrict necessary services because of their budget restraints.

MARKET MOVER TIPS

- Watch the Congress and the administration to gauge if truly effective measures are being taken to control America's annual budget deficit. If they are not, then expect interest rates to continue at 7% to 8% or higher for long-term Treasury bonds. Bond rates would periodically rise toward 9%; and when this happens, be sure to lock in yields.

- Watch the financial conditions of major states and cities to see if they're getting their budgets under control. If the state in which you live and whose tax-exempt bonds you buy does not have a credit rating of AA or AAA, then confine your municipal bond purchases to insured bonds.

- Commercial real estate will remain in a slump for the foreseeable future as it suffers from its binge of overbuilding. Avoid real estate investment trusts (REITs) except for those that you or your broker know are solid, such as some of the health-care REITs.

- Quality bond investments—Treasuries and corporates—will be good long-term portfolio additions in the nineties because INFLATION, which has eroded their values in the past, will be far less of a problem in the near future.

DID YOU KNOW THAT?

Our national debt dates back to Colonial times. The United States had borrowed heavily to finance the Revolutionary War, and by the time Alexander Hamilton became our first secretary of the treasury, the country was approximately $79 million in debt: $12 million was owed to foreigners; the federal government's domestic public debt accounted for about $42 million; and the various state governments owed another $25 million. Hamilton crafted a fiscal policy by proposing that all of these debts be combined and paid off by the federal government by issuing bonds paying 6%. His aim was to make the United States the best credit risk in the world. He also proposed setting up a new national bank patterned after the Bank of England. He faced strong opposition from Thomas Jefferson and Aaron Burr on both counts. They felt federal concentration of power was dangerous and favored giving the bulk of power to the individual states. Nevertheless, most of Hamilton's extraordinary monetary plan was adopted, with modifications, by the Congress in the early 1790s.

CHAPTER 25

Credit Crunch

■ ■ ■

A significant reduction of bank lending and the rationing of loans to businesses is called a credit crunch.

Credit crunches happen most often during recessions but may be brought on by other factors. In the fall of 1990, following the invasion of Kuwait by Iraq, there was serious concern among analysts and economists that America would suffer a severe credit crunch. Banks had been badly shaken by the collapse of junk bonds—those troublesome, highly leveraged transactions that the banks themselves had made to help finance corporate takeovers and leveraged buyouts (LBOs). In addition, many banks had made large loans to real estate developers only to see their real estate collateral drop so sharply as to be almost unsalable. Subsequently, many S&Ls and some banks were forced to close or were taken over under the supervision of banking regulators. The Fed averted a severe credit crunch by lowering short-term INTEREST RATES, which in turn encouraged banks to make loans.

Credit crunches of a recent vintage occurred in 1966, 1969–70, 1973–74, and 1978–81. Most were brought on by a banking regulation that put a ceiling on the interest rates that banks could pay depositors. Not surprisingly, depositors put their money where rates were higher—primarily money market accounts. This loss of bank deposits is called disintermediation, because banks are supposed to intermediate between depositors and borrowers. When banks lose this function through disintermediation, they are forced to slow down their lending operations and ration their loans.

POSTDEREGULATION CREDIT CRUNCHES

Since the deregulation of financial institutions in the early eighties, banks and S&Ls are no longer constrained by ceilings on the interest rates they can pay their depositors. Thus ended disintermediation as a cause of credit crunches, but it led to other problems, primarily the granting of risky loans.

Free to pay market rates for deposits, banks began to compete with each other and with other financial institutions for money. As a result, a large number of risky loans were made by a great many banks that should have known better. By the end of the eighties, there were so many dubious loans that it became apparent that highly leveraged transactions, junk bonds, and poor commercial real-estate loans had landed our banking system in serious trouble.

The seeds of a credit crunch were sown during this period because when the loan portfolio of a bank carries a high number of risky or bad loans, the bank is forced to slow down the number of loans it makes and grant them to only the most creditworthy customers. All other loans are put on hold or *rationed* out in order to build cash reserves to cover future loan losses.

The current low rate of inflation is another factor behind the credit crunch since real estate is not appreciating in value as much as it did in the late seventies and early eighties. Mortgages are more risky, and in many cases real estate is now worth less than the size of the loan issued a few years earlier.

At various times in the past, credit crunches have also been brought on by the Fed itself, when, in an effort to control INFLATION, it has discouraged banks from making loans by using its OPEN MARKET OPERATIONS to raise short-term interest rates.

CREDIT COMMITMENTS

A popular solution to the ill effects of loan rationing brought on by credit crunches is a type of revolving credit known as credit commitment. A bank credit commitment is an agreement between a bank and a company to which the bank agrees to make a loan at any time it may be needed, up to a specific amount and within a specified time period. Most of these agreements commit the bank for a time period of several years. Donald P. Morgan, an economist at the Federal Reserve Bank of Kansas City, analyzed credit commitments in an article in the September/October 1990 issue of *Economic Review*. Morgan noted that ''in recent years, a growing number of businesses have been able to insulate themselves from rationing with bank credit commitments.''

One might conclude that such broad coverage of credit needs through the use of bank commitments has made credit crunches a thing of the past. Small firms, however, are less likely to be covered by these credit commitments and thus are still subject to loan rationing in a credit crunch period. Furthermore, Morgan noted that ''small businesses are a vital force in the U.S. economy . . . firms with fewer than 500 employees accounted for over half of employment and 45 percent of sales in 1986.'' Moreover, ''In the construction, wholesale trade, and service industries, fully 80 percent of the output originated at small businesses.''

HOW IT'S REPORTED

Bank loan data are provided weekly and monthly by the FEDERAL RESERVE. To the layman these figures do not obviously forecast credit crunches, but the media often reports economists' views on any significant changes. Chart 17A, covering 1987 to 1991, shows how the credit crunch reduced the growth of all outstanding U.S. debt—except that owed by the federal government and the lenders themselves—to less than 4%.

WHY IT'S IMPORTANT

The new banking crisis has created a new breed of cautious bankers who are slowing down the number and size of loans they make to both consumers and corporations. These lenders are increasing the required income levels and demanding larger down payments from home buyers. Corporations, too, must show strong cash-flow statements in order to get loans; banks are also putting dollar limits on the size of corporate loans. The conservative trend in banking is spilling over into insurance companies, who are also making it tougher to get loans. Credit crunches are not just tough on the individuals and businesses who need loans; they dampen economic recoveries because there is less credit available for corporate expansion and consumer spending.

MARKET MOVER TIPS

- At the first sign of a credit crunch, the Fed lowers short-term interest rates to encourage banks to make loans to smaller borrowers. Lock in yields in Treasury bonds, long-term CDs, and AA-rated corporate bonds because rates will fall further.
- Blue-chip growth stocks thrive in a low-interest-rate environment. Buy individual stocks or invest in a blue-chip growth mutual fund.
- At the first sign that the Fed is intervening to ease a credit crunch, buy bank stocks because their cost of borrowing will drop (the Fed will ease short-term rates) and yet the banks will continue to be able to make loans at high rates. Caution: Many banks, including the most well-known and largest, have had their credit ratings lowered because of poor real

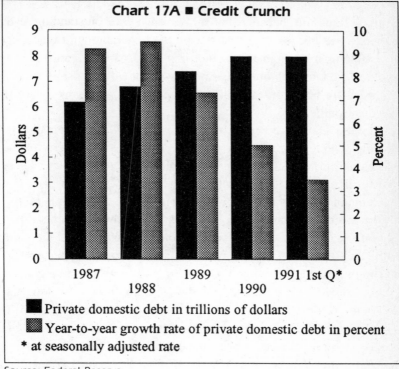

Chart 17A ■ Credit Crunch

■ Private domestic debt in trillions of dollars
■ Year-to-year growth rate of private domestic debt in percent
* at seasonally adjusted rate

Source: Federal Reserve

estate and corporate loans. Select carefully among regional banks that are recommended by *Value Line* or Standard & Poor's.

■ If you're seeking a loan, get it at the start of a credit crunch before loan money dries up and/or be prepared to put up a larger down payment.

DID YOU KNOW THAT?

The biggest credit crunch in the country's history was resolved by a stubborn and prominent investment banker, J. P. Morgan. In 1907 a wave of panic hit Wall Street as investors unloaded $800 million of securities within a short period of time. This started the credit crunch. Bank runs became almost everyday events. Even huge institutions were not immune: the run on the venerable Knickerbocker Trust Company began in the morning of October 22 and by two o'clock the bank ran out of cash and was forced to close its doors. Crippled by bad loans and dishonest practices, the banks were in serious trouble.

Morgan loaned the stock exchange $25 million to prevent its closing. Next, he decided to pressure the leading bankers to join forces and prevent a total financial collapse of the country. These powerful men met at Morgan's New York mansion on Tuesday evening of election day to work out a rescue plan. Apparently, they needed some convincing. Morgan locked the presidents of the nation's leading banks in his private library, refusing to let them out until they agreed to a plan. Only after they agreed to put up $25 million to rescue the ailing bank system and contribute to a general fund to meet further emergencies did Morgan unlock the door and let them go home.

When news of the meeting reached the public the next day, the stock market recovered. When someone criticized Morgan for being so controlling, he replied, "I'm not in Wall Street for my health." Morgan's comment has become an oft-repeated sentiment in investment circles.

CHAPTER 26

Leading Economic Indicators

■ ■ ■

This grouping of key indicators tends to change direction before *the general economy moves from an expansion to a recession, or vice versa.*

Perhaps in no other field is the eternal search for a way to foretell the future more intense than in economics. Because there is no crystal ball, mind-boggling amounts of data are collected, processed, and presented by the U.S. Department of Commerce and by other government agencies. The composite index of leading economic indicators is an effort to select those economic series that tend to change in *advance* of changes in the BUSINESS CYCLE.

WHAT IT COVERS

Components are selected for the leading economic indicators index on the basis of the economic concept that profits are the primary mover in a private enterprise economy. Expansions and recessions are thereby caused by changes in the outlook for profits: when the outlook for profits is favorable, businesses expand production and investment, and when the outlook for profits is negative, businesses retrench. Or as Calvin Coolidge, a president noted for saying very little, remarked to a gathering of esteemed economists: "Business will be better or worse."

However, no single economic statistic is strong enough in its predictive ability to be a reliable harbinger of changes in the business cycle. Consequently, the Department of Commerce uses eleven advance indicators each month to create the index of leading economic indicators. These eleven indicators share two characteristics:

1. Each offers a broad coverage of the economy and is not limited by geographical or industry limitations.
2. Each is available promptly each month and is not subject to large subsequent revisions.

The leading indicators reflect the status of the labor market based on employer hirings and firings; the buildup of orders, contracts, and inventories that impact on future production; the prices of materials that reflect shortages or gluts; the availability of funds in credit markets; and the optimism or pessimism of prices of stocks. The eleven individual components are

1. average weekly hours of manufacturing production workers
2. average weekly initial claims for state unemployment insurance
3. manufacturers' new orders in 1982 dollars for consumer goods and materials industries
4. vendor performance, *i.e.*, the percentage of companies receiving slower deliveries
5. contracts and orders in 1982 dollars for plants and equipment
6. new private housing building permits (aka HOUSING STARTS)
7. change in manufacturers' unfilled orders in 1982 dollars for durable goods industries
8. monthly change in prices of crude and intermediate materials

9.   stock prices of five hundred common stocks
     (1941–43 = 10)
10. MONEY SUPPLY—M2—in 1982 dollars
11. index of consumer expectations (aka consumer confidence
     index; 1966 = 100)

These eleven indicators have indeed shown advance warnings of changes—including recessions—in the economy, as reflected in chart 18A. Nevertheless, the indicators are not perfect. In 1984 and again in 1987, the leading indicators declined although no recession followed. These "false alarms," however, do not impair the basic value of the index as a guide to the future. Chart 18B is a reminder that the leading indicators aren't tea leaves; they cannot predict disasters, such as war. In chart 18B you can clearly see that the indicators had not turned down until after war broke out in the Persian Gulf.

As seen in chart 18B, in August and September of 1992 the leading indicators fell back to back. It was the third decline since March of 1992, and a signal that the economy was still sluggish and the recovery weak. By looking at the breakdown of the components of the index, which are often listed in newspapers, one could see that the largest contributing factors to the decline were lower prices for crude and intermediate materials and a shorter average workweek for production workers in manufacturing. Falling consumer expectations and higher first-time claims for unemployment insurance as well as backlogs in durable goods and lower orders for plants and equipment also caused the leading indicators to fall.

HOW IT'S REPORTED

The leading economic indicators are posted monthly. The statistics are presented in percentage format against a base year, 1982, set equal to 100.

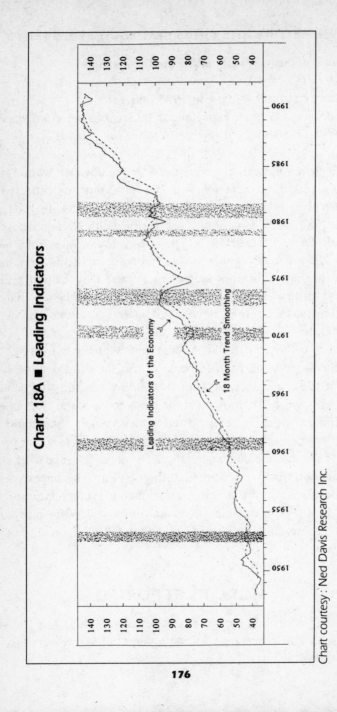

Chart 18A ■ Leading Indicators

Leading Indicators of the Economy

18 Month Trend Smoothing

Chart courtesy: Ned Davis Research Inc.

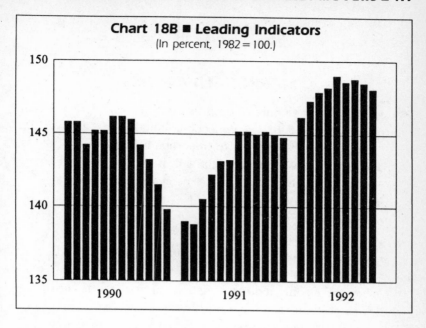

Chart 18B ■ Leading Indicators
(In percent, 1982 = 100.)

WHY IT'S IMPORTANT

On January 31, 1991, *The Wall Street Journal* reported that the leading economic indicators posted a rise in December 1990, offering the "first glimmer of hope in half a year, rising 0.1% in December for its only increase since June." This was cited as "slight" evidence that the recession might be a mild one. But the hopeful signs of the slight pickup in December were dimmed by the January results, reported in the *Journal* on March 4, 1991, which revised the December indicators to a 0.1% decline and posted January's 0.4% decline. From this it was reported that the economic weakness continued, but the downturn was slowing.

Economics is not an exact science, yet the leading economic indicators are valuable in forecasting the direction of the economy. All that is required is some patience until the "bigger picture" is visible. Studying the leading indicators as well as the business cycle and its component economic series provides a far better investment insight than can be obtained without these indicators.

MARKET MOVER TIPS

■ Around the beginning of each month, *The Wall Street Journal* prints a chart of the leading economic indicators. It gives the big picture and alerts you to important changes in the direction of the economy. Clip and use it as a basis of comparison as each of the other economic statistics are reported throughout the month. New evidence of the economy's direction is also revealed by the GDP, CAPACITY UTILIZATION, and other economic data. In general, the leading indicators foretell the economy's direction by three to six months.

■ When the leading indicators flatten out and start to turn down, postpone starting a new business and expect a recession to begin within three to six months. At this time start to switch from cyclical stocks, such as chemicals, autos, and steel producers to recession-resistant industries, such as food and beverage and utilities.

■ Recessions bring lower interest rates, so lock in high yields with seven- to ten-year Treasury notes and A-rated corporate bonds.

DID YOU KNOW THAT?

Some Wall Streeters believe that holidays are as good an indicator of stock market activity as any other data. In 1987 Robert Ariel, a member of the finance faculty at Bernard M. Baruch College in New York, published a study showing that there's about a 75% chance that the market will rise on the last trading day before most major holidays. He was not the first to note the trend. Arthur Merrill, author of *Behavior Prices on Wall Street*, published in 1966, studied stock prices dating back to 1897 and found that the DOW JONES INDUSTRIAL AVERAGE rose on the trading day preceding each of the eight annual holidays an average of 67.9% of the time. The Dow average on all trading days was up only 52.5%. The holidays to watch for are: New Year's Day, Washington's Birthday, Good Friday, Memorial Day, Independence Day, Labor Day, Thanksgiving, and Christmas.

CHAPTER 27

Dow Jones Industrial Average

■ ■ ■

A price-weighted average of thirty actively traded blue-chip stocks, primarily industrials, the Dow average is quoted in points, not dollars.

On April 18, 1991, a *Wall Street Journal* headline proclaimed, "Dow Jones Industrials Crack the 3000 Mark." The *Journal* went on to state, "Nine months after the Dow Jones Industrial Average came within a whisper of closing above 3000, the widely watched market indicator sailed across yesterday with room to spare." The Dow rose 17.58 points to a record 3004.46.

What is the Dow Jones Industrial Average (DJIA), and why has it gained such importance in the financial consciousness of the United States and of the world? Is the Dow Jones Industrial Average itself a market mover, or is it simply a reflection of the changes in stock prices?

The DJIA is the most common, shorthand way of saying whether the "stock market" went up or down in price for a given day, week, month, or year. When you hear on the evening news that "the market went up six points today," it means the Dow Jones Industrial Average rose six points over the previous day. In this sense it is a reflection of the market's movement, but like a poll announced on the day of an election, it can influence the market movement as well. Individual investors watch—and react—to the DJIA, growing concerned when it falls and elated when it rises even when they don't own the individual stocks that are used to calculate the DJIA.

The Dow, the oldest measure of market performance and the most widely quoted of all economic indicators, has been around since the 1880s, when Charles H. Dow, a financial analyst, drew up a list of the average closing prices of eleven stocks for his "Customer's Afternoon Letter," which he sent to his clients. Dow, a conservative New Englander, was born in 1851. He worked on the *Springfield Republican* newspaper before going to New York to seek his fortune. For a while he owned a seat on the New York Stock Exchange. Eventually he and his partner, Eddie Jones, founded the Dow Jones Company, publisher of *The Wall Street Journal*. In 1916 the original list of eleven stocks grew to twenty industrials. In 1928 the average was expanded to the present number of thirty stocks. Today, the editors of the *Journal* decide which stocks in the Dow should be dropped and which ones will replace them.

WHAT IT COVERS

The DJIA covers thirty major companies whose stock is traded on the New York Stock Exchange (NYSE). They are widely held blue-chip companies, primarily in manufacturing but also in mining, communications, finance, retail, and service industries. These thirty stocks account for approximately 25% of the market value of all companies listed on the NYSE. The stocks are averaged arithmetically, based on the price per share of each company; this gives more weight to the movements of those companies with high prices per share than those with low prices per share. The Dow is actually determined by adding up the prices per share of all thirty stocks at the end of a trading day and then dividing by a special divisor. In 1928 this divisor was thirty, but over time some of the companies have split their stocks. When this takes place the divisor is changed. Over the years the divisor has shrunk. In 1986 it fell below 1.0; as of August 1991 it stands at 0.505. If the price per share of the thirty combined stocks adds up to $1,500 at the end of the day, dividing by 0.505 would produce a Dow Jones closing average of 2970.3.

The Dow Jones Industrial Average, the stocks included, and the divisor are listed daily in *The Wall Street Journal*. As of November 1992, the DJIA was comprised of these stocks:

Alcoa	Goodyear Tire
Allied Signal	IBM
American Express	International Paper
AT&T	McDonald's Corporation
Bethlehem Steel	Merck and Company
Boeing	Minnesota Mining & Manufacturing
Caterpillar	J. P. Morgan
Chevron	Philip Morris Companies
Coca Cola	Procter & Gamble
Disney (Walt)	Sears, Roebuck
E. I. DuPont	Texaco
Eastman Kodak	Union Carbide
Exxon Corporation	United Technologies
General Electric	Westinghouse Electric
General Motors	Woolworth

For many years the Dow Jones Industrial Average hovered around 100, peaking at 386 in 1929 just before the Great Crash. After the crash and the Great Depression, it slowly climbed back up, and during World War II it hit a high of 700. It reached 1000 in 1971 and fell back to 570 in 1974. In August 1987 the Dow posted an all-time high of 2722.42, but two months later on October 19, the Dow plunged a record-breaking 508 points to 1738.74. Since that second record-breaking crash, the Dow has moved irregularly to the historic high of 3004.46 on April 18, 1991. (See chart 19A.) By November 1992, the Dow was hovering in the 3200s.

The DJIA is so important to the financial consciousness of the nation that every effort is made to keep it a consistent measuring tool. ''We don't make a habit of fiddling with the makeup of the industrial average, because consistency along with longevity are among its important attributes,'' said Norman Pearlstine, managing editor of *The Wall Street Journal,* on May 3, 1991. Over time, however, changes have had to be made in the component companies. IBM has been put into the Dow, taken out, and then put back in.

Pearlstine was quoted on May 3 upon the occasion of the addition of three stocks—Caterpillar, Disney, and J. P. Morgan—and the removal of Navistar, Primerica, and USX Corporation. The editor went on to point out that the average has always been a dynamic index, not a static artifact, and that over the past sixty-two years more than two dozen stocks had been replaced. The May 1991 change was designed to reflect the growing importance of the service sector in the U.S. economy. J. P. Morgan was the first banking company included in the average, and Disney, with its leading theme parks and TV and movie production, served to reflect the importance of the service area in today's American economy.

WHY IT'S IMPORTANT

The Dow is designed to reflect the broader, underlying price trend of the market as a whole. It is often criticized, however, because a high-priced stock, such as IBM, has a greater influence on the index than a lower-priced one, such as AT&T. Other critics maintain its coverage is too narrow, since it is based on just thirty blue chips and only on NYSE issues. Due in part to these shortcomings, other stock market measurements, reflecting a broader aspect of the market, have become popular. You can, however, use the Dow Jones Industrial Average as a method of tracking long-term ups and downs

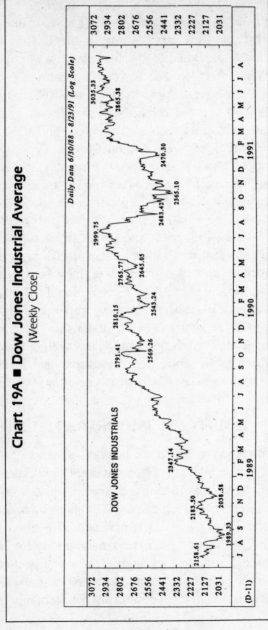

Chart 19A ■ Dow Jones Industrial Average
(Weekly Close)

Daily Data 6/30/88 - 8/23/91 (Log Scale)

DOW JONES INDUSTRIALS

3072		3072
2934	3035.33	2934
2802	2865.38	2802
2676		2676
2556		2556
2441		2441
2332	2470.30	2332
2227	2365.10	2227
2127	2483.42	2127
2031		2031

2999.75

2765.77
2810.15   2645.05

2791.41   2543.24
           2569.26

2347.14

2183.50
              2038.58
2158.61
           1989.33

J A S O N D J F M A M J J A S O N D J F M A M J J A S O N D J F M A M J J A
1989   1990   1991

(D-11)

184

on the market, although it is a more accurate gauge when it's used in conjunction with the S&P 500 and the WILSHIRE 5000.

The Dow itself reacts to many market movers, as chart 19A demonstrates. Note that right after Iraq invaded Kuwait in August 1990, the Dow took a three-month nosedive. Yet, after America entered the war and after President Bush declared an allied victory, the Dow rose steadily, breaking through the illusive 3000 mark on April 17, 1991, as we were welcoming home the first troops from the Gulf War.

MARKET MOVER TIPS

■ Don't be alarmed or misled if the Dow makes a big move either up or down. The shift may be caused by a significant move in a single stock. To ascertain how important the price of an individual component stock is to a given day's change in the average, take the stock's price change for that day and divide it by the divisor. For example, if IBM drops by 3 points on a given day, divide by 0.505. You'll then know that IBM contributed minus 5.94 points to the change in the DJIA for the given day. (For a discussion of the Dow Theory, which is based on the price changes in the Dow Jones average, turn to page 255.)

■ Keep in mind that although the DJIA is the most widely publicized index by the financial media, it still only reflects the movement of thirty stocks. The S&P 500 and the Wilshire 5000 offer a far wider reading of the market.

■ Use the Dow to track long-term ups and downs of the market; try to buy after the Dow has had a severe drop of 4% to 5%.

DID YOU KNOW THAT?

Most of the stocks in Charles Dow's first version of the index were these railroad stocks:

Chicago & North Western
Delaware, Lackawanna & Western
Lake Shore Line
Louisville & Nashville
Missouri Pacific
New York Central

Northern Pacific
Pacific Mail
St. Paul
Union Pacific
Western Union

Then Dow worked toward creating an index consisting of only industrial stocks. He published this list a few years later:

American Cotton
American Sugar
American Tobacco
Chicago Gas
General Electric
Laclede Gas

National Lead
North American
Oil Distilling & Cattle Feeding
Tennessee Coal & Iron
U.S. Leather
U.S. Rubber

CHAPTER 28

Standard & Poor's
500 Stock Index

■ ■ ■

This index measures changes in the stock market based on the average performance of five hundred widely held common stocks.

Standard & Poor's maintains a daily index of stock prices that dates back to 1928. The first index had only ninety issues. The S&P 500 as we know it today was introduced in 1957. Representing approximately 70% of the total market value of American stocks, it is one of the U.S. Commerce Department's leading indicators and is key in forecasting future business conditions.

WHAT IT COVERS

Until 1988 the S&P 500 tracked the price movement of four hundred industrial company stocks, twenty transportation stocks, forty financial company stocks, and forty public utility stocks. Today, however, there is more flexibility in these subdivisions in order to more accurately reflect our increasingly diverse economy. Approximately 61% of the issues are listed on the New York Stock Exchange, another 35% are traded on National Association of

Securities Dealers Automated Quotation System (NASDAQ) over the counter, and the remainder on the American Stock Exchange. Each stock is market-value weighted: the individual stock's closing price on a given day is multiplied by the number of its outstanding shares. The weighting of each stock by the number of shares outstanding provides a realistic measure of value because each stock influences the index in proportion to its importance.

The S&P 500 is presented against the base years of 1941–43, which equal 10. In the prosperous fifties the S&P 500 had an annual average percentage change of +19.4%, steadily moving over the course of the decade from the high teens to 60. During the eighties the S&P 500 increased an average of 17.5% annually, moving from a low around 100 in 1980 to a high of nearly 340 in 1987. On April 17, 1991, when the Dow topped 3000, the S&P 500 also climbed 2.83 to a new high—390.45.

HOW IT'S REPORTED

Committees at Standard & Poor's Corporation, a New York City financial advisory, rating service, and publishing company, select the stocks, adding and removing companies to ensure that the five hundred stocks represent all sectors of the economy and to adjust for mergers, takeovers, bankruptcies, and so on. (Often a stock will jump in price when it's announced that it has been added to the S&P index.) The S&P 500 is reported daily in most newspapers (see chart 20A). Like the DJIA, news reports frequently give a percentage change to give the reader a better perspective on the numbers.

WHY IT'S IMPORTANT

The S&P 500 can be used by individual and institutional investors as a broad measure of the rise and fall of the overall stock market, and also as a yardstick against which to measure the performance

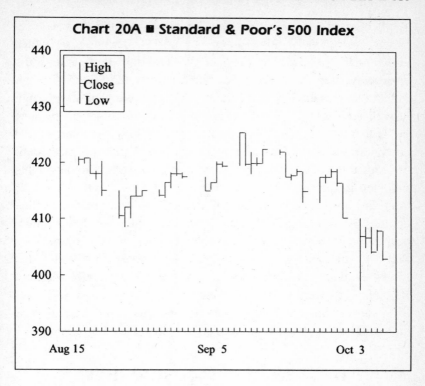

Chart 20A ■ Standard & Poor's 500 Index

of their own (or other) portfolios. The S&P 500 is considered such an accurate measurement of the stock market that the U.S. Department of Commerce uses the S&P 500 as one of its components in its composite index of LEADING ECONOMIC INDICATORS.

THE DOW VERSUS THE S&P 500

The DOW JONES INDUSTRIAL AVERAGE may be the oldest measure of the stock market, dating back to the 1880s, but it is no longer considered by most to be the most accurate indicator of the total economy. The average is arrived at by calculating the per share closing prices of thirty blue-chip stocks. (See chapter 27, "Dow

Jones Industrial Average.'') Thirty stocks, no matter how well selected, are still only thirty stocks in a much wider universe, which is one of the reasons why the S&P 500 measures the market more accurately. Also, the companies that comprise the S&P 500 better reflect our present economy. Small high-tech companies with high growth rates are generously represented, as are some of the new fields that are key to our economic strength, such as biotech and computer software. In addition, the market-weighting method of arriving at the S&P 500 gives a precise measure of the money value involved in the stock market's rise and fall.

During the takeover frenzy of the late eighties, many old-line companies with long-established positions in the Dow Jones Industrial Average were taken over or bought out in leveraged buyouts (LBOs). This sent their stock prices rocketing higher and accounted for a great deal of distortion in the Dow average. General Foods and RJR Nabisco were two such examples. Of course, the S&P 500 loses some companies to takeovers or bankruptcy, but the impact of individual companies is far smaller in a universe of five hundred.

DOW AND S&P 500: HOW THEIR PERFORMANCE DIFFERS

The Dow Industrials are thirty large-capitalization, blue-chip stocks, while the S&P 500 offers a broader measure of the whole market. Over time investor enthusiasm tends to shift from one of these areas to the other and back again. Although the two indexes generally move along the same track, they do diverge when one or the other area of the market gains a greater share of investor enthusiasm. (See chart 20B.) The Dow is always more volatile because it's narrower and may make dramatic highs or lows, which are unconfirmed by the S&P. In these situations investors need to be cautious about reaching conclusions based only on the action of the Dow.

Chart 20B ■ Dow Jones Indices & Standard & Poor's 500 Index

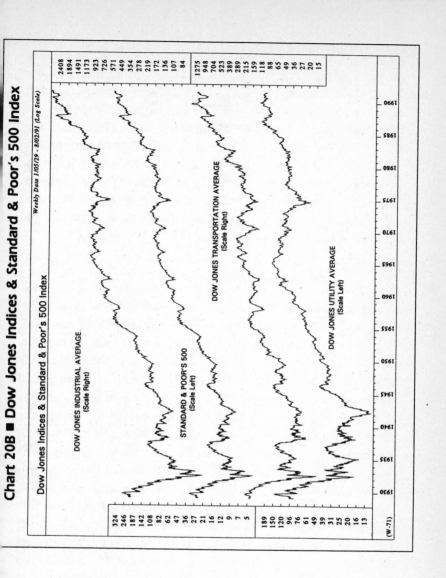

Dow Jones Indices & Standard & Poor's 500 Index

Weekly Data 1/05/29 - 8/02/91 (Log Scale)

DOW JONES INDUSTRIAL AVERAGE.
(Scale Right)

STANDARD & POOR'S 500
(Scale Left)

DOW JONES TRANSPORTATION AVERAGE
(Scale Right)

DOW JONES UTILITY AVERAGE
(Scale Left)

(W-71)

191

INSTITUTIONAL PERFORMANCE AND THE S&P 500

Most institutional investors—pension funds, money managers, mutual fund portfolio managers—measure their individual performance against that of the S&P 500. The index is indeed a formidable competitor and difficult to outperform. According to Lipper Analytical Services, during the five-year period ending December 31, 1988, the average total return of 1,009 equity mutual funds was 68.23%, while that of the stocks listed in the S&P 500 was 102.84%.

OTHER S&P 500 PRODUCTS

Standard & Poor's has licensed several products that track the S&P 500. These include index mutual funds, whose portfolios consist of the same stocks that comprise the S&P index. It would be cumbersome and difficult for an individual investor to replicate the S&P 500, yet it is possible to "buy" this index. An index mutual fund is one whose portfolio matches that of a broad-based index—in this case, the S&P 500—and whose performance simply mirrors the index as a whole. Many institutional investors and professional money managers put money in index funds on the theory that trying to beat the market averages over the long haul is difficult. Investments in these index funds keep pace with the market as a whole.

There are two advantages to index funds: they provide a high degree of performance predictability versus the market as a whole, and they are available at low cost. Index fund expenses are low since management fees and operating costs are low; the fund does not need much management, and its portfolio is seldom turned over.

There are, of course, disadvantages as well. Because the fund is committed to following the stocks in the selected index, this passive approach is not satisfying in a poor market. Even in a flat market, a more actively managed mutual fund may provide better results.

Therefore, index funds are best for those who invest long-term and are prepared to ride out market swings.

MARKET MOVER TIPS

■ Compare the performance of the S&P 500 with that of the Dow before drawing any conclusions about the overall market. The Dow may be making new highs or lows without confirmation by the S&P. In this case the Dow may not be giving a true picture as to what the whole market is signaling.

■ To measure the performance of your own portfolio or the money manager or financial planner who manages it, check it against the S&P 500 every quarter or six months. Your stock mutual fund can also be compared to the index.

■ If the S&P 500 drops 2½% to 3%, it is a buying opportunity for all but the very conservative investor.

DID YOU KNOW THAT?

A sustained rising period in the market is known as a *bull market*, whereas a *bear market* describes a sustained falling market. The most popular theory about the origin of these terms is that bears attack their prey by swinging their paws in a downward motion, while bulls toss their horns upward in attack.

In bear markets stock prices typically fall 30% or more, and the fall lasts anywhere from several months to two years. A small bear market visited Wall Street from the beginning of 1981 until the end of August 1982. The longest bear market was in 1929: it lasted twenty-two months and stock prices declined around 47%.

CHAPTER 29

The Wilshire 5000

■ ■ ■

This index measures the performance of more than six thousand U.S. stocks.

WHAT IT COVERS

Established in 1974 by Wilshire Associates of Santa Monica, California, the Wilshire 5000 Equity Index tracks the total dollar value of more than six thousand stocks—all of the companies listed on the New York Stock Exchange, the American Stock Exchange, and all over-the-counter companies traded on NASDAQ. (The ''5000'' figure is outdated.)

The Wilshire 5000 is a market-value–weighted index; it is designed to represent the total value of all U.S. stocks: 82% New York Stock Exchange, 4% American Stock Exchange, and 14% over-the-counter. Because it is market weighted, price movements of companies with large market values are given more weight than those with small market values.

HOW IT'S REPORTED

On January 13, 1975, *Barron's* became the first journal to publish the Wilshire index. Now the index is carried by the Associated Press wire service and appears daily in *The Wall Street Journal*, *The New York Times*, the *Los Angeles Times*, and the *Washington Post*.

The index reflects the market value based on the capitalized structure of companies as of December 31, 1980, when the total market value was more than $1.4 trillion. At its recent level of 4067.78 (as of November 1, 1992), the index indicates that the entire U.S. stock market is currently worth over $4 trillion. Since December 31, 1980, the total value of all U.S. stocks has increased by 185%, from $1.4 trillion to $4 trillion.

WHY IT'S IMPORTANT

The Wilshire 5000 Equity Index can be used in conjunction with the DJIA and S&P 500 to track the movement of the market or to assess the value of your own portfolio. This index derives its major importance as a market mover because of the all-encompassing nature of its measurement—it is the widest single measure of the movement of stocks.

MARKET MOVER TIPS

- Use the Wilshire 5000 to confirm movements in the S&P 500 and the Dow Jones Industrial Average.
- If the Wilshire keeps dropping for a six-month period (or longer), check to see if the cause is that a large number of companies have been replaced by leveraged buyout debt or were acquired by other companies. If not, expect economic troubles ahead.

DID YOU KNOW THAT?

The stock market sometimes plunges for extremely odd reasons, situations that have nothing to do with the economy. These declines appear as "blips" on the indexes. One such drop, known as the "Ice Water Panic," took place on May 14, 1898, at the two-hour Saturday morning session of the New York Stock Exchange. The day before, Roswell P. Flower, the former governor of New York, left his Wall Street brokerage firm early to spend the weekend at his Long Island country club. That evening he ate a big dinner of ham and raw radishes and drank a lot of ice water—all of which his doctors said led to his fatal heart attack.

News of Flower's death spread during the night, and the next day all the stocks Flower owned—Brooklyn Rapid Transit, Peoples Gas, Rock Island, Federal Steel, New York Air Brake, Atchison, and International Paper—crashed. There was little reason for the stocks' fall because the companies actually lost nothing by Flower's death. Yet, 400,000 shares of Flower's stocks and another 350,000 shares of other companies having no connection with him, were sold at a loss by a nervous public. Many were quickly bought up by savvy brokers for the Vanderbilts, Rockefellers, J. P. Morgan, and other well-to-do Americans. In the end, over $100 million was lost within two hours simply because one man drank too much ice water.

PART V

...

GLOBAL MARKET MOVERS

The age of telecommunications has shrunk the world considerably. We can now find out what's happening on the Tokyo stock market almost as easily as we can get the price of IBM or General Motors stock in our own country. This ease of information gathering means that global market movers—economic happenings taking place in countries other than our own—affect us as well. Key market movers, such as the price of oil and the value of the U.S. dollar here and abroad, affect many other market movers in this section and others. Global market movers include:

Oil prices
Group of Seven
Global stock markets
Balance of trade
Foreign exchange rates
Value of the dollar
Eurodollars

Global market movers can have a tremendous impact on, and are themselves affected by, U.S. INTEREST RATES, INFLATION, and unemployment. Some are monitored closely by the FEDERAL RESERVE, which attempts to intervene for the good of the U.S. economy. Others, like Eurodollars, are largely beyond the control of the Fed. Whether you invest in other countries or multinational companies or are concerned about American foreign policy and the economic, social, and political consequences of America's balance of trade, a global view of market movers is vital to a true understanding of U.S. economics and our financial markets.

CHAPTER 30

Oil Prices

■ ■ ■

World oil prices are the single most important commodity within the whole spectrum of market movers. As J. P. Getty, founder of the Getty Oil Company, was fond of saying, "The meek may inherit the earth—but not its mineral rights." Oil is preeminent because it's far easier to use than any alternative fossil fuel; only nuclear power plants can compete effectively in producing power. Nuclear power, however, has not yet been used for automobiles, and some experts say it never will. Our lone nuclear-powered passenger ship, the *Savannah*, had to be scrapped because people refused to sail on it, although we do have nuclear submarines. The long and the short of it is that oil is cleaner and cheaper than coal and more easily transported than natural gas.

For abundance of supply, ease of transportation, and quick deliverability, we count on oil. Heavily. Since World War II worldwide oil consumption has soared from 10 million barrels per day in 1950 to 65 million barrels per day in 1990. During that same time span there have been a number of oil panics. The consequences of each of these events—from the 1951 nationalization of Iranian oil properties of the British Petroleum Company to the 1979 revolution in Iran and the coming to power of Ayatollah Khomeini—were sharp rises in prices and the redoubling of efforts on the part of the industrial nations of the world to reduce their dependence on oil.

According to the American Petroleum Institute, the American economy presently consumes 1.45 barrels of oil for each thousand dollars of goods and services produced. In 1978 that figure was 2.2 barrels. The three key factors behind the reduction in oil consumption are increased efficiency (for example, the mileage of the car fleet is increasing by 2% to 3% a year), the substitution of natural gas or coal for oil by industries, and slower economic growth throughout the world.

Oil consumption is always reduced during periods of recession: Factories operate at a lower rate; some are even shut down. Air travel is cut back, and business and consumers are more frugal in all of their expenditures. During the first six months of 1991, for example, oil demand in the United States was 4.1% lower than in the same period in 1990. Demand for oil will increase, says the American Petroleum Institute, when the economy grows by at least 3% annually.

Today, to some extent, prices are determined by a cartel, the Organization of Petroleum Exporting Countries, more commonly referred to as OPEC. (A cartel is an agreement, written or unwritten, between producers to fix prices, share markets, or set production levels. Market competition and/or antitrust laws often undermine cartels, as is the case with OPEC.) About 65% of the world's oil reserves are in the Middle East and the Arab countries of the region dominate OPEC. To the extent that the OPEC nations cooperate and do not cheat on their production quotas, they are able to exercise control of world oil prices.

OPEC was established in 1960 to try to coordinate oil production among the leading exporters. Its success as a cartel is questionable.

In 1974, after oil prices quadrupled within just a few weeks, OPEC became a household name, but by 1980 OPEC's success was dependent on Saudi Arabia, the world's largest and dominant producer. Saudi Arabia generally used its influence to hold down production from other producers such as Algeria and Venezuela, thereby keeping oil prices as high as possible.

Not all exporters belong to OPEC. Among those who do not are Norway, Britain, Mexico, and the C.I.S. Because these "outsiders" are major producers, OPEC can not entirely control oil prices. Production from non-OPEC countries reached a high in 1988 at 41.6 million barrels a day. Although two-thirds of current world oil production comes from non-OPEC countries, primarily the U.S. and the Soviet Union, these two countries have only one-fourth of the world's identifiable oil reserves. Most of the rest lies with the current members of OPEC: Saudi Arabia, Iran, Iraq, Kuwait, UAE (United Arab Emirates), Qatar, Venezuela, Nigeria, Indonesia, Algeria, Gabon, and Ecuador.

HOW OIL IS PRICED

Oil is priced in two ways: in the spot market (immediate delivery) and in the futures market (delivery within the coming eighteen months). The two largest oil-trading markets are the New York Mercantile Exchange (Nymex) and the International Petroleum Exchange (IPE) in London. A third and smaller market is the Singapore International Monetary Exchange (Simex). Prior to 1988, London's IPE traded only in large tanker-size lots of 500,000 barrels; this restricted trading in London to the big oil companies that could manipulate and control the market. In 1988 London's IPE introduced a 1,000-barrel trading lot, which allowed small traders to become involved and made the IPE market more responsive to free market fluctuations. Today, so-called "Wall Street Refiners" such as Bankers Trust Company and the Salomon Brothers' subsidiary Phibro are—like Exxon and Chevron—major players in the world oil markets.

When price changes are reported, three types of crude oil are mentioned in the press: Brent North Sea crude oil, which is traded in London; Arabian sweet crude, traded in the United States; and West Texas intermediate, also traded in the United States. Brent's prices are slightly cheaper because the purchaser must bear the additional transportation costs to reach the United States.

WHY IT'S IMPORTANT

To the investor in stocks and bonds or their mutual fund equivalents, the fluctuating prices of crude oil in these world markets is of great importance. When Saddam Hussein's Iraqi army occupied Kuwait on August 2, 1990, the resulting price fluctuations were a dramatic example of this.

As Iraq invaded Kuwait, gasoline prices at the pump immediately rose, causing financial hardship to many Americans and raising the ugly prospect of simultaneous inflation and recession (stagflation). The DOW JONES INDUSTRIAL AVERAGE fell for a three-month period and then leveled out. When the Persian Gulf War officially started in January 1991, oil prices fell dramatically from a peak of $41 per barrel to $26 per barrel; traders foresaw a quick end to the war and

Table 7A ■ Oil Price Fluctuations Following Invasion of Kuwait

Date	Action	Price/ Barrel
August 1990	Iraq invades Kuwait	$19
September– December 1990	Concern over possible war grows	$41
January 1991	Operation Desert Storm begins	$36
February– March 1991	War winds down and ends	$19
August 1991	One year after invasion	$21

a return to an oil market characterized by a worldwide glut and oversupply. In January the DJIA started rising again, and on April 17th it broke through the 3000 mark.

For the individual investor trying to fathom the future of stock and bond markets, oil prices are a market mover of the highest importance. When world oil prices are around twenty dollars a barrel, or within a 10% range (eighteen to twenty-two dollars), the industrial economies of Europe, Japan, and the United States can prosper. Inflation is low and economic growth can occur provided other favorable economic forces are operating.

MARKET MOVER TIPS

■ When the price of oil approaches thirty dollars and appears as if it will stay in the high twenties, expect recessions in most parts of the world. At this point it's wisest to get out of most stocks—with the exception of blue chips and stocks of oil and oil-service companies. Check *Value Line* for recommendations on oil stocks. Some suggested stocks are:

Atlantic Richfield	Haliburton
Baker Hughes	Philips Petroleum
Chevron	Schlumberger
Exxon	Texaco

■ When oil prices are high, A-rated bonds and bond mutual funds with A-rated issues are preferable to most stocks.

DID YOU KNOW THAT?

Standard Oil, the country's first major oil company, was founded by a man with little formal education but with a passion for keeping track of every penny he earned. John D. Rockefeller, a pious Baptist, worked first as a bookkeeper and then became a partner in a Cleveland produce business before moving into the burgeoning oil industry. Recognizing that the way to control the industry was to handle the refining process, he built the largest refinery in Cleveland in 1863, and two years later another one. By 1870 his company, Standard Oil of Ohio, was making its own barrels and running its own fleet of tankers. Through shrewd and sometimes unscrupulous practices, Rockefeller ruthlessly crushed competitors, so that by 1880 the company dominated the oil business. By 1910 the market value of Standard Oil was $600 million.

The richest man in the world when he died in 1937, Rockefeller was at once the most generous and the most frugal. He gave more than $530 million to charities during his lifetime; yet for years he crossed the Hudson River by ferry, passing out dimes to the passengers, admonishing them to save each and every one.

CHAPTER 31

Group of Seven

■ ■ ■

*The Group of Seven is composed of the seven largest capital-
ist nations, whose heads of state meet informally and quite
frequently to discuss general economic issues.*

On January 1, 1991, an article appeared on the business page
of *The New York Times* carrying this headline: "Group of 7 Opens
Talks on Outlook." The following day, *The Wall Street Journal* ran
the headline "Faster Growth, Rates Drop Seen by Group of 7."
Who is the Group of Seven? The name may make them sound like
something out of the Wild West or the radical sixties, but the Group
of Seven is made up of the United States and its six main industrial
allies. They are market movers who affect the global economy and
financial markets.

The group actually began as the Group of Five and was made up
of the United States, Japan, Britain, France, and West Germany.
Today Canada and Italy are members and the C.I.S. would like to
be. The special importance of the group dates from the early seventies, when fixed exchange rates between the world's currencies were
abandoned in favor of what is known as a floating rate system. (See
chapter 35, "Value of the Dollar.") Since the beginning of the

floating rate system, the Group of Seven has functioned as a kind of shadow agency, providing assistance, advice, and sometimes massive intervention in currency trading in order to keep the world on an even economic keel. The group has three major tasks:

1. Containing INFLATION when world economies become overheated with strains on capacities—when CAPACITY UTILIZATION is over 90%.

2. Attempting to control trade surpluses and deficits between the major industrial countries so that they are neither too large nor too disruptive. For example, if Japan exports great numbers of its automobiles and VCRs to the United States and Europe, creating massive import surpluses for those countries, the Group of Seven nations will explore ways to get Japan to open its markets and import goods from the same countries to which it is exporting goods. This will to some extent equalize the balance of trade between the leading nations. (See chapter 33, "Balance of Trade.")

3. Preventing financial collapses such as the one that occurred on Wall Street in October 1987 from spreading into a worldwide financial problem or a global recession. For instance, the Group of Seven will instruct its central banks to provide sufficient credit and liquidity to stockbrokers and investment bankers so they can carry their inventories of stocks and not be adversely affected by a troubled market in another part of the world. This prevents what is known as the domino effect, the collapse of several markets in the wake of a major market's collapse. (See chapter 32, "Global Stock Markets.")

With these and other goals on its agenda—such as promoting noninflationary growth and assisting the economies of less-developed countries in Africa, South America, Asia, and the Middle East—the Group of Seven meets on an annual basis. At its 1991 meeting in London, Mikhail S. Gorbachev, president of the Soviet Union, stole the show, although he was not a member of the group. His plea for sympathy and help was met with a warm response, and the promise of continued dialogue and some inexpensive technical advice. The Group of Seven promised to listen regularly to Gorbachev on his country's huge economic problems and to press the International Monetary Fund and other world organizations to give his country technical advice to help with the various currency, market, and deficit issues the U.S.S.R. faced.

Although not every meeting of the group makes waves, a number have been significant. One meeting that turned out to be a key market-moving event was the Plaza Accord of September 1985, during which the governments agreed that the dollar's exchange rate was too high and should be pushed down. This helped American exporters to increase sales and soon made U.S. real estate, products, and even stocks lower in price, appealing to foreign investors and tourists.

The Group of Seven is the only unofficial, cooperative control mechanism in the area of international currency exchange rates and foreign debt. For example, if the U.S. dollar begins to fall in value against the Japanese yen, its fall will be monitored by the group, which will then decide if the fall is disruptive or severe enough to require intervention on the part of the world's central banks. If members of the group decide to intervene to keep the dollar from a dangerous free-fall, then the members will buy dollars and sell their own currencies or exchange blocks of currencies, known as "swaps." In the final analysis the Group of Seven is the closest thing today to a worldwide central bank.

Meetings of the group are always reported fully in the press, so you can get insights into what developments are troubling the world's central bankers and what remedies they are planning to take. In this way the Group of Seven meetings in and of themselves are often market movers.

MARKET MOVER TIPS

■ Many stock and bond investments involve a judgment about the economic strength of foreign countries as well as future currency values. With the European unification in 1993, European economies are expected to experience rapid growth over the next few years. Information reported on the Group of Seven meetings will inform you as to which economies are the strongest. A small portion of your stock portfolio can be invested in stocks of American multinational companies that earn a large percent of their income in Europe; stocks or ADRs (American Depository Receipts) of promising foreign companies; or shares in an international mutual fund.

■ If your reading of the Group of Seven meetings leads you to believe the dollar may fall in value, then invest in a foreign bond fund to earn a high total return from interest income, plus the change in currency values.

DID YOU KNOW THAT?

The grandfather of the Group of Seven was the United Nations Monetary and Financial Conference held in 1944 in the small New Hampshire town of Bretton Woods. At this conference officials from forty-five noncommunist nations agreed on a system of international exchange rates and liquidity. It was the first time that a formal world agreement with rules for an international monetary system had been drawn up. Under the Bretton Woods agreement exchange rates of all members were fixed in terms of gold or the dollar. The conference also resulted in the creation of the International Monetary Fund and the International Bank for Reconstruction and Development.

CHAPTER 32

Global Stock Markets

■ ■ ■

Electronic technology has so shrunk the world that the movement of one nation's stock market is almost immediately reflected in another's. The most dramatic example of this interrelationship occurred during the October 1987 market crash in the United States. The selling panic that hit the New York Stock Exchange on October 19 reverberated around the world as Asian and European stock markets opened and closed during the twenty-four-hour period following the U.S. debacle. Investors in all parts of the globe viewed the damage in New York and immediately thought about what would happen if the same storm hit their own stock market. The Hong Kong market actually closed; the Frankfurt, London, and Zurich markets in particular suffered large losses.

A different situation occurred at the beginning of Operation Desert Storm. In mid-January 1991, after a bruising decline that began with the invasion of Kuwait, the U.S. stock market began an impressive rise and by mid-April was up 19%. America's recession, which had begun in July of the previous year, had been accelerated by the outbreak of war and by fear that oil prices would rise dramatically. By spring economists felt the recession in the United States had bottomed out and that the nation was about to enter the recovery phase of the BUSINESS CYCLE.

By spring 1991, however, a number of European countries were facing recessions. Yet those foreign stock markets also rose (by 12% to 15% in some cases) during the same period that the American market was rising. What caused the rise in Europe? Why did the global markets seem to "dance together"? As the *Economist* of April 20, 1991, asked: "If Europe's economic (and hence profit) cycles are currently much less synchronized with America's than usual, why do its stock markets dance so closely in step with Wall Street? . . . With European economies just starting to slow, is not Europe's rally premature?"

One reason that stock markets in different countries and others are moving more closely together these days is that so many nations have opened up their stock markets to foreign investors, and a growing number of major corporations now list their shares on more than one country's stock exchange. (See chapter 47, "European Community.") In the United States we're accustomed to exchanges that list primarily American stocks, yet this is not the case in Europe. There the listings are far more international; in fact, on some European exchanges about one-third of their listed stocks are foreign. Half the volume on the London Stock Exchange in 1990 was in non-British shares.

"Global dancing" is also a result of the close international and economic ties among large multinational companies. As the *Economist* noted, "America accounts for about one-fifth the profits of big British companies, a third of Swiss firms' profits and almost two-fifths of the profits of top Dutch companies."

In the case of the spring 1991 rally, the Gulf War provided yet another reason for the apparent union of movements between global markets. All major markets were focused on a common problem—

namely, the future price of oil. Beginning with the invasion of Kuwait on August 2, 1990, the price of oil began to rise until it eventually reached a high of $41 per barrel. Investors, economists, and politicians in every oil-using nation began calculating what the high price of oil would do to their gross national products. (See chapter 30, "Oil Prices.")

Although the simultaneous rise in global stock markets in reaction to the events in the Persian Gulf was a one-time event, the correlation between global markets is a fact of life. As trade barriers between nations fall by the wayside and international trade increases, imports into one country will increasingly stimulate exports into another, and this "widening linkage," as economists call it, will bring national economies closer together.

The study by the Organization of European Community Development (OECD) on the connection between global stock markets bears out this trend. The report indicates that the relationship between London and New York stock markets has changed from a coefficient of 0.45 before 1973 when foreign exchange rates were fixed, to 0.59 in the latter half of the eighties. (A coefficient of zero indicates there is no connection between two markets; a coefficient of one indicates that the two markets move in perfect unison.) As the *Economist* explains, "Put crudely, this implies that price movements in New York 'explain' 59% of London's movements. Since 1973, America's correlation with most other markets has risen: France increased from 0.28 to 0.44; Japan from 0.19 to 0.42, and Germany from 0.39 to 0.45. These correlation coefficients clearly demonstrate the growing interconnections between the world's stock markets."

In the nineties the United States has a unique opportunity to lead the rest of the world, not only politically but also economically. As America's economy expands and if it can do so without corrosive inflation, world stock markets will move along with the United States more closely than ever because of America's importance to the economies of Europe and Asia. The strength in the VALUE OF THE DOLLAR will raise profits of European and Asian companies that export to the United States, and world stock markets will respond to these rising profits. But there's also a downside. INFLATION in America, which is the result of undisciplined spending and borrowing by government and consumer alike, would dissipate the opportunities that the strong dollar and political leadership have brought.

The proposed NORTH AMERICAN FREE TRADE AGREEMENT and the EUROPEAN COMMUNITY will further impact the movements of global stock markets. The PRESIDENT OF THE UNITED STATES and the GROUP OF SEVEN will intervene whenever possible to try to avoid any ill consequences of "global dancing."

MARKET MOVER TIPS

■ Because the links between the stock markets of America and her major trading partners in Europe and Japan will be closer in the future, if anything begins to adversely or positively affect the stock market of any of our trading partners, look for its shadow to fall on the American stock exchanges.

■ The linking of global stock markets is much stronger during times of high volatility such as the crash of October 1987. During calmer times the linkages may seem less dramatic, but don't let short-term stock market movements in one industrial country or another blind you to the underlying fact that they are all strongly interrelated.

■ Don't buy stocks in the United States when the market in either Japan or London is suffering a severe drop, unless you want to buy on dips.

■ When a major foreign stock market drops, it's wise to be cautious about U.S. investments. Japanese investors own a broad spectrum of U.S. investments, particularly real estate. Any move to liquidate their real estate would intensify a drop in real estate prices in this country.

DID YOU KNOW THAT?

Foreign stock markets affected us as far back as World War I. In late July 1914 exchanges shut down, one after the other, to prevent mass liquidations and plunging stock prices. Toronto, Madrid, Vienna, Budapest, Brussels, Antwerp, Berlin, and Rome closed first. On July 30 exchanges in Paris, St. Petersburg, and all of South America closed. When the London Stock Exchange did not open the morning of Friday, July 31, the New York Stock Exchange was, as Henry G. S. Noble, president of the exchange said, "the only market in which a world panic could vent itself." Minutes before the opening bell that morning, the exchange's governing committee voted to suspend trading "in order to forestall what would surely have been a ruinous collapse." The exchange did not fully reopen until the middle of December. Even then, price and trading restrictions on certain stocks were in effect until the spring of 1915. Never before or again has the NYSE been closed for so long.

CHAPTER 33

Balance of Trade

...

The dollar difference between America's imports and exports of merchandise is measured by the balance of trade.

Think about the items you and your neighbors own or consume: Italian shoes, French perfume, Japanese VCRs, Chinese clothing, German cars, Swiss chocolates, Colombian coffee, Irish salmon, French wine. Americans purchase these items not simply because they're exotic, but because they are either superior to American products or less expensive, or both. America, like all other industrialized nations, is heavily dependent upon imports as well as exports. International trade permits each nation to concentrate their resources and skills on those goods it can produce most efficiently.

One yardstick of our nation's health is its trade balance. If U.S. trade with the rest of the world adds up to a *surplus*—we export more goods than we import—it means our goods are competitive on the international scene. If there's a *deficit*—fewer exports than imports—it may mean that our products are not as desirable as those of foreign countries. A surplus is generally regarded as a favorable balance of trade while a deficit is unfavorable. Through most of the eighties and into the nineties, the United States has been operating under a balance of trade deficit.

WHAT IT COVERS

The Commerce Department provides monthly figures on our exports and imports of merchandise. It includes movable goods, such as automobiles, foodstuffs, and apparel. The amount, given in dollars, is often referred to in the press as the U.S. merchandise trade deficit or merchandise trade surplus.

Exports include domestically made goods and reexports, items that are imported and then exported without substantial change to the item. The amount is valued at the place of export: although the dollar value includes the cost of transportation within the United States, insurance, and any other costs to deliver the merchandise to the ship or plane, it does not include overseas transportation costs or any other expenses beyond the U.S. port.

Imports include goods for immediate consumption as well as those stored in the Customs Department's bonded warehouses and in U.S. foreign trade zones.

WHAT'S NOT INCLUDED

Payments abroad for services and tourism are not included.

WHY IT'S IMPORTANT

The balance of trade measures our competitiveness in world markets. This competitiveness also affects the VALUE OF THE DOLLAR. And the amount we produce for export also impacts on employment: a surplus in the trade balance (or a reduction in the trade deficit) helps the economy grow and provides employment; a deficit does the opposite.

There are some economic advantage to imports, as well. Imports tend to keep INFLATION down; they directly compete with American products and prevent American manufacturers from raising prices too much. Imports also fill in a gap or shortage in given items caused by a drought, unexpected rise in demand or consumption, a walkout, or long-term strike.

Economists study the trade gap figures carefully to discover:

- if we are importing substantially more cars, VCRs, trucks, clothing, and other goods from overseas than we are exporting
- how many jobs have been lost to overseas manufacturing plants that are more efficient and/or have lower labor costs
- if our educational system is failing to prepare trained workers and management to compete in the future

HOW IT'S REPORTED

The U.S. trade deficit (or surplus) is reported in billions of dollars. In 1991 the trade *deficit* rose in May to $4.57 billion from $4.51 billion in April. Economists attributed the increase to the lingering effects of the recession. In the spring of 1991, the faltering domestic economy had put a lid on imports. Exports were thought to be leveling off because of slowdowns in some of the economies of U.S. trading partners. Chart 21A shows exports and imports: the gap between these two figures represents the deficit.

MARKET MOVERS TIPS

- When the U.S. trade deficit is dropping, it begins to strengthen the dollar, bolstering our Treasury market because foreigners are eager to buy our bonds. Watch for a lowering trade deficit and invest in long-term Treasuries, those with five- to ten-year maturities.

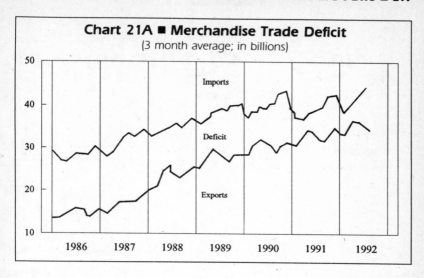

Chart 21A ■ Merchandise Trade Deficit
(3 month average; in billions)

■ When America's trade deficit is lower, ask your broker which industries and companies are benefiting from higher exports.

DID YOU KNOW THAT?

In Colonial times we also had a trade deficit, since the colonists imported more from Britain than they exported. From 1747 to 1765, the value of our exports to Britain doubled, from about £700,000 to £1.5 million. At the same time, Colonial imports from Britain rose even more, from about £900,000 to over £2 million. At that time Britain was unable to produce nearly enough food to meet the needs of its rapidly growing population, and so it turned to the colonists, who were happy to export to the mother country. Consequently, prices for wheat, flour, port, and tobacco rose between 35% and 80% and the standard of living among nearly all the colonists was high. Ordinary citizens were able to buy luxury items—ranging from Irish linen and lace to Wedgewood dishes that previously only the well-to-do merchant class had been able to afford. The newly rich were known as the ''swells.''

CHAPTER 34

Foreign Exchange Rates

■ ■ ■

Foreign exchange rates measure the number of units of each foreign currency that the U.S. dollar will buy.

The importance of foreign exchange rates—and monitoring the changes in currencies—has increased in direct proportion to the growth of trade between nations. As major industrial nations have moved toward opening their local markets to one another and promoting free trade, the foreign exchange markets of the world have likewise grown in importance.

THE FOREIGN EXCHANGE MARKET

The foreign exchange market is to currencies what the stock market is to stocks: it's where these items are traded. Banks buy and sell in this market for their clients—importers, exporters, traders, for example—who want to exchange currencies. Unlike most stocks, which are actually traded on the floor of an exchange, such as the New York Stock Exchange, the foreign exchange market is not a physical place but an extensive electronic network connecting thousands of computers and telephones. As currency traders buy and sell, the rate for every one of the world's currencies, including the dollar, is revised all day long. (The minimum trading unit is $1 million.)

Whereas most tourists exchange currencies by using cash, their ATM cards, or traveler's checks, most businesses exchange currencies through their banks. Businesses rarely make physical exchanges of dollars for lire or pounds; their positions are merely entered into their accounts.

For many years the relative weights of the various world currencies were measured against gold and/or silver. In other words, a British pound was worth x amount of gold; the Japanese yen worth y amount of gold, and the U.S. dollar worth z amount of gold. The use of the gold standard made comparing two currencies relatively simple. In the early seventies the nations of the world stopped using the gold standard and all currencies began "floating" against one another.

The supply and demand for foreign and U.S. currencies comes from an enormous number of sources: importers, exporters, multinational corporations, tourists, traders, and speculators operating in the foreign exchange markets. Central banks, such as the Federal Reserve banks in the United States or the Bank of Japan, may want to raise or lower the value of their currency. These central banks believe that an abrupt drop in the value of their nation's currency will raise the price of imports, perhaps creating a flood of unwanted foreign imports and increasing inflationary pressures. An abrupt rise in value of their currency makes exports more expensive to foreign buyers, who would then turn to other countries for products.

HOW IT'S REPORTED

The daily closing prices for the world's currencies are listed in *The Wall Street Journal* and other newspapers.

For each foreign currency, exchange rates are posted for converting the dollar into that currency and for exchanging that currency for the dollar. For example, when you look at a table of exchange rates, you might see a quotation for yen per dollars of 137.18, and for dollars per yen of .007290. This means it takes 137.18 yen to buy a dollar, and .007290 dollar buys a yen.

HOW EXCHANGE RATES MOVE MARKETS

Currencies are not exchanged only because nations wish to export or import goods or services. Currencies are also exchanged in order to make investments in other nations' stock markets, or in their bonds and treasuries. Naturally, this flow of money amongst nations for investment purposes also causes the value of currencies to rise or to decline.

A nation's high INTEREST RATES is one cause of foreign, rather than domestic, investment. The economies of all countries do not rise and fall in unison, and each nation may be in a different phase of the BUSINESS CYCLE. So when another country has a stronger economy than the United States, it usually pays higher interest rates on its government bonds or paper. Conversely, sometimes economic growth and interest rates are higher in the United States than abroad.

Investment money throughout the world seeks the highest rate of return. For example, if U.S. Treasury bills offer a return of 5.5% and treasury bills in Sweden yield 12%, investors will invest money in Sweden rather than the United States. Although there is no danger that the government of Sweden will default on their treasury obligations, there is a danger, albeit not a very big one, that the Swedish krona will fall in value against the dollar during the time the investor owns Swedish treasuries.

The potential investor in Sweden's treasury bills has two choices: one, keep the money in the United States and be content with a 5.5% yield; two, buy Sweden's treasury bills and ''sell short'' another currency, one that moves up and down with the krona, to try to protect against a drop in the value of the krona. To sell short a krona, a trader *borrows* $1 million in krona and sells them. If the krona falls in value against the dollar, the trader buys them back at a lower price and makes a profit. This profit balances out the loss he suffers on the Swedish treasuries due to the fall of the krona. (This sell-short technique is often used to take advantage of an anticipated decline in the price.)

The principle to keep in mind is that investors seek the best rate of return in whatever currency offers it. For instance, if the FEDERAL RESERVE raises U.S. interest rates so they are above those of Germany and Japan, then investment money will flow to the United States. If Germany is perceived as a better place to buy bonds and make stock market investments, then money will flow there. Therefore, an investment in any currency must be considered in light of the probable future value of its currency in the foreign exchange market.

MARKET MOVER TIPS

- When the U.S. dollar is strong, it's a good time to purchase shares in individual foreign stocks; your dollar will buy more of these foreign assets.

- When U.S. interest rates are low and CDs and Treasuries are paying yields of 6% or less, invest in a multimarket mutual fund and take advantage of higher foreign interest rates. Most large mutual fund "families" offer a fund that invests in U.S. government securities, foreign government securities, CDs, and sometimes high-grade corporate securities in many countries. Multimarket funds differ from global bond funds in that they concentrate their portfolios on short-term, fixed-income securities, whereas global bond funds usually have longer-term securities. Because multimarket funds invest in securities of many foreign countries as well as the United States, they tend to have higher yields than U.S. money market funds and CDs.

- If the dollar is falling and you're planning a trip to Europe six months in advance, you may want to lock in the cost of your foreign exchange by purchasing a CD denominated in Swiss francs or German marks, the two strongest currencies in Europe. Most U.S. banks are now permitted to sell CDs denominated in foreign currencies.

■ Purchase stocks in multinational corporations when the dollar is low; foreign earnings will translate into higher dollar earnings. Multinationals are companies with more than one-third of their earnings derived from overseas, such as Colgate-Palmolive, PepsiCo, Philip Morris, and most large pharmaceutical companies.

DID YOU KNOW THAT?

Europe may eventually have a single, common currency. Because each country's currency fluctuates in value, much of the process of doing business with European nations requires keeping track of a large number of different rates of exchange. To help resolve this problem, the EUROPEAN COMMUNITY (EC) has established a common monetary unit called the European Currency Unit (ECU). This unit defines the official value of each member's currency. The ECU is already being used for banking transactions, and there are ECU-denominated CDs and bonds. (In 1990, 14 billion ECU bonds were sold, and in the first quarter of 1991 alone, investors gobbled up 13.5 billion ECU bonds. One ECU equaled approximately $1.17 in June 1991.) The ECU may eventually be a currency like the franc or the pound.

If institutional money managers shift assets into the European Community, it could weaken the dollar and force the United States to keep rates higher than they otherwise would. In this case the ECU, if it becomes attractive in the foreign currency market, could be the first serious rival to the dollar in world finance. The EURODOL-LAR market—composed of dollar-denominated obligations outside the United States and a key source of international liquidity for banks around the world—could begin to dry up.

The ECU—pronounced "*ai*-kew" or referred to by its initials— takes its name from a French gold coin of the thirteenth century. *Ecu* means "shield" in French.

CHAPTER 35

Value of the Dollar

■ ■ ■

*The value of the dollar represents the price of the U.S.
dollar in the foreign exchange market vis à vis other nations'
currencies.*

The dollar rises and falls in relation to the currencies of other
countries. The rate of exchange for the dollar, its value, expresses
its purchasing power in another country's marketplace. When
Americans buy a dinner in Barcelona, champagne in Paris, or lace
in Ireland, the current exchange rate for the dollar determines the
cost. A tourist's calculations are a small example in microcosm of
what happens all over the world among bankers and businesses.

If a U.S. department store sells shoes made in Italy, the store
has to pay for the shoes in Italian lire. The U.S. storeowner must
"exchange" his dollars for lire, and since currencies continually
fluctuate in value, the store owner may discover that the shoes cost
more or less from year to year—and not because the manufacturer
raised the price. If it takes more dollars to buy the same amount of
lire, the store owner will have to pay more for the shoes. In this
case the dollar is said to have fallen in value.

HOW IT'S REPORTED

In addition to the daily fluctuations of the dollar in the exchange market that are reported in the newspaper, the FEDERAL RESERVE and the International Monetary Fund, among others, publish indexes of the dollar's value on a weekly and monthly basis.

WHY IT'S IMPORTANT

These changes in the dollar affect our economy in several distinct ways. First, the value of the dollar determines how competitive our goods are in the export markets. With a low dollar we can sell more goods abroad. This boosts American production and INFLATION. A falling dollar raises the prices of foreign goods and results in an increase in American import prices.

When the U.S. dollar rises in value, U.S. exports become more expensive to foreigners, and at the same time, imports become less expensive to Americans. This can lead to a rise in the UNEMPLOY-MENT RATE and increase the U.S. trade deficit. A deficit exists when a nation imports more than it exports. (See chapter 33, "Balance of Trade.") The reverse is also true. Throughout the eighties and nineties, America has had a trade deficit, as opposed to a surplus. A *falling* dollar would decrease the trade deficit, but probably not result in a surplus.

Some sort of equilibrium is obviously desirable, to keep prices of goods low, curb inflation, and help our factories produce goods for export and provide employment.

WHAT DETERMINES THE VALUE OF THE DOLLAR

Exports and imports, foreign investment, and inflation all affect the dollar's value.

Table 8A ■ Effects on the Value of the Dollar

	Strong Currency	Weak Currency
Exports/Imports	Demand for U.S. products means demand for the currency required to pay for them, *i.e.,* U.S. dollars.	Low product demand means lower demand by foreigners for U.S. dollars.
Foreign Investment	When U.S. Treasuries offer high yields, foreigners will want U.S. dollars to buy those securities.	Low interest rates mean less demand for U.S. dollars to buy American securities.
Inflation	When U.S. inflation is low, foreigners have confidence in U.S. securities and real estate.	When inflation is high, foreigners will invest in other countries.

THE ROLE OF THE FEDERAL RESERVE

The FEDERAL RESERVE intervenes in foreign exchange markets to protect the dollar. Although the dollar trades freely as do other major currencies, the Fed intercedes to avoid "disorderly conditions" such as sharp rises or falls. The Federal Open Market Committee (FOMC), which supervises FED FUNDS trading, is also responsible for carrying out policy objectives in foreign exchange markets. (See chapter 21, "Federal Funds.")

Since the early seventies, when the fixed exchange rate system was abandoned in favor of a floating rate system, the Fed has actively bought and sold dollars and other major foreign currencies in an effort to keep the trading in U.S. dollars orderly. The central banks of other major industrial nations also intervene in the foreign exchange market to assist their currencies. These central banks and the Fed often cooperate in order to keep all international currencies relatively stable and balanced. (See chapter 31, "Group of Seven.")

When the Fed (or another central bank) intervenes, it buys and sells its own currency to prevent too strong a rise or too steep a drop. For example, if the dollar is falling in value against other currencies, the Fed might borrow $1 billion in deutschemarks from Germany's central bank, DeutscheBank, and then using these borrowed DMs, it would buy dollars. Taking $1 billion out of circulation does two things: one, it creates a demand for dollars, and two, it helps hold up the value of the dollar because it's in shorter supply. The existence of international currencies such as the EURODOLLAR, which are not subject to intervention by a central bank, can limit the effectiveness of the Fed's—or any central bank's—intervention.

There are several developments that could cause massive buying or selling of dollars. If these events look like they will result in a free-fall in the value of the dollar or a temporary shortage of dollars in the exchange markets, the Fed would intervene. They include these four scenarios:

1. U.S. Treasury bill rates rise above 12% in response to the Fed's tightening of the money supply in order to control inflation. (This happened in 1981 and 1982.) Such high INTEREST RATES cause a massive, worldwide demand for dollars by foreign investors, and the dollar rises sharply in value.

2. Foreigners perceive that U.S. debt is mushrooming without any effort being made to control our budget. This perception causes investors to sell the dollar. Too much selling could lead to what is called a free-fall in the dollar's value.

3. A severe recession causes the Fed to lower interest rates in order to promote spending in the United States, and lowered rates could prompt foreign investors to sell their dollar investments and move their money to other currencies.

4. If Germany were to reach the end of its costly unification effort with East Germany and restart its vigorous industrial growth, global investors might then begin selling U.S. investments and switching their dollars into deutschemarks.

WHAT FED INTERVENTION MEANS

Fed intervention is a market mover, although it is one many investors are unaware of. Yet you can watch for news of it in the financial press and then follow the market mover tips at the end of this section.

If you hear that the dollar is falling and the Fed is *not* intervening, you may assume that it's not worried about higher prices for U.S. imports. Similarly, if the Fed stands aside and allows the dollar to rise, the Fed is not concerned that our exports will be too costly.

If the Fed is actively intervening to stem a fall or slow down a rise in the value of the dollar, it may be an indication of a change in Fed policy, in which case it may soon lower or raise interest rates.

MARKET MOVER TIPS

■ Read what the "Fed watchers" (economists and analysts who track the Fed's actions) say about the value of the dollar. This will help you make investment, business, and travel decisions.

■ The dollar is regarded as a "safe haven" currency. In times of war or other international disruptions, global money managers often shift their funds into dollars.

■ After 1992 when the EUROPEAN COMMUNITY (EC) is scheduled to become fully operational, there is a possibility that Europe will form a hostile "trading bloc" that will keep out or reduce American imports. There is no certainty that this will happen, but a weak and falling dollar, with or without Fed intervention, will be an early warning sign. (See chapter 47, "European Community.")

■ If the Fed begins to intervene strongly in dollar trading, its next move may be to raise or lower interest rates. If yields are currently high, lock them in by purchasing long-term CDs, Treasuries, and A-rated corporate bonds. If rates are low, stay in short-term T-bills, CDs, or money market funds to have liquid money available for reinvestment when rates rise.

DID YOU KNOW THAT?

The largest-denomination U.S. currency is the $100,000 bill. However, it won't ever end up in anyone's wallet! It's used only in transactions between the Treasury Department and the Federal Reserve. Bills of $10,000 are in general circulation, although they have not actually been printed since 1944. No $5,000, $1,000, or $500 bills have been printed since 1969. The $100 bill, with a portrait of Benjamin Franklin, is the largest denomination now being issued.

CHAPTER 36

Eurodollars

■ ■ ■

Eurodollars are deposits denominated in U.S. dollars located in a bank or branch bank outside the United States and not subject to U.S. banking regulations.

Eurodollars are a form of dollar deposits and loans that, though not subject to the control of our FEDERAL RESERVE, nevertheless play a role in the United States as well as the global economy. Because of some risks—there is no Federal Deposit Insurance Corporation (FDIC) coverage, for example—Eurodollar rates are a fraction higher than rates in domestic U.S. banks.

Many foreign banks and foreign branches of U.S. banks accept deposits in dollars and give the depositor an account denominated in dollars. These dollars are called Eurodollar deposits, a term that came about when the market was located primarily in Europe; Eurodollars may be owned by individuals, corporations, or governments located anywhere in the world. Although most Eurodollar deposits are still held in major European financial capitals, the business has spread to the Bahamas, Bahrain, Canada, the Cayman Islands, Hong Kong, Japan, Panama, the Netherland Antilles, and Singapore. Banks in the Eurodollar business compete directly with U.S. banks in seeking these dollar-denominated deposits. In 1981 domestic and foreign banks were allowed to open "international banking facilities" (IBFs) in the United States; the dollars deposited in these IBFs are also Eurodollars.

Most Eurodollar deposits are in large amounts (often jumbo CDs of $100,000 and higher) and are made by foreign, domestic, and multinational corporations, by foreign central banks, U.S. domestic banks, and by wealthy individuals. These deposits have a fixed term that can range from overnight to five years. Most Eurodollar transactions mature in six months or less.

Banks receiving Eurodollar deposits use them to make loans denominated in dollars to corporations, foreign governments, domestic U.S. banks, and other large borrowers. The Eurodollar market is considered *the* international capital market of the world, with U.S. corporations financing foreign operations, foreign corporations funding both foreign and domestic business, and foreign governments funding projects. In 1987 it was estimated that there were approximately 1 trillion Eurodollars in circulation.

Another important use of Eurodollars is as an alternative to FED FUNDS. For example, a U.S. bank with a reserve deficiency may borrow Eurodollars instead of purchasing Fed funds. A domestic bank with an excess of funds may loan in the Eurodollar market as an alternative to the loaning of Fed funds. These loans circumvent the actions and intentions of the Federal Reserve in regulating America's MONEY SUPPLY, since it has no jurisdiction over Eurodollars.

Eurodollar loans are usually priced at LIBOR (London interbank offer rate) plus a spread. The amount of spread over LIBOR depends on market conditions. When loan demand is slack, the spread may widen to LIBOR plus 2½%. You can find Eurodollar rates listed in the "Money Rates" column of *The Wall Street Journal*. In October 1992, LIBOR rates were listed at 3¼% for one month, 3⁷⁄₁₆% for three months, and ranging up to 3½% for one year. Fed funds were listed at 3½% high, 2½% low, 2½% near closing bid, 3% offered.

Eurodollars are extremely attractive to U.S. banks since Eurodollar deposits are free of U.S. banking regulations, which impose restrictions on margins—borrowing—and on reserve requirements, the percent amount of a bank's funds that must remain on deposit in a Federal Reserve bank. With Eurodollars, banks sidestep the requirement to keep on hand non-interest-bearing cash reserves against Eurodollar deposits. (Commercial banks' deposits in the Federal Reserve do not earn interest.) There are virtually no restrictions on INTEREST RATES that can be paid on Eurodollars or charged on loans; thus banks in the Eurodollar market can operate on narrower spreads or profit margins between dollar borrowing and lending rates than banks in the United States.

There is also no required FDIC assessment, a costly expenditure for U.S. banks. Another advantage for banks doing Eurodollar business is that they can set up offices where tax rates are low. For instance, Eurodollar deposits and loans negotiated in London may actually be booked in the Cayman Islands and therefore benefit from the islands' lower tax rate.

Foreign regulatory authorities are quite naturally reluctant to regulate the Eurodollar business. They fear that doing so would drive this lucrative business away, thus reducing the income tax revenue and jobs for their country. Even if the United States could get a group of foreign countries to participate in a regulatory plan, such a plan would be worthless unless all countries of the world agreed not to accept the Eurodollar business.

It is important to keep in mind that today more than ever, the U.S. dollar is a global currency that can flow through the U.S. banks to and from foreign banking centers with or without the restraints of the United States banking regulations. In essence then, there is no central control over this money and no Federal Reserve to balance the trade between Eurodollars and goods and services. This impacts on FOREIGN EXCHANGE RATES and the VALUE OF THE DOLLAR, and it is essentially beyond the Fed's control. However, stocks, commodities, and products in international trade from chemicals to automobiles all can be traded and exchanged with great facility because of the existence of the worldwide Eurodollar market. The Eurodollar market actually separates the U.S. dollar from the United States banking system and makes it a truly international currency.

MARKET MOVER TIPS

■ When inflation in this country is high, the Federal Reserve reacts by tightening credit in order to keep interest rates high. Investors with large sums can get even higher rates on Eurodollar CDs under these circumstances because these funds are not restricted by Fed regulations.

■ The growth in Eurodollar banking reflects the growth of the U.S. dollar as a dominant international currency. If this leadership role begins to be lost to Euroyen, Eurodeutschemarks, or Europounds, it will create some serious problems for the United States.

DID YOU KNOW THAT?

A national bank issuing paper currency was established in France in 1716. The idea was John Law's, a Scottish financier who established, with the support of the king, a national bank as part of a scheme to reduce the public debt and stimulate French industry and trade. At the same time Law established a stock company, the Mississippi, to capitalize the French colony in Louisiana. By merging the bank and the stock company, Law unleashed a rash of dizzying speculations and stocks rose to ridiulous prices, and then crashed. By 1720 the whole banking and monetary system had collaped and Law left France in disgrace.

PART VI

...

PEOPLE MARKET MOVERS

Often one wonders, can any one person make a difference? The answer in terms of the financial markets is a resounding yes. This section covers a variety of people, from economic guru Henry Kaufman to flamboyant TV personality Louis Rukeyser, as well as positions of enormous economic influence, such as the chairman of the Federal Reserve.

The people who move markets include

Chairman of the Federal Reserve
President of the United States
Elaine M. Garzarelli
Robert J. Farrell
Richard Russell
Barton M. Biggs
Henry Kaufman
Edward Hyman
Chairman of the Ways and Means Committee
Louis Rukeyser

The words and actions of all of these market movers are covered in the press. By paying attention to their predictions and actions and understanding the financial consequences, you're significantly closer to a broad understanding of the movement of financial markets and the American BUSINESS CYCLE.

CHAPTER 37

Chairman of the Federal Reserve

■ ■ ■

The chairman of the board of governors of the FEDERAL RE-SERVE, which oversees the policies of the twelve regional Federal Reserve banks, is not only the spokesman of the Fed, he is also its chief policy-making officer.

When the nation began slipping into a recession in 1990, all eyes turned to Alan Greenspan, the current chairman of the Federal Reserve, who is not only a brilliant economist but a careful *thinker*. His pronouncements on the economy, INFLATION, INTEREST RATES, and the VALUE OF THE DOLLAR are attended throughout the world.

For example, during the recession, a *Wall Street Journal* story of January 23, 1991, noted: "Greenspan Says More Rate Cuts May Be Needed. . . . Mr. Greenspan told the House Budget Committee that the money supply, which had fallen into disfavor among many Fed policy makers as a guide to the economy, has assumed a greater role because it is a good way to gauge the persistence of the credit crunch." (See chapter 25, "Credit Crunch.") The article noted that the Federal Reserve was cutting interest rates in order "to spur growth of the money supply." Greenspan indicated that this should be sufficient; if not, Greenspan reported, "further action would be required."

Greenspan's clear, authoritarian words meant that interest rates were lowered and the Fed would watch the MONEY SUPPLY to see if credit began to expand. If it didn't, then the Fed would use other means to achieve its ends.

On the following day *The New York Times* carried a report on page 1 of the business section: "More Signs of a Slump, Greenspan Indicates Fed May Act Soon." In it, Robert T. McGee, chief economist for the Tokai Bank Ltd., stated, "The [Federal Reserve Bank] report strongly supports the case that the Federal Open Market Committee will approve additional easing steps." McGee said his view was strengthened by statements to this effect by the Fed's chairman, Alan Greenspan, in appearances before Congress the day before and again that morning. Mr. Greenspan told the Senate Banking Committee that the Fed would act in a "shorter rather than longer" period to spur greater lending and borrowing.

In January 1991 Alan Greenspan made the markets move. The same *Times* article reported: "Both the stock and bond markets reacted positively to the Fed chairman's comments. Traders said the prospect of lower rates helped push up the Dow Jones Industrial Average, which ended the day up 15.84 points. And prices of Treasury notes and bonds also rose and yields fell. But the dollar, whose value is eroded by lower rates, dropped against most leading currencies."

Greenspan made page one of *The New York Times* on July 11, 1991, with the headline: "Greenspan Named for New Term as Chairman of Federal Reserve." The journalist noted that Greenspan's current term was due to expire August 11 and that "mild jitters (had) developed in the financial community in recent weeks when no word from the White House was forthcoming." President Bush appeared with Greenspan in the White House press-room for the announcement and said, "The respect that Alan Greenspan has around the world and in this country, particularly in financial marketplaces, is unparalleled." When the press asked Bush about the occasional complaints from some top administration officials that Mr. Greenspan had slowed down economic expansion by keeping interest rates too high, President Bush replied that the chairman was "strongly committed to growth."

The *Times* summarized the chairman's key role in the direction of the economy: "The nation's large budget deficit prevents the President or Congress from using tax and spending policies to influence the economy, and that leaves Mr. Greenspan far and away the most important economic policy maker in the Government." The *Times* reported that the Federal Reserve's "considerable influence over interest rates [makes it] a main factor in the state of the economy."

After the news conference Greenspan responded to reporters' questions, repeating what some have called his "mantra": he would "try to maintain the maximum sustainable long-term economic growth that is possible," while at the same time keeping inflation under control. The Dow Jones Industrial Average responded favorably to the reappointment of Greenspan and his commitment to a low rate of inflation. About a week later, on July 16, 1991, Greenspan told a House banking subcommittee that the recession was nearly over and inflation was easing. *The New York Times* in its coverage of Greenspan's appearance called him "the Government's most important economic policy maker."

Enough said. Fed Chairman Greenspan is definitely a market mover.

Never underestimate the power of any Federal Reserve chairman—not only Alan Greenspan—to make things happen, to move the economy in one direction or another. Paul Volcker, during his tenure as chairman, was determined to wipe out unnecessary inflation—and he did.

GREENSPAN'S BACKGROUND

Alan Greenspan was sworn in August 11, 1987, as chairman of the board of governors of the Federal Reserve System. In this capacity he also serves as chairman of the Federal Open Market Committee, the system's principal monetary policy-making body.

Greenspan was born March 6, 1926, in New York City. He received a B.S. in economics (summa cum laude) in 1948, an M.A. in economics in 1950, and a Ph.D. in economics in 1977, all from New York University. Prior to his appointment as chairman of the Federal Reserve, Greenspan was chairman and president of Townsend-Greenspan and Company, Inc., an economic consulting firm in New York City. He has also served as chairman of the President's Council on Economic Advisers under President Ford, as a member of President Reagan's Economic Policy Advisory Board, and as senior adviser to the Brookings Panel on Economic Activity. In recent years he has served as a corporate director for Aluminum Company of America; Automatic Data Processing, Inc.; Capital Cities/ABC, Inc.; General Foods; J. P. Morgan; Mobil Corporation; and the Pittston Company.

MARKET MOVER TIPS

- The chairman is required to appear before Congress every six months to report on the state of the economy and the outlook for monetary policy. Follow carefully his testimony as well as all other statements he makes. If you don't get a clear idea of what he is saying, then read the newspaper accounts in *The Wall Street Journal, The New York Times*, and your local financial press. TV coverage with interpretations by experts is also useful.
- When the chairman of the Fed reports that inflation is easing, it's a good time to buy bonds and longer-term Treasury notes

(five to ten year) to lock in current yields. An easing rate of inflation results in lower interest rates.

■ A lower rate of inflation (and subsequent lower interest rates) is also good for growth stocks because their total returns (dividends plus price appreciation) are more desirable when rates paid on bonds are lower.

DID YOU KNOW THAT?

President Wilson not only had trouble getting men to serve on the first Federal Reserve Board, but also getting his nominations passed by the Senate. Wilson's selections were popular among the nation's banking leaders but not with the progressives, who wanted men without any connections to Wall Street. A nasty fight ensued with two men actually declining the appointment: Richard Olney, secretary of state under Grover Cleveland, and Harry A. Wheeler, former president of the U.S. Chamber of Commerce. In their places Wilson named Charles S. Hamlin, a Boston democrat, and Thomas D. Jones, director of the International Harvester Company. Despite pressure from Wilson, the Senate refused to accept Jones because International Harvester, universally hated by farmers and progressives, was under indictment. Jones, who had not been eager to serve, eventually withdrew his nomination. This was Wilson's first defeat before the Senate. Jones's replacement, Frederic A. Delano, president of the Monon Railroad, was easily confirmed. On August 10, 1914, the board was officially sworn into office, with Charles S. Hamlin as chairman.

CHAPTER 38

President of the United States

■ ■ ■

The president of the United States, by virtue of the fact that he is the leader of the world's most powerful nation, is a market mover—even when his actions and intentions have little to do with the economy. For instance, the president's health can affect stock prices: Eisenhower's ileitis operation, Reagan's bullet wound, and Bush's thyroid condition all sent the DOW JONES INDUSTRIAL AVERAGE south, albeit not for very long. Presidential announcements on a variety of topics are more critical: for instance, the market fell when President George Bush announced the decision to send troops into the Persian Gulf. Likewise, a president's decisions (or lack of them) concerning the economy are market movers.

Throughout American history strong presidents have seized opportunities for leadership, for directing the course of the country and its economic policies. Perhaps the most notable example of this type of market mover was Franklin D. Roosevelt, who made a number of decisions that propelled the country out of its worst depression, although it took World War II to complete the job he began in 1933.

Even when a president does nothing, he can move markets. Some historians would say that Herbert Hoover's lack of action was a market mover. Although well intentioned, he let the nation drift into the depression. Hoover proved one of Will Rogers's sayings: "Even if you're on the right track, you'll get run over if you just sit there."

Wall Street tends to be happier with Republican presidents, who have traditionally been more biased toward business and less apt to raise taxes to pay for social reforms and welfare programs. Ronald Reagan's tax program, which helped the rich by reducing the top federal income tax bracket to only 28%, made it possible for Wall Street to flourish—so much so in fact that the eighties became known as the decade of excess and greed. However, soon-to-be President Clinton enjoyed "a level of business support unusual for a Democratic nominee," according to a *New York Times* article on October 13, 1992.

George Bush, although a Republican, presided over a more troubled United States, one that faced financial problems at federal, state, and local levels. According to a *New York Times'* survey of the economy under nine presidents (Truman through Bush), President Bush presided over the lowest GDP growth and nonfarm job growth, the second lowest disposable income growth, and tied with Eisenhower for last place in industrial production growth during his term.

President Clinton's mandate to reduce the deficit, speed up the economic recovery, shore up the country's infrastructure and improve the U.S. health care system ensure that he, too, will be an important market mover, impacting INTEREST RATES, and INFLATION. Even before he was elected president, Clinton demonstrated a dramatic ability to move the market. In an October 13, 1992 *New York Times* article entitled "Money Managers Considering the Clinton Effect" it was reported the Clinton's announcement of his support of the NORTH AMERICAN FREE TRADE AGREEMENT moved the market.

According to the article, "the next day the Mexican Bolsa climbed 65 points, or 4.7 percent, even as most of the world's major markets plunged." The same article reported that Clinton's announcement that he favored price controls on prescription drugs resulted in a $3 fall over the next two days of the already troubled Merck & Company pharmaceutical stock, a $3.4 billion paper loss for investors. The day after President Clinton was elected, the Dow fell 29.44 points due to a sharp fall in the prices of blue chip stocks. In each of these cases, Clinton's market moving ability was due to investor's *predictions* about President Clinton's impact on the economy.

Expectations of President Clinton's ability to help the economy ran from optimistic to pessimistic in the first days after the election. And as is usually the case, other market movers, such as HENRY KAUFMAN, consultant and former chief economist at Salomon Brothers were consulted by the press. (See chapter 43, "Henry Kaufman"). No matter what position one took, everyone agreed: the President of the United States exerts tremendous impact on vital economic factors. Interest rates, inflation, the North American Free Trade Agreement, multinational companies, foreign markets, and the VALUE OF THE DOLLAR will all be affected to some degree or another by the President of the United States—no matter whom the President happens to be at the time.

THE FEDERAL RESERVE

There was a distinct impression both at home and abroad that the FEDERAL RESERVE was much more influenced by the Bush administration than it had been by past administrations. Paul Volcker, who was Fed chairman through the eighties, was more independent in his pursuit of anti-inflationary policies than is his successor, Alan Greenspan. Greenspan *is* dedicated to lowering the U.S. inflation rate, but he appeared to be more of a team player in the Bush administration than was Volcker in the Reagan days.

If the United States finds itself in a crunch, forced to choose between lowering interest rates to remedy a serious economic slump and keeping them high to avoid a recovery that brings in its wake a higher rate of inflation, President Clinton's relationship with the head of the Federal Reserve would have serious repercussions. Every president desires low interest rates during his administration so business will boom and employment will be high during his term. Many economists, however, feel that it is when the Fed panics and lowers interest rates too much during a recession that inflationary pressures build up; these pressures are difficult or impossible to control after the economy starts its recovery.

THE FUTURE OF EUROPE

The unification of Europe in 1993 is creating a massive, common European market, not only providing new groups of consumers but also establishing new competition and perhaps even hostile trading blocs. Economists and central bank officers attending the Federal Reserve's annual summer conference in late August 1991 argued that the forty-year-old free-trade system, in which some ninety-plus nations jointly agreed to lower tariffs simultaneously, appears to be giving way to regional trading blocs that are emerging in Europe, North America, and Asia. (The United States has already formed a North American trade zone with Mexico and Canada, and Japan has made similar overtures to its Asian neighbors.) The new blocs can use tariffs to keep out imports from countries that are not members. If world trade is limited to regional blocs that exclude one another, America would certainly suffer. The president's leadership in this area is critical: he could use his position as leader of the United States to influence the world to continue its commitment to free trade and lower tariff barriers. (See chapter 48, "North American Free Trade Agreement," and chapter 47, "European Community.")

MARKET-MOVING CONCEPTS TO BEAR IN MIND

If the president fails to keep a united Europe from turning its back on the rest of the world, there is a strong possibility the value of the dollar will continue to drop, as will the growth rate for the U.S. economy. Keep in mind a fundamental economic equation: the more nations that trade with each other, the more prosperity is created for all of them. If the world divides itself into hostile trading blocs, then world prosperity will suffer. It is quite possible that only the president of the United States is in a strong enough leadership position to avert such a disaster.

DID YOU KNOW THAT?

The labels given by our presidents (or by journalists and historians) to presidential programs or leadership styles characterize how these leaders affected the country and its economy:

Andrew Jackson	Jacksonian Democracy
James K. Polk	Manifest Destiny
Andrew Johnson	The Reconstruction President
William McKinley	Live and Let Live
Theodore Roosevelt	The Square Deal
William H. Taft	Dollar Diplomacy
Woodrow Wilson	New Freedom
Franklin D. Roosevelt	The New Deal
Harry S. Truman	The Fair Deal
Dwight D. Eisenhower	Modern Republicanism
John F. Kennedy	The New Frontier
Lyndon B. Johnson	The Great Society
Richard M. Nixon	Imperial Presidency
Gerald R. Ford	Custodial President
Ronald W. Reagan	Reaganomics

CHAPTER 39

Elaine M. Garzarelli

■ ■ ■

Elaine M. Garzarelli is one of Shearson Lehman Brothers' leading market analysts. Her superstar status is based on numerous accurate market predictions that consistently benefit the investors who follow her advice. According to Coopers and Lybrand, an accounting firm hired by Shearson to study Garzarelli's record, investors who took her advice between 1982 and 1987 wound up beating the stock market by an annual average of five percentage points. Ms. Garzarelli is a sector analyst—one who concentrates on selecting those industry groups which will outperform or underperform the overall market. She also manages Shearson's $500 million Sector Analysis Portfolio mutual fund. In the first three months of 1991, the fund was up 22% versus 11.6% for the DOW JONES INDUSTRIAL AVERAGE.

Garzarelli graduated from Drexel University in 1972, where she majored in economics. As an undergrad she worked at the Philadelphia brokerage firm of A. G. Becker. As the story goes, her boss set her in front of a computer and told her to figure out what makes the stock market go up and down. She eventually developed her own system of thirteen "Garzarelli indicators," which she still uses.

In 1982 Garzarelli and her by-then well-known forecasting system joined Shearson Lehman Brothers. Soon after, she began making appearances on "Wall Street Week" and other financial television shows, earning the worldwide reputation she enjoys today.

Elaine Garzarelli's major calls regarding the direction of the market have for the most part been extremely accurate and have given her a devoted following among professional traders, money managers, and others on Wall Street. In 1982 Garzarelli predicted the beginning of the new bull market five months ahead of its start— not easy to do—permanently endearing her to Shearson and its clients. In 1987 she appeared on CNN and called the crash of 1987 about a week before it happened—in time to get her clients out of the market. She also predicted the strong 1991 market.

Garzarelli's predictive accuracy extended to an extraordinary call during the Persian Gulf crisis. While the whole financial world trembled and pushed clients to move into cash, she advised investors to buy stocks. By the middle of March, the Dow Jones Industrial Average was up between 12% and 13%, and Garzarelli's followers were beaming.

Some of her recent and breathtaking calls on the stock market are recorded in Ms. Garzarelli's own words in the July 8, 1991, issue of *Sector Analysis*, her fund's newsletter: "Our indicators remain in bullish territory, at a 67% reading, after reaching a buy signal in late September [1990] at 2380 on the Dow. The previous sell signal was on August 7, 1990, at 2770."

The two "calls" she mentions in her report—to sell when the Dow was at 2770 and to buy when it was at 2380—are the kinds of predictions that make Elaine Garzarelli a market mover.

Garzarelli advised clients regarding the 1991 recession: "Considering the current economic statistics, we believe the recession bottom has occurred and that investing in economically sensitive stocks—cyclicals—will provide investors with returns far superior to those available from recession-resistant stocks.''

Garzarelli continued by providing a list of the industries, and specific companies in those industries, that her technical studies told her to select. It is this kind of direct advice that makes Garzarelli a sound guide to the investor. Her predictive abilities, broadcast to the public, have made Garzarelli a significant market mover.

MARKET MOVER TIPS

■ Study the work of Elaine Garzarelli by contacting a Shearson Lehman stockbroker who has access to her *Sector Analysis* report. Major turns in the stock market as well as the economy are forecast from time to time, and those forecasts are almost always right. If, for instance, she recommends cyclicals, it may indeed be time to buy such stocks while their prices are still low.

■ If you do not have access to the Shearson Lehman research, watch Garzarelli on ''Wall Street Week'' or other financial TV shows. Garzarelli thrives on publicity, and you can often see, hear, and read her pronouncements in the media and press.

CHAPTER 40

Robert J. Farrell

■■■

Robert J. Farrell, senior vice president and chief market analyst at Merrill Lynch Pierce Fenner and Smith, is one of the most respected analysts in America. His judgments and market calls are, in and of themselves, market-moving events. Stock analysts and economists throughout the country read Farrell's reports as soon as they're printed, and follow his words when broadcast by the media. He's good: in 1982, for instance, when the bull was just stirring out of the pen, Farrell predicted that consumer goods stocks would be the big leaders in the coming bull market. He was right.

Institutional Investor, the prestigious publication that focuses on securities research and the portfolio managers of the major mutual funds, holds an annual poll to determine the "All-American Research Team." This poll is to securities analysts what the Super Bowl is to football players. For the last fourteen years, Bob Farrell has ranked number one in the "Market Timing" category.

Farrell's entire career has been spent with Merrill Lynch, where he started as a research trainee. As an undergraduate at Manhattan College, he majored in economics and finance, graduating in 1954. He received an MS in investment finance from the Columbia Graduate School of Business in 1955.

Farrell is a technical analyst. In the investment world there are two quite distinct approaches to studying the stock market: technical analysis and fundamental analysis. The latter studies the factors that influence a company's earnings in order to forecast its future stock-price movement. Fundamentalists focus on a company's assets, earnings, sales, products, research, management, its position within the industry, and its balance sheet and income statement.

A technical analyst studies the factors that impact on the movement of stock prices rather than on the specifics of any individual company's earnings. Technicians, as technical analysts are called, look at the price and volume movements of stocks using charts and computers to find price trends that they believe will foretell future price movements. Generally, they do not focus on the financial position of a company. Among the charts that technicians use are the DOW JONES INDUSTRIAL AVERAGE, STANDARD & POOR'S 500, the WILSHIRE 5000, and the advance-decline ratio of each day's trading on the New York Stock Exchange. (The advance-decline ratio measures the number of stocks that have advanced and the number that have declined over a given time period.)

By using these and other technical indicators, market technicians such as Robert Farrell try to forecast future stock prices and determine what market or investment strategy should be followed.

One of Farrell's specialties and an area in which he has pioneered as a market strategist is his "sentimental indicators." These indicators measure whether investors and their advisers are bullish or bearish on the market. Farrell's position purposely goes against popular sentiment: As long as stock market sentiment indicates that investors and their advisers are negative and fearful about investing, the stock market will rise and confound them. Conversely, when investors become confident and optimistic, Farrell says, it's time to sell and become negative about the market. Based on this theory, Farrell, on July 29, 1991, in his *Market Analysis Comment* wrote why he was bullish on the market: "The Consensus Inc. survey of bulls on stocks is still at a reasonably subdued level of 38 percent, this would likely have to rise to the 50–70 percent range to be a clear-cut negative indication. The Investor's Intelligence survey of bearish advisory services increased again last week to 33.9 percent, this is up from 24.5 percent in late June."

Farrell's *Market Analysis Comment* is distributed to professional investors only and is generally not available to the public. This may be just as well since it's not an easy read. But the above extract provides a glimpse of the kind of thinking that lies behind so many of Robert Farrell's accurate calls on the stock market.

Although Farrell is most frequently referred to as a market technician, he does combine some fundamental theories with the technical, especially when looking at long-term strategies. He was quoted in a 1991 issue of *Forbes* as saying, "The most profits come from recognizing the right themes, not by saying where the Dow will be." He also comments on individual industries and stocks, explaining in *Forbes* his theory that a major bull market can start only after the stocks that were leaders in the prior bull market are no longer the winners.

MARKET MOVER TIPS

- Robert Farrell's opinions on the stock market are available in a simplified, distilled version at Merrill Lynch offices around the country. He also appears on "Wall Street Week" and other financial TV shows and is quoted in the financial news. Become familiar with his opinions and use them as a guide for investing in blue-chip stocks and for switching out of the market and into CDs, money market funds, and Treasuries.
- If you find you enjoy following Farrell's predictions, invest in

a mutual fund family that offers you the chance to switch from stock funds to bond funds to money funds for free or a minimal fee. With a small amount of your investment dollars, track Farrell. If after several months you're making money, add to your "Farrell-tracking funds" portfolio.

CHAPTER 41

Richard Russell

■ ■ ■

Richard Russell of La Jolla, California, is the founder and publisher of *Dow Theory Letters*, one of the most widely read and respected financial advisory newsletters in the country. Leading institutional investors, money managers, analysts, and individual investors have been following Russell's pronouncements on the market since the newsletter was established in 1957. Russell's loyal following is largely due to his accurate calls on the direction of the market, although many people also enjoy his wry and witty comments on economic policy and politics—and his favorite restaurants.

Russell, like ROBERT FARRELL, is a technical analyst. Technical analysis is a method employing various indicators, charts, and computer programs to track stock price trends. It focuses on the behavior of the market, industry groups, and the stocks themselves—their price movements, volume, trends, and patterns—rather than on the fundamentals of the individual or collective companies. He bases his market calls on two technical theories: the Dow Theory, and the Primary Trend Index, which is his own proprietary theory.

THE DOW THEORY

The Dow Theory, used by Russell and other technical analysts, operates on the premise that the past action of the stock market is the best indicator of its future. In other words, a stock's price movement is largely due to factors outside a company's control. The Dow Theory also supports the notion that much of the stock market movement is psychologically, not economically based.

Russell uses the Dow Theory as a predictive technique to forecast the direction, up or down, of the overall stock market. He studies charts covering the movement of the DOW JONES INDUSTRIAL AVERAGE, the Dow Jones Transportation Average, and to a lesser extent the Dow Jones Utility Average, to determine the direction of the market.

Although Russell is the most-respected practitioner of the Dow Theory today, he is not its pioneer. The Dow Theory was established in the nineteenth century when Charles Dow began publishing *The Wall Street Journal*. Dow and his followers saw the stock market as consisting of two types of "waves": the *primary wave*, which is a bull or bear market cycle lasting several years, and the *secondary wave*, which lasts a few weeks to a few months. A single primary wave may contain twenty or more secondary waves. The primary trends in the market must be confirmed by a singular movement in the Dow Jones Industrial Average and the Dow Jones Transportation Average. A significant trend is not reached until both of these Dow Jones indexes reach new highs or lows. If they don't, the theory goes, they will fall back to their former level; in such a case the movement is a secondary wave.

When Russell began his advisory service in 1957, the number of people who practiced technical analysis of the stock market was comparatively small. Then, as now, there were chart readers, but they primarily studied individual stock charts in an effort to get a buy or sell signal for a particular stock. Russell, on the other hand, rediscovered the body of knowledge surrounding Dow's theory and began using it to forecast rises and falls in the market as a whole.

In 1958 the public and Wall Street professionals first became aware of Russell's rediscovery of the Dow Theory through an article he wrote for *Barron's* entitled "Dow Theory Revisited."

THE PRIMARY TREND INDEX

Russell also uses a second technical indicator, the Primary Trend Index (PTI), to confirm the conclusions drawn from the Dow Theory. The results are published in each issue of Russell's newsletter.

Because the body of knowledge about the Dow Theory is available to anyone who cares to study it, Russell felt that eventually enough correct readings of the theory would be made so that the Dow would lose its value as a market predictor. For this reason he searched for some years to find a new technical tool, known only to himself, which would assist him in confirming his conclusions drawn from the Dow Theory. The result of his research was the amalgam of eight action indices, which he called the Primary Trend Index.

Here, in his own words, from the November 29, 1989, issue of *Dow Theory Letters* is the way Russell first conceived and developed the idea:

> I started worrying about "too many cooks spoiling the broth." Or to put it another way, I was worrying that too many analysts were following the same indicators. I decided to work on an indicator of my own, an indicator that only my subscribers and I could follow. . . . I tried combinations, new indices, variations, ratios, moving averages, you name it. I spent three years dreaming up and testing new barometers and indicators. In my research I came to one unshakable conclusion: My "new indicator" would have to be based on the action of

the market as opposed to indices of sentiment, financial, economic. The reason I insisted on action-of-the-market indicators is that they eliminated all subjective analysis. For instance, if advances are greater than declines on a given day, that's a fact. There's no guessing or interpretation there. The fact tells you something definite about what the market did that day.

Working on that premise, I developed an amalgam of eight indicators whose combined actions revealed the underlying direction of the market. I tested this index over three years . . . it ALWAYS revealed the underlying correct direction of the market. . . .

I've computed the PTI daily since the late 1960s, and I've included a chart of the PTI in every *Letter* since 1971. I've said this before and I blush to repeat it, but most of the mistakes I've made in the market over the last 20 years have been in believing I knew better than my PTI what was happening in the market. . . . One more thing. The PTI is proprietary. I have never revealed its formula. I felt if I did reveal this ''secret'' that the PTI could gather a following and thereby lose its value.

MARKET MOVER TIPS

- Unlike some of our other ''people'' market movers, whose research is available only to the firm they work for or its clients, Richard Russell's advice and predictions are given to the subscribers of his newsletter.
- Russell's newsletter informs investors exactly when (according to Russell) they should be in cash, stocks, bonds, Treasuries, or gold.
- Russell is often quoted in *The Wall Street Journal, Barron's,* and other financial publications. He also appears on ''Wall Street Week'' and speaks at financial seminars.

CHAPTER 42

Barton M. Biggs

■ ■ ■

Market movers are not always people well-known to the general public, but they are people that economists listen to very carefully. Analysts, portfolio managers, savvy investors, and key policymakers in Washington, D.C., also heed their predictions. Although the research of some of these key people is not readily available to the public, their conclusions are frequently reported in the media.

Barton M. Biggs is the chief investment strategist at Morgan Stanley and Company, the leading investment banking firm in the United States. Morgan Stanley also engages in investment advisory and management activities for clients with a very high net worth and acts as a broker for large institutional clients. Barton Biggs' comments on the U.S. and foreign stock markets are made available to the firm and its clients through a weekly publication, *U.S. Investment Perspectives*. Within its seventy-odd pages are summaries of

Morgan Stanley's comments, economic predictions, and research on individual stocks. Copies of *U.S. Investment Perspectives* are highly prized, and the most popular section is Biggs' commentary.

Biggs is not a conventional market mover. He does not cause the market to rise or fall as soon as he says something, but he is so well respected that his opinions usually become part of the judgment-making process for leading investment managers. When Biggs turns negative or optimistic, people listen. He combines intelligence, wide sources of information, and plain common sense, as illustrated by his comment on the Japanese market in the July 10, 1991, issue of *U.S. Investment Perspectives:*

> Is the Japanese Supermoney Spigot Running Dry?
>
> I believe the weakness in the Japanese stock market is not just a local event but has implications—perhaps even dire implications—for the world economy and for other equity markets.
>
> With their supermoney, Japanese buyers were willing to pay way up, for almost everything from Renoirs to Pebble Beach and Rockefeller Center.
>
> The Japanese establishment is trying to organize an orderly, gradual end . . . of the biggest speculative boom . . . of all time. For the sake of all of us, I hope they succeed, but the long history of men, markets, and bubbles is against them.

In the July 31, 1991, issue, Biggs addressed the question of whether the market is bullish or bearish. He noted, "One of the reasons I have been feeling more bullish is that there is so much bearishness around." Biggs continued by speculating on the argument that frequent-flyer coupons were virtually going to "bankrupt the airlines one by one, destroy the airplane manufacturers, bruise the banks with another round of loan defaults and . . . be the straw that breaks the camel's back. Anyway, I still think there is going to be a global summer rally. And Chicken Little was wrong."

MARKET MOVER TIPS

- The research of behind-the-scene market movers like Barton Biggs is often difficult for the public to locate. His writings are generally available only to a special list of clients and associates. However, check with your broker, money manager, or banker to see if they receive any of this material.
- Watch for interviews in the financial press and appearances on "Wall Street Week" and other television programs.

CHAPTER 43

Henry Kaufman

■ ■ ■

Henry Kaufman is founder and president of Henry Kaufman and Company, Inc., a New York City money management and financial consulting firm. Before "going on his own" in 1988, Kaufman was a managing director of Salomon Brothers, Inc., as well as that firm's chief economist. Kaufman spent time earlier in his career as an economist at the Federal Reserve Bank of New York. At Salomon Brothers, Kaufman worked under the guidance of Sidney Homer, a universally admired expert on bonds. Kaufman described Homer, now deceased, as a "brilliant, insightful, and classical man." Sidney Homer, who was also regarded as one of Wall Street's great wits, said of his own career that he made his first trade in bonds by swapping Mesopotamian 5% bonds for Babylonian 6%. This line is oft quoted among bond traders today.

During Kaufman's career at Salomon, he rose to worldwide prominence, and his forecast of future movements in the bond market were widely followed. His most sensational—and accurate—prediction was voiced in August 1982 when the U.S. economy was in the midst of the worst recession since the end of World War II. Kaufman, who had earned the nickname "Dr. Doom" because of his dire economic outlooks and predictions of higher and higher INTEREST RATES, changed his opinion on August 17: He stated that Treasury bond rates, then yielding 12.25%, would fall sharply; Kaufman predicted they would drop to 9% to 10%. He also predicted that the FED FUNDS rate would drop from 10% to a low of 6% to 7%.

Kaufman spoke, the world listened. Wall Street reacted. *The Wall Street Journal* reported that stock prices soared a record 38.81 points on the DOW JONES INDUSTRIAL AVERAGE: "Much of the buying panic was credited to an optimistic prediction by Salomon Brothers analyst Henry Kaufman that interest rates would fall sharply in the next twelve months." In reaction, it was reported that short-term interest rates did fall and the prime was cut from 14.5% to 14%. Because Kaufman had so accurately predicted the recession, his sighting of the end of the recession was taken seriously, even though he was the only economist doing so.

Throughout his years at Salomon Brothers, Kaufman was one of the most respected and heeded economists of the eighties. He warned against the rising tide of debt, which limited the flexibility of our banks, corporations, and the Treasury itself. He was among the first to speak out against the folly of exchanging corporate equity (common stocks) for junk bonds. His words of caution were heeded by some, but the fever of unrestrained "takeover mania" of the late eighties caused many to ignore his warning.

After Kaufman left Salomon, there were changes in how his advice and opinions were reported. Today, Kaufman gives major speeches analyzing banking, governmental, and financial situations and problems. For example, on the American economy, he spoke at the 1990 Financial Conference:

The American economy and the financial system is at a critical juncture. No significant economic revival can take place until many of our convalescing financial institutions have been rehabilitated. No quick fix is possible. . . . This time, a more tolerable but still frustrating period is unfolding, but it is the price we have to pay for reversing the long period of financial excesses and for moving toward an improved economic and financial environment later on in this decade.

The day after Bill Clinton was elected President of the United States, Henry Kaufman's views were reported in *The New York Times*. Attesting to the fact that "Mr Kaufman . . . speaks for the nation's bond markets as much as anyone," the *Times* reported Kaufman's views that Clinton could be an effective President if, in the *Times'* words, "he adheres to a cautious economic policy." Kaufman was reported as believing that the administration would fail if it pumped too much money into the economy and thus encouraged INFLATION. Kaufman stated, "The Federal Reserve should bring down interest rates another half percentage point. But the Fed will only do this is there is no danger of higher inflation."

Economists are listening to Henry Kaufman—and that moves markets.

MARKET MOVER TIP

■ Watch the financial press for reports and coverage of Kaufman's speeches. He always spells out the real financial problems of our economic system, and he never minces words. There is a great deal of economic "noise" within the media, but the clear voice of Henry Kaufman puts our financial future in perspective. If you want to know whether to prepare for recovery, recession, inflation, or deflation, Kaufman's words are an excellent guide.

CHAPTER 44

Edward Hyman

■ ■ ■

The *Institutional Investor* has rated Ed Hyman the number one economist on Wall Street for eleven consecutive years. Hyman heads the International Strategy and Investment Group, Inc. (ISI), a New York firm that manages $800 million in bond funds. Although he is less well-known to the public than ROBERT FARRELL of Merrill Lynch and ELAINE GARZARELLI of Shearson Lehman Brothers, Hyman has a loyal following among institutional investors, who regard him as a top economist and bond portfolio manager.

Ed Hyman's ability to accurately forecast the direction of the market and of INTEREST RATES is based on a unique genius for selecting the right economic numbers to study and then coming to the right conclusions. Along with his partner, Nancy R. Lazar, Hyman and his staff spend each weekend—especially Sundays—phoning department store executives, automobile and general retailers, and other business leaders in order to gather the latest reports on sales, credit, consumer confidence, and other economic data *before* it's reported to the press in the conventional economic series.

ISI's research is published weekly, and much of it is updated on a minute-by-minute basis. ISI's *Weekly Economic Data* for July 8, 1991, noted:

- Despite the drop in Payroll Employment, June's Employment report was strong, suggesting that Personal Income rose 0.8% and that the Leading Indicators increased 0.8%, which would make for the fifth consecutive increase. The economy has rebounded, but we expect weaker reports this fall.
- Auto sales were a bit stronger in June but our contacts at department stores report weaker sales.
- Note: Both the CRB [Commodity Research Bureau Index of Commodity Prices] and Nikkei Dow [the DJIA equivalent in Japan] are back to their 1987 lows, suggesting that world interest rates are too high.

Hyman's prose may be enjoyable only to economic majors, but his following, his track record, and his reputation make him a major market mover.

MARKET MOVER TIP

- Note Hyman's private forecasts about interest rates and the economy. When ISI reports interest rates are going to come down, lock in the yields that are currently available. When they forecast rising rates, it's a good time to get into money funds and Treasury bills (ninety days) so that you can have money readily available to invest as yields on CDs, corporate bonds, and Treasuries move up.

CHAPTER 45

Chairman of the Ways and Means Committee

■ ■ ■

Market movers are not always economists or denizens of Wall Street. Dan Rostenkowski is a Democratic member of the House of Representatives and has held his seat for over three decades. Today, as chairman of the Ways and Means Committee, where all new tax legislation is proposed and written, Rostenkowski is one of the most powerful men in Congress.

Although the chairman of the Ways and Means Committee is always a market mover by virtue of his position, Rostenkowski has taken a particularly active role. His part in writing and getting the Tax Reform Act of 1986 passed made him a market mover with clout. It began in 1985 when Senator Bill Bradley and Richard Gephardt, a member of the Ways and Means Committee in the House, began to promote a new tax reform bill aimed at flattening out all tax brackets and eliminating many of the most abusive tax shelters, which had put the rich into the farming, cattle, and equipment-leasing business. When the Bradley/Gephardt proposal came along, Rostenkowski, who felt the country was ready for tax reform, decided it was an issue on which he was willing to take a significant political risk to gain commensurate political reward. He quickly put himself squarely behind the new legislation. Using all of his political skills to promote the Tax Reform Act, Rostenkowski even appeared on television, urging the public to "write Rosty" and give him their reactions.

Rostenkowski is neither a lawyer nor an accountant, yet he brokered, badgered, and engineered tax reform through the House and provided much of the clout necessary for its passage in the Senate. When Rostenkowski was done, the country had a new tax bill and the system received the most thorough overhauling it had had in years.

As long as he is chairman of the Ways and Means Committee, Rostenkowski will continue to be a market mover regarding tax legislation. And taxes have a direct effect on PERSONAL INCOME, consumer spending, CONSUMER CREDIT, and other economic series.

MARKET MOVER TIPS

■ Higher taxes in the top brackets are good for tax exempt securities such as municipal bonds.

CHAPTER 46

"Wall Street Week"
—Louis Rukeyser

■ ■ ■

Louis Rukeyser, the host of the television program "Wall Street Week," is thought by many to be America's most popular economic commentator. Rukeyser, who has been at the helm of "Wall Street Week" since its inception in 1970, prides himself on his unique blend of information and entertainment—combining puns with ideas and pitting expert against expert. *Playboy* magazine described him as a man born "with a ticker tape in his mouth."

Rukeyser's approach seems to work. An estimated 10 million people watch his television program every Friday evening—that's more than twice the size of *The Wall Street Journal*'s circulation.

Joining Rukeyser's program each week are key people in U.S. and international finance, business, and government. Three panelists, chosen from a rotating group of twenty-six, are also featured. The show's experts-as-guests have included Peter Lynch, John Templeton, Pat Weaver, John Kenneth Galbraith, Paul Volcker, Milton Friedman, Grant Tinker, Alan Greenspan, T. Boone Pickens, Roger

Smith, and Donald Regan—all of whom are market movers themselves.

Among the statements made on "Wall Street Week" that have proven to be market movers are these:

- In an interview with panelist Martin Zweig on October 16, 1987, Zweig stated he saw a stock market "crash" as imminent; three days later, "Black Monday," the Dow went into a record-breaking free-fall that sent the stock market into a tailspin.
- An uncanny prediction in October 1981 by stock analyst George Lindsay claimed that America's prevailing bear market would end on August 26, 1982. He turned out to be off by thirteen days. On August 13, 1982, the Dow rose to 786.92, setting off the bull years of the eighties.
- In a series of interviews in the early eighties with Chase Manhattan's Willard C. Butcher and Citicorp's Walter Wriston, Rukeyser pointedly and aggressively asked them about the possibility of future defaults on major overseas loans.

Are the experts and their suggestions consistently correct? It's difficult to know. The show's producer does not release any statistical follow-up on the performance of the stocks or industries recommended by the panel and guests.

Does Rukeyser move markets? Yes—although again, it's difficult to determine precisely how much. Yet if you talk to people interested in finance, most of them will admit to watching the show now and then if not regularly. Many investors across the nation jot down the names of stocks recommended on "Wall Street Week," and many viewers no doubt purchase these stocks during the following week. Some stockbrokers, who may laugh at Rukeyser, nevertheless watch the show in order to do their homework on the stocks mentioned on the Friday newscast. By the following Monday morning they are prepared to answer their clients when they call wanting to know if they should buy a "Wall Street Week" stock.

Even if the precise degree to which Rukeyser moves markets is unknown, we do know he and his program have heightened America's awareness of the world of Wall Street.

MARKET MOVER TIPS

- Watch "Wall Street Week." Nowhere else can the average investor hear the advice of so many talented professionals— and at no cost. Although many of the experts and members of the panel are on other news programs, they seem to speak with unusual freedom on "Wall Street Week."

- If you watch financial news shows on a regular basis, you'll gather an amazing amount of information, automatically track economic trends, and build your financial vocabulary and awareness. The key to smart investing is to be up to date, and the media can help.

- Remember this cautionary note: investment tips heard on TV and radio are also heard by millions of others. They're no longer a hot new idea.

- Temper any urge to rush out and buy every stock that is mentioned by remembering the advice of the pros, who say, "Sell on the news."

Financial TV Shows

"Wall Street Week"
PBS
Hosted by Louis Rukeyser, this weekly show discusses the week's stock market activity and follows up with questions from viewers. A noted financial expert is questioned by the program's panel.

"Adam Smith's Money World"
PBS
"Adam Smith" is a pen name for a financial author. His weekly program features excellent graphic presentations of a current business topic followed by discussions with experts.

"Nightly Business Report"
PBS
This half-hour show, Mondays through Fridays, covers topical business news and the stock market. It includes excellent information on overseas and domestic markets.

"Moneyline"
PBS
This half-hour show, Mondays through Fridays, covers stock market news and late-breaking financial stories. Stock tips and financial insights are valuable to serious investors.

"Wall Street Journal Report"
CBS
During this half-hour weekly show, a team of reporters covers current business and consumer news. Topics are of general interest and often include news about individual industries.

CNN
Cable
Continuous coverage of the financial markets weekdays from 6:00 A.M. to 6:00 P.M. The ticker tape runs constantly at the bottom of the TV screen, so investors can check a stock's price.

PART VII

...

EVENT-DRIVEN MARKET MOVERS

Major happenings such as wars, assassinations, and economic or financial scandals also push the market. Sometimes they act like wild cards with sudden and unpredictable consequences. By studying the market's responses over the decades, however, we've come to understand their long-term consequences. Six different types of events and their impact on the financial world are examined in this section:

European Community
North American Free Trade Agreement
Unexpected events
War (or the Threat of War)
Scandals in the financial community
Quirky indicators

Unlike most other market movers, these do not help us forecast our position within the BUSINESS CYCLE. Instead, they sometimes result in "false" readings, such as consumer confidence rising in 1990 after the American victory in the Persian Gulf, although the recession was not yet over. Sometimes these market movers register as mere blips on the screen, working their way through the financial markets and then correcting themselves in a matter of hours or days. And some of these event-driven market movers, such as the EUROPEAN COMMUNITY, NORTH AMERICAN FREE TRADE AGREEMENT, and war have a significant long-term impact that affect our personal financial holdings. The knowledgeable investor must be able to "predict" the short- and long-term consequences of these market movers in order to stay ahead of the game.

CHAPTER 47

European Community

■ ■ ■

The European Community, also referred to as the Common Market, is a group of twelve European nations that have joined to form an area free of internal tariffs.

December 31, 1992, was a momentous New Year's Eve for Europeans. The next day the twelve nations that make up the European Community (EC)—France, Germany, Great Britain, Italy, the Netherlands, Belgium, Luxembourg, Ireland, Spain, Portugal, Denmark, and Greece—joined together to form an integrated economic community called the European Community. It's a day that Europeans had been working toward since the end of World War II. The EC will bring about the free, unencumbered movement of people, goods, services, and capital across the borders of twelve countries. To achieve this economic unity, the EC has removed all tariffs between member nations.

The twelve member countries have a total population of 340 million people, making it the largest single marketplace for goods and services in the world. By way of comparison, the United States has 245 million consumers, and Japan 130 million. The united market of Europe is expected to produce $4.5 trillion in goods and services, putting it in second place to the United States, whose GNP in 1990 was \$5.5 trillion, and ahead of third-place Japan.

The twelve nations agreed that for their mutual benefit the following internal freedoms would begin on January 1, 1993:

1. **Free movement of persons:** European Community nationals and foreign tourists will no longer be stopped at borders between the member states. They will be able to travel as freely as they do within their own nations; students and workers will also be able to study and/or work at any place within the EC.

2. **Free movement of goods:** Goods will travel freely between member nations without the constraints of tariffs, border checks, or administrative paperwork.

3. **Free movement of services:** Airlines will offer a wider number of destinations within the EC, service and safety will improve, and costs will be lowered. The transportation of goods will become more efficient and cost-effective because internal paperwork will be eliminated and border restrictions will be reduced or eliminated. European television will offer more channels and programs as technology for the entire EC is upgraded. Telephone service will be similarly improved.

4. **Free movement of capital:** Citizens of the twelve countries will be able to move their currency and financial assets within the EC without restriction. Both corporations and individuals will be able to transfer funds freely in the EC, and investment and borrowing will be similarly free of cross-border restraints.

WHY THE EC IS IMPORTANT
TO THE UNITED STATES

Many of the United States' most important trading partners are members of the European Community. International trade between the United States and these countries has been comparatively free and easy. Yet even as free trade flourished, there were disagreements. If the EC moves in the direction of greater exclusivity, and if the differences of opinion between the United States and the EC turn to open hostility, the United States will lose some of its most important markets.

The future is still uncertain. There have been hostile as well as conciliatory speeches by European political leaders. Nevertheless, the possibility of a "Fortress Europe" with external tariffs and quotas remains a possibility. Some say this is why the United States has entered into the NORTH AMERICAN FREE TRADE AGREEMENT, which—if it is ratified—will unite the markets of Canada, Mexico, and the United States.

Because the direction of the post-1992 Common Market is still uncertain, we can only consider the possible outcomes and compare the impact of each on our currency, stocks, and bonds.

The Best Scenario

Europe remains friendly and trade between the United States and the EC continues to be as free as it is now, in which case investors could expect these conditions to continue:

1. The U.S. dollar remains the reserve currency of the world and continues to be held by EC and other nations as a store of value.

2. Stocks in the United States continue to attract European and other foreign investors as long as they do not become overvalued or damaged by internal conditions in the United States, such as rising INFLATION or a deep recession.

3. U.S. bonds continue to be bought and held by foreign investors as long as United States INTEREST RATES attract these investors.

The Middle Scenario

Relations between the United States and the EC are strained, but many of the free trade arrangements remain intact. Then these developments can be expected:

1. The U.S. dollar remains in its preeminent world position as a reserve currency for the world, but is subject to "free-falls" in value of 10% during those times when our economy goes into a recession or our inflation rises above the inflation rate of the EC and other industrialized nations.

2. U.S. stocks are subject to even greater volatility as foreign investors tend to "dump" our stocks when they feel uncertain about our currency.

3. A greater uncertainty about our dollar may make our trading partners less willing to buy our Treasuries. This could lead to higher interest rates in the United States and slower economic growth.

The Worst Scenario

The European Community becomes a regional trading bloc, a Fortress Europe, which severely restricts U.S. imports. If this occurs, these conditions can be anticipated:

1. The dollar might no longer be the world's reserve currency. The VALUE OF THE DOLLAR would depend on the strength of our own trading bloc consisting of the United States, Canada, and Mexico.

2. Our stocks could have considerably less appeal to foreign investors, who are drawn instead to the stock markets of Europe and the developing Eastern European nations. If these areas promise greater economic growth, investment by foreigners in the United States would decline.

3. Bond prices in the United States could suffer. First, a lower dollar would make imports more costly, and our rate of inflation would rise, which is always bad for bonds. Foreign investors would be less willing to buy long-term U.S. Treasury bonds, and this would force the United States to raise interest rates to attract investors.

MARKET MOVER TIPS

■ As the European Community begins to move into high gear, watch the media for clues to the direction European leaders are taking with respect to the three scenarios described above. If it appears as though the worst-case scenario may come to pass, buy CDs denominated in German deutsche-marks or in ECUs (European Currency Units). These will offer protection against any serious fall in the value of the dollar.

■ If the middle-case scenario unfolds, expect the United States to strengthen its ties to its North American trading partners and use this as leverage in its trade arrangements with the EC. Call your broker about recommendations for investments in Mexico and Canada. Teléphonos de México ADRs (TMX on the New York Stock Exchange) has already risen in price in anticipation of this event. Look for mutual funds that include Canadian and Mexican stocks in their portfolios.

■ In the event that the best-case scenario evolves and free trade continues to flourish between the United States and the EC, U.S. stocks will be good buys. Invest in a blue-chip mutual fund or individual blue chips and multinational companies. (Multinationals have the advantage of already doing extensive business with European countries.)

■ Even if you're not a stock or bond investor, be sure to stay tuned—the upcoming events in the European Community will affect all of us, our jobs, and our businesses.

DID YOU KNOW THAT?

Most European currency can trace its origins to ancient times.

Deutschemark. As the standard monetary unit of West Germany, the deutschemark was instituted in 1948 to distinguish it from the East German mark. The word *mark* originally referred to a weight measurement—in the ninth century A.D. it was valued at two-thirds of the Roman pound. The first mark coin was struck in Lübeck in 1506. The deutschemark is divided into a hundred pfennigs. The pfennig was a medieval silver coin.

Drachma. The main unit in Greece, the drachma, is divided into a hundred lepta. In ancient Greece the drachma was a silver coin as well as a standard weight measurement. The word meant handful. *Lepton* was the name of a smaller amount of weight.

Escudo. The name of the Portuguese currency means shield. It is divided into a hundred centavos. The first escudo appeared in 1537.

Franc. The French franc was first issued as a gold coin in 1360, and it is believed it took its name from the coin's inscription in Latin: "*Francorum Rex,*" or king of the Franks. This was the official title of Jean le Bon, or John the Good, who was king of France when the coin was struck. The franc is divided into a hundred centimes. The centime was first struck in 1795 by the revolutionary government as part of the country's new decimal system.

Luxembourg and Belgium also use the franc and centime for their currency.

Guilder. In the Netherlands the guilder was first struck in 1601. The guilder was originally a gold (*gulden*) coin.

Krona. The name of this Danish coin means crown. It has been the official monetary unit in Denmark since 1895, when it was issued as a silver coin.

Lira. The currency of Italy, the lira is divided into a hundred centesimi. The name is derived from the Roman *libra*, or pound. Although it was used in medieval times as an accounting term, it was not struck as a coin until 1472, when it was issued by Doge Nicholas Tron of Venice.

Peseta. The currency of Spain derives its name from *peso*, or weight, and dates back to the eighteenth century. The peseta was introduced in 1497 during the monetary reforms of King Ferdinand and Queen Isabella; it is divided into a hundred centimos.

Pound. The first one-pound piece was struck in silver in 1642. The present pound, which is also a coin, was struck in 1983 to replace the one-pound paper note. In 1986 the British introduced a two-pound coin. The pound is divided into a hundred pennies. The penny was originally a silver coin dating back to the eighth century and probably copied from the Roman *novus denarius*, or new denier. The decimal penny was introduced in 1971.

Punt. The Irish pound. It is divided into a hundred pighne, or pence.

CHAPTER 48

North American Free Trade Agreement

■ ■ ■

A proposed accord among the United States, Mexico, and Canada, the agreement would form a continental free-trade zone, similar to the European Common Market.

The United States has long been an advocate of a world in which trade between nations moves freely, so that each country can compete in an open, global marketplace. Yet external pressures are coming to bear on this long-held attitude: as the unification of Europe into a common market draws nearer, fears grow that a unified Europe—with a captive marketplace larger than North America—will become exclusive, even self-sufficient, and will reduce its trading activities with the rest of the world, including the United States.

The Bush administration, therefore, pushed for a trade agreement that will create a unified North American marketplace. In mid-1991 Congress granted the president a two-year extension to negotiate the treaty. President Clinton has until June 1993 to present a trade agreement to Congress that they must either accept without amendment or reject.

With this take it or leave it mandate, and with the majority of the Congress in favor of an agreement, negotiations went forward full-blast under President Bush's leadership. President Clinton endorsed NAFTA with reservations. The degree of his enthusiasm and support will be a major market mover in and of itself. (See chapter 38, "President of the United States.") Both Mexico and Canada have many compelling reasons to support the agreement, and all three countries have been working to meet the 1993 deadline.

The major issues on the table are these:

- access to each country's markets and elimination of tariff barriers
- protection of copyrights, patents, and trademarks
- freedom to enter each other's energy markets for oil and gas production and cross border pipelines
- liberalizing rules for investment in each country
- allowing trade to flow freely within the trade union

A major obstacle was surmounted when Mexico passed a law protecting patents of both industrial and intellectual property. American pharmaceutical companies were especially concerned about protection for their patents.

Other hurdles are still to be overcome, including Mexico's reluctance to have foreign competition within their energy and transportation industries. Likewise, Canada doesn't want foreign firms competing in its broadcasting, newspaper, and publishing areas. Although Canada and the United States already have a free trade agreement, Canada wants easier access to the U.S. banking system. In the United States, labor unions worry about a flood of cheap Mexican labor undercutting higher-paid U.S. workers. President Clinton is concerned about protecting the environment and American workers. These are only a few of the points yet to be resolved.

As we go to press, the odds for passage of the North American Free Trade Agreement (NAFTA) are very good. Exactly how NAFTA will move our markets will depend upon the final agreement negotiated, how North America interacts with the European Community, and whether world trade divides into regional trade blocs or remains open. Yet NAFTA is already a market mover: on July 1, 1991, *The New York Times* reported that "Mexico held its position as the world's top-performing market, as investors continued to bet that it would benefit from economic reform and a free-trade agreement with the U.S. and Canada . . . [as] many other of the world's markets . . . fell."

If NAFTA is established, major Mexican and Canadian companies will be listed on the New York and American stock exchanges or over the counter. Capital and investments should flow more easily throughout the continent, which may lead to banks with branches in all three countries. If so, cross-border investments will be facilitated.

Finally, low-cost Mexican labor will be a significant first step in bringing American industries such as apparel and textile production back to North America. Later, as this pool of labor becomes more skilled, North American automobiles may again rival in quality those of Germany and Japan.

MARKET MOVER TIP

■ Talk to your broker about suitable investments in Mexican and Canadian stocks that will benefit from NAFTA. Consider individual stocks or single-country funds.

DID YOU KNOW THAT?

Few countries have as many natural resources as Canada. Its forests cover about half its land surface and more than half of them are commercially productive, used for making lumber, pulp, and paper. It is also the world's leading producer of nickel and zinc and the second-most-important producer of uranium. It ranks third in the world in the production of cobalt, platinum, and gold and fourth in aluminum and lead. Canada is also home to two of the world's most-productive fishing grounds.

CHAPTER 49

Unexpected Events

■ ■ ■

Certain unexpected events cast their shadows on the New York Stock Exchange and other financial markets. Since these events are each unique, it's not possible to rely on the general rules or theories that can be applied to changing economic indicators. However, by becoming familiar with the historical reactions of financial markets to a variety of unexpected situations, you can better judge how markets might react to future events.

Whether an event is world shaking, such as the 1991 coup in the U.S.S.R. (and its aftermath), a major new oil discovery, or serious internal troubles within a major corporation, the effect is soon reflected in the financial markets. The fundamental thing that makes market prices change is the investor's perception of the future. When, for instance, the economy is headed into a recession after a period of expansion, investors perceive that the Fed will follow its usual path and lower INTEREST RATES. During unexpected events perceptions are shaken up, and for a period of time conjecture simply causes confusion.

When a pharmaceutical company has several exciting new products awaiting approval by the Food and Drug Administration, analysts and investors perceive that there will be higher sales and greater profits for the company in the future and so the prices of the stock are bid up. Higher profits is an expected event. But if the pharmaceutical company's new drugs were developed to treat cancer, and cancer was made obsolete by a miraculous cure, the prices of the company's stock would fall.

Typically when the unexpected occurs, investors must react very fast—or not react at all. Sometimes it is best not to react—not to sell—because often these events merely create blips in market prices; within time, the situation and the prices stabilize. Even dramatic and sudden events such as the coup in U.S.S.R. are predicted now to have only short-term effects on the market.

You can be certain that any important event will be covered by the press. Economists, financial analysts, and a host of experts will offer their opinions, advice, and predictions. By understanding the fundamentals of the economic series, you can make an informed opinion about the value of these experts' statements.

WORLD POLITICAL EVENTS

August 19, 1991. Right wing hard-line communists held Soviet President Mikhail Gorbachev under house arrest and were in the process of taking over the government. As stock markets opened around the world, they fell precipitously. Tokyo's Nikkei average fell 1,357 points or 5.95%; Germany's DAX index fell 155 points, or 9.4%; and when trading was finished on the New York Stock Exchange, the DOW JONES INDUSTRIAL AVERAGE had fallen 70 points, or 2.4%.

The VALUE OF THE DOLLAR rose as investors around the world

sought the safe haven of American currency, and gold was up as well. Investors in the stock market perceived a new world equation in which militant communism would again be a powerful and troublemaking force in the world. At the very least they saw a mass exodus of Russian and Eastern European refugees pouring into Western Europe. (See chapter 50, ''War or the Threat of War.'')

By August 21, 1991, the coup had collapsed after a dramatic two days in which the world worried that communism might be back in the driver's seat. When news that the coup had failed reached investors on Wednesday, the Dow Jones Industrial Average soared 88 points, or 3.02%. Once this more predictable situation prevailed, traders and investors around the world reacted: the German DAX index climbed 44 points, or 2.87%, and earlier, in Tokyo, the Nikkei average had recovered by 364 points, or 1.68%.

Because the American economy was fairly insulated from the Soviet Union, the coup was not seen by economists as a disastrous event over the long term. A stronger dollar would weaken exports, which would be more expensive to foreigners; and agriculture might be impacted by the unpredictability of the future of grain sold to the Soviet Union. On the whole the effect on our markets was expected to be mild. Still, when it was over investors breathed a sigh of relief.

November 22, 1963. On this day President John F. Kennedy was shot in Dallas, Texas. As the news came across the wires, the stock market reacted almost immediately: The market had been undergoing a small rally, with the Dow Jones up 3.31 points at 1:00 P.M, but at 2:00 P.M. the news hit Wall Street, creating a flood of sell orders and causing the Dow Jones Industrial Average to fall 21.16 points, the worst drop since Black Monday, May 28, 1962, when the Dow fell 34.95 points. Trading earlier in the day had been relatively light: At 2:00 P.M. only 4.43 million shares had been traded, but by 2:07 P.M., when the New York Stock Exchange halted trading, 2.2 million additional shares had been sold, pushing the day's volume to 6.63 million. (The day before, the trading volume was 5.67 million shares.) After the exchange closed, it took the tape forty-two minutes to complete the orders that had already been placed.

September 26, 1955. This day is remembered by veterans of the market as the day Ike had his heart attack after playing thirty-six holes of golf in Denver's high altitude. President Eisenhower's illness brought about the largest dollar loss since 1929 on the New York Stock Exchange. Volume was the highest in twenty-two years and the DJIA lost nearly 32 points, down from a high of 487.45. During November President Eisenhower returned to the White House, and the market quickly moved up. The Dow closed the year at its high, 488.4, up 20.8%, reflecting the nation's and Ike's good health. In June of the next year, Eisenhower had an ileitis attack and the market again reacted, but in proportion to the severity of the illness: there was a one-day, great drop in volume, and it quickly recovered.

FINANCIAL EVENTS

June 19, 1991. The Columbia Gas System, a leading supplier of natural gas to utilities located in the Northeast, announced the suspension of dividends on its common stock and said that it might have to declare bankruptcy if it was unable to renegotiate its contracts with bankers and gas producers. When the announcement was made, a share of Columbia Gas dropped from $35.50 to close the day at $20.75, representing a price loss of 40%.

Columbia Gas's news came as a shock to most of the investment community; it had not anticipated the event, and the 40% drop in the company's stock price reflected an effort on the part of investors to adjust to the new development. Later, the company did indeed go into Chapter 11 bankruptcy.

INTERNAL CORPORATE PROBLEMS

September 4, 1991. News about a corporation's financial outlook often impacts immediately on the price of its shares. This was true for Browning-Ferris after company officials said profits for the fourth quarter would be 15% to 25% lower than the third quarter and profits for fiscal 1991 would be 12% to 15% below 1990. The company is the second-largest hauler of U.S. trash.

After the information appeared in a filing with the Securities and Exchange Commission, the stock tumbled $3.875, or 15%, to $21.875 per share on heavy volume. The September announcement was the latest in a series of bad news from the company.

The problems the company faced were partially recession based: the recession had cut hauling and dumping volumes; businesses and the public were working to reduce their garbage through recycling, and some large Browning-Ferris dumps had either closed or cut back the amount of trash they could accept. With each negative announcement more and more investors concluded that a turnaround for the company was not in sight. Adding to the market-moving event were negative comments about the company from several garbage-industry analysts.

Heavy selling of a company's stock by top management or, in the case of a family-owned business, by members of the family, is sometimes seen as a negative sign, which it may or may not be. The perception in the case of insider selling is that these people know something negative about the company. In the Browning-Ferris debacle the company's chief financial officer, R. John Stanton, Jr., disclosed on September 4 that during the three weeks prior to his announcement, he had sold half of his stock in the company for about $1.7 million—and at a price substantially above what it was on September 4. These and other announcements over the year undermined investor confidence in Browning-Ferris and its management.

CHANGES IN CORPORATE OWNERSHIP

Sometimes market events force stockholders to make quick financial decisions. This was the case during the late eighties when a series of takeovers swept through corporate America. The troubled Federated Department Stores was an excellent example of an event-driven change in an individual company's stock.

- On January 11, 1988, Federated shares closed at $34.75.
- During that week Donald Trump announced he was buying a large block of common stock in the company. Stock prices fell slightly.
- On January 25 Robert Campeau made a bid for the company at $47 per share.
- On March 2 Federated entered into a merger agreement with R. H. Macy. Macy offered a cash tender at $77.35 per share, but for only 80% of Federated's shares.
- In April Campeau bid $87.50 per share.

The Campeau offer was one that Federated could not refuse. What did Federated have that Campeau wanted so badly? Federated's assets were far more valuable than its stated book value of $29.50. The company's true value was based in downtown real estate in leading cities throughout the United States; shopping-center leases in important locations; the value represented by Bloomingdale's name (Bloomingdale's flagship store with its international recognition was a prize sought by both Campeau and Macy); and major department-store properties with prestigious names such as A&S, Burdine's, Filene's Basement, and Rich's. These values, which were not represented by the stated book value, attracted both Campeau and Macy into the bidding war. After an initial decline in value, the stock prices more than doubled in three months.

These examples show quite clearly how events—especially surprise events—move overall markets as well as the markets in individual stocks. Of course, some events, such as a continuing weakness in a commodity in which there is a glut, can be foreseen. Other events, however, come as "almost" complete surprises. It is these surprise events that can be very costly or beneficial to investors. (See also chapter 51, "Scandals in the Financial Community.")

MARKET MOVER TIPS

■ To protect your investments from surprise events, don't be greedy—take profits on a continual basis.

■ When the whole world seems to agree about something— THINK that they may be mistaken.

■ Buy stocks and bonds for their solid values and the income and/or growth they provide. If they are sound investments, they are likely to be unaffected by an event or will recover fairly quickly.

■ If you own investments adversely affected by an event-driven market mover, follow the advice of the late Wall Street veteran, Harold L. Rosenthal, who said: "Sell down to the sleeping point." The sleeping point varies, depending upon your risk tolerance; it may mean one-third, one-half, or all of a position.

DID YOU KNOW THAT?

Events only rarely cause the New York Stock Exchange to close at midday. Trading was halted just twenty-six minutes after the news services reported that President John F. Kennedy had been shot. The early close was unusual for the big board. Although it had closed occasionally for funerals of dignitaries, there were only two other emergency closings during the century. In 1933 a prankster put tear gas in the exchange's ventilating system. On September 16, 1920, the NYSE closed at noon after an explosion outside J. P. Morgan and Company, located at 23 Wall Street, killed thirty people.

CHAPTER 50

War or the Threat of War

· · ·

Someday," as Carl Sandburg once said, "they'll give a war and nobody will come." Someday, of course, has not yet happened, and wars—whether official or unofficial, invasions or military coups—are still very much a part of our world, affecting us in many ways. Wars also have a critical impact on the financial markets.

News of war or a military crisis almost inevitably makes stocks fall. Then at some point during the conflict itself or shortly after it's over, they rally.

Results of a study by Ned Davis Research, Inc., of Nokomis, Florida, found that the DOW JONES INDUSTRIAL AVERAGE generally falls prior to or at the beginning of a military crisis but bounces back within a month or so. (See table 9A.) During the first week after the bombing of Pearl Harbor, the Dow dropped 6.5%, one month later it was up 1.4%. The greatest recovery occurred with the Cuban Missile Crisis in 1962. The Dow fell 9.4% but bounced back within a month, up 15.6%. The bombing of Libya was an exception. When

Table 9A ■ Crisis Events, DJIA Declines, and Subsequent Performance

Event	Event Dates	Reaction Dates	%	—Months From Low— 1	3	6
U.S. Invasion of Panama	12/17/89–1/4/90	12/15/89–12/20/89	-1.9	-3.2	+1.9	+7.7
U.S. Bombing of Libya	4/15/86–4/16/86 11 p.m.–12 a.m.	4/15/86–4/21/86	+2.6	-4.3	-4.1	-2.7
U.S. Invasion of Grenada	10/25/83 +	10/24/83–11/7/83	-2.7	+4.9	-2.8	-4.1
Falkland Islands	4/2/82–6/14/82	4/1/82–5/7/82	+4.3	-7.5	-10.2	+19.4
USSR Invades Afghanistan	12/26/79 +	12/24/79–1/3/80	-2.2	+6.7	-4.4	+8.4
Arab Oil Embargo	10/19/73–3/18/74	10/18/73–12/5/73	-18.2	+11.2	+10.7	+5.3
U.S. Troops in Cambodia (Also Liquidity Crisis)	4/30/70 +	4/29/70–5/26/70	-14.4	+9.0	+20.5	+23.7
Cuban Missile Crisis	8/24/62–10/28/62	8/23/62–10/23/62	-9.4	+15.6	+21.4	+28.1
Korean War	6/25/50	6/23/50–7/13/50	-12.0	+9.0	+15.7	+23.4
Pearl Harbor	12/7/41	12/6/41–12/10/41	-6.5	+1.4	-6.9	-4.4
Fall of France (German Blitzkrieg Dunkirk)	5/10/40–6/22/40	5/9/40–6/22/40	-17.1	-.6	+10.0	+4.5

Table courtesy: Ned Davis Research Inc.

the news broke on April 15, 1986, the Dow actually rose 2.6% and then one month later fell 4.3%. Of the eleven military crises examined by Ned Davis Research, on average the Dow rallied 3.8% from the low within one month, 4.7% within three months, and 9.9% within six months.

THE BAKER-AZIZ TALKS

Sometimes there need only be talk of a war to move the market. That was the case with the Baker-Aziz talks. On January 9, 1991, in Geneva, with just six days remaining before Iraq's deadline to pull out of Kuwait, U.S. Secretary of State James A. Baker met with Iraqi Foreign Minister Tariq Aziz in what the world felt was a last-ditch effort to head off war in the Persian Gulf. Around the globe people waited anxiously for any hint of the outcome.

The meeting in Geneva began at 5:00 A.M. Eastern Standard Time. Had the two men met and quickly adjourned, there would have been plenty of time for those who wished to do so to enter their buy or sell orders (based on the outcome of the talk) before the opening of the New York Stock Exchange at 9:30 A.M. Eastern Standard Time. But instead of slamming out of the meeting in anger, the two men kept talking, right through the opening of the New York Stock Exchange and well into the morning, New York time.

The only news that leaked out was from a White House "spokesman" who said the talks were "substantive." That one word was all the markets needed. The Asian markets had already closed, the European markets were about to close, but in New York, the word "substantive" led to public optimism that there would be peace: the bond and stock markets took off. Treasury bonds rose 1½ points (a very sizable rise for Treasuries even though in dollars it's only $15 per $1,000 bond). Based on a feeling of relief and hope that the war could be avoided, the Dow Jones Industrial Average rose nearly 40 points. At the same time, the price of crude oil, which had been high because of fears of a disruption of Persian Gulf oil supplies if war broke out, plunged as peace seemed at hand. The VALUE OF THE DOLLAR fell against the deutschemark and the yen because if the world remained at peace, these two strong currencies would maintain their world dominance, while the dollar, regarded as a safe haven in times of turmoil, would be less attractive as an investment.

Suddenly, it all fell apart. As the public listened to Secretary of State Baker's news conference just before 2:00 P.M., stock prices started to fall. *The Wall Street Journal* reported what happened: "The stunning reversal came the moment U.S. Secretary James Baker . . . said he had made no progress in persuading Iraq to withdraw from Kuwait. U.S. stock and bond prices began plummeting as soon as Mr. Baker said: 'Regrettably . . . I heard nothing that suggested to me any Iraqi flexibility whatsoever.' "

The Dow Jones Industrial Average, which had been up more than 40 points earlier in the day, plunged 54 points *two hours later*, ending the trading day with a total drop of 39 points. The market mover in this case was one word: "regrettably." That's all it took for stocks and bond prices to fall, oil prices to rise, and the dollar to gain in strength against other currencies.

This, then is an example of what can happen to the financial markets when our perceptions about the future are abruptly jolted by a major event. We saw a similar situation in late August 1991 when a military coup temporarily replaced Mikhail S. Gorbachev, president of the Soviet Union.

THE KREMLIN SHAKE-UP

On Monday, August 19, 1991, the world's financial markets reacted sharply and immediately to the news that a group of hard-line communists had led a coup against President Gorbachev. At one point during the day, the Dow Jones Industrial Average dropped 106 points. It closed the day with a loss of 69.99 points, its largest drop since the beginning of the Kuwait crisis. (On August 6, 1990, soon after the Iraqi invasion of Kuwait, the Dow dropped 93.1 points.)

At the same time, the American dollar rose 3% against other currencies as the uncertainty of the situation sent investors looking for a safe currency. OIL PRICES jumped as traders speculated that a civil war in the Soviet Union, which produces an enormous amount of oil, might disrupt its oil exports. Prices of grain (corn, wheat, and soybeans) dropped sharply on commodity exchanges, reflecting concern over whether U.S. grain sales to the Soviet Union would be disrupted and/or not be paid for.

Defying the general downward trend of stocks, were military and aerospace stocks; this was due to the belief that U.S. cuts in military spending might be reversed. The United States was reminded, once again, that war is possible. Among those stocks that were up for the day were McDonnell Douglas, Loral, Northrop—all military and aerospace stocks—and Exxon, Chevron, and ARCO.

The Soviet situation came about just as the FEDERAL RESERVE's top policymakers were getting ready to go to Washington, D.C., for one of their periodic meetings to decide on whether to change short-term INTEREST RATES. There was some speculation that the coup would force the Fed to lower rates once again in order to overcome a possible decline in consumer spending caused by fear of war or a renewed cold war. Earlier the same month (August 1991) the Fed had lowered short-term rates to stimulate the recession-weakened economy.

THE PERSIAN GULF WAR

Military and aerospace stocks also performed well during the Persian Gulf War, in part because this war was televised. Americans saw on their TV screens just how well weapons manufactured in this country performed. It might seem logical, therefore, to purchase stock in the companies that produced our missiles. Yet the effect of war on the market is never exactly the same.

Before selecting stocks in which to invest in any wartime situation, these questions should be addressed:

1. Will the _____ war end quickly and decisively? If the answer is yes, there may be no need to replace weapons used out of inventory.
2. Will the country or countries where the fighting takes place be destroyed, as Germany was in World War II? If so, certain companies may be called in after the war to rebuild the country's infrastructure, medical-care facilities, schools, and so on.
3. Is the United States (and its allies) willing to commit ground forces to the war and thus risk losing many soldiers? If the answer is no, then a war may require larger quantities of sophisticated missiles and equipment

If the crisis is fairly localized, as was the case with the Kremlin shake-up in August 1991 and the T'ienanmen Square massacre in June 1989, the impact is very short term. For a crisis to impact on our economy and create an abrupt slump in business and consumer confidence, either the action has to be closer to home or U.S. troops have to be involved. Fortunately, such large-scale action *appears* to be unlikely.

MARKET MOVER TIPS

■ War jitters lift the dollar because it's regarded as a safe haven. A stronger dollar increases the price of American exports to foreign countries, causing a rise in the UNEMPLOYMENT RATE, and hurts stocks of multinational companies that rely heavily on revenue from abroad. When the dollar is strong, foreign income is worth less when converted into dollars. (See chapter 35, "Value of the Dollar.")

■ If war brings about a fear of higher prices, particularly for oil and other staples, yields on long-term Treasury bonds tend to rise and investors are wise to lock in those yields.

- The sharp falls in the stock market that occur at the outset of a war present a buying opportunity: quality stocks are often cheaper than they were before a crisis.
- Terrorism can hurt certain industries, regardless of where it takes place. Hotels and resorts in strategic locations suffer. General trade between those countries involved is adversely affected, and so is the shipping industry. Airlines, some cruise-ship lines, and other travel-related companies experience a drop in business.

DID YOU KNOW THAT?

The Erie Canal was an indirect result of the War of 1812. During that war much of the land action took place along the Canadian border, highlighting the need for better transportation in upstate New York. As peacetime prosperity returned to the country, De Witt Clinton, who'd been mayor of New York City for nineteen years and governor of the state for nine, sponsored the Erie Canal, which enabled commerce from the Great Lakes area to be channeled through the New York harbor. The canal, built without any help from the federal government, cost $7,602,000. On October 26, 1825, when the waters of Lake Erie were admitted into the canal at Buffalo, the news was sent to New York City by firing off cannons in sequence down the Hudson River. New York City replied in kind, and the roar of the cannons went back up the river. Before the canal was dug, it cost $125 a ton to move freight between Albany and Buffalo. Immediately after its completion that rate dropped to $5 a ton.

CHAPTER 51

Scandals in the Financial Community

■ ■ ■

Scandals may be nothing new on Wall Street, but they never seem to stop shocking everyone—the public as well as the financial community. The most seasoned, cynical traders and brokers can be heard to say, "I can't believe they'd do that!" as the news of fortune hunters cutting corners comes over the tape. Mark Twain understood the temptation of a fortune better than most: "I'm not opposed to millionaires," he said, "but it would be dangerous to offer me the position."

To protect the public from unscrupulous operators, President Franklin D. Roosevelt established an industry watchdog: the Securities and Exchange Commission (SEC). Unfortunately, there's a lot to watch. The commission hasn't been able to prevent some scandals from moving the markets.

MICHAEL MILKEN

This one-time king of junk bonds, and the prime force behind the creation of the $200 billion junk bond market, wreaked havoc in the bond markets and elsewhere when his activities came to light. His forced departure from Drexel Burnham Lambert, Inc., in late 1988 set a chain of events in motion that ended with Drexel filing for bankruptcy on February 18, 1990. Over five thousand people lost their jobs.

One of the earliest signs of trouble in the junk bond market popped up in the spring of 1989 when Drexel failed to rescue one of its bigger deals: Integrated Resources, Inc., the financial services company. Integrated had sold real-estate tax shelters, a business that died with tax reform in 1986. The company tried to regroup by diversifying with capital provided by junk bonds. But the company had heavy losses, and Drexel allowed Integrated to default on $1 billion of commercial paper. In what some people saw as poetic justice, Integrated filed for bankruptcy the same day as Drexel Burnham Lambert.

It was some time before Milken was found guilty. In September 1990, when the news that he'd admitted to six securities-related crimes hit Wall Street, prices for junk bonds fell 8.36% compared with 5.1% for stocks. The firestorm that raged through the junk bond group pushed down the prices on the highest-quality to a price level of 88% to 94% of their original value. At that time, junk bonds were valued *on average* at just 68.5% of their initial price. Many poor-quality bonds suffered the ultimate indignity of "no bid."

As bond prices dropped, skittish investors took big losses and redeemed their shares in junk-bond mutual funds. The Fidelity High Income Fund, for example, shrunk in size from $1.8 billion to just over $1 billion.

Eventually the junk-bond market recovered, but the beating the bonds took in the scandal-related decline left permanent scars. Tax-payers were hurt, too: many of the savings-and-loan institutions taken over by federal regulators held larger portfolios of junk. The decline in the value of those portfolios resulted in an increase in the taxpayer's share of the cost of rescue of the S&L system. Insurance companies also suffered, with several closing their doors. Again, the bailout costs eventually hit the taxpayers, and the situation could grow worse. The final story on the insurance industry is unwritten.

DENNIS LEVINE

The Mike Milken scandal came to light largely through a chain of events that began with Dennis Levine. In the summer of 1986, the largest insider trading case to date came to the public's attention. Levine, managing director of Drexel Burnham Lambert, pleaded guilty to making $12.6 million on inside trades. He apparently conducted his trades thought the Bahamian branch of Swiss-owned Bank Leu of the Bahamas. Prior to serving his two-year jail sentence, Levine pointed the finger at several others: one of those was Ivan F. Boesky.

IVAN F. BOESKY

In November 1986 Boesky agreed to give up $50 million in insider-trading profits and pay fines of $50 million. The SEC defines insider trading as the illegal profiting from information about corporate takeovers before that knowledge has been publicly announced. Boesky was a specialist in risk arbitrage—the buying and selling of stocks in companies that appear ready to be taken over by another company. Over the course of ten years, Boesky made an estimated $200 million through this procedure.

Arbitrage based on public information is not illegal, but the use of secret tips or insider information, as Boesky sometimes did, is against SEC rules. In this case, the SEC charged that Boesky had contracted Dennis Levine, the takeover specialist at Drexel Burnham Lambert, to provide insider information. Levine, through his own network, had advance information about takeover bids, and Boesky apparently promised to pay Levine a percentage of profits for his tips plus a $2.4 million lump-sum payment.

SALOMON BROTHERS SCANDAL

After the close of trading on August 14, 1991, Salomon Brothers, Inc., one of the nation's leading investment banks, made an announcement that shocked the country. It revealed that three of its top officials had known since April that the firm had engaged in illegal bidding practices in the almost sacred U.S. Treasury note auction.

The following day, Salomon, Inc., the parent of the investment banking firm, watched its stock drop by $4.75 a share and close the day at $26.87, for a 15% drop and a loss of $532 million. A week later the stock was down to $22 per share. Between August 9 when the scandal broke and August 23, the stock fell 38%.

Salomon had outstanding debt of about $7 billion, and there was talk that the debt would be downgraded by one of the independent bond-rating services. Resignations of the firm's top three managers, including John H. Gutfreund, the firm's famous chairman and chief executive and ultimate party-goer and -giver, and the quick appointment over the weekend of Warren Buffet, chairman of Berkshire Hathaway and known to many as Mr. Clean, helped save the company's stock from more-drastic price declines.

Later that month, however, Moody's bond-rating service downgraded Salomon's debt rating by a small degree—from A2 to A3. It remained in the high-grade category, but the downgrading "hurt Salomon's prestige" according to *The Wall Street Journal*, and forced the company to increase its borrowing costs.

The latest fallout from the firm's bond-bidding scandal was desertion by several large, important clients. A number of state pension funds, including Connecticut and California, as well as the prestigious World Bank, suspended doing business with Salomon. The scandal not only caused an immediate drop in the company's stock prices but also sent a shudder through the investment community: if the sacrosanct Treasury auction isn't safe from scandal, what is?

JAPANESE SCANDALS

On July 9, 1991, news broke that the Tokyo Nikkei index had dropped by 3.15% to 21,764, a decline of 412 points. This was a new low for the year and followed on the heels of a drop of 722 points. The severe decline in the Japanese stock market was in response to emerging scandals of illegal trading practices in Japan.

The biggest cause of the fall was the news that Nomura Securities Company, Japan's giant brokerage house, had made huge payments to special customers to cover their stock losses. Apparently other brokerage firms engaged in similar payback policies. One of Nomura's paybacks included Hitachi Ltd., the country's leading electronics firm, as well as a government-affiliated pension fund. At the same time, the firm was hit with charges of doing business with Susumu Ishii, the former head of Japan's second-largest organized crime syndicate.

When the news hit the tape, stock prices on almost all the major Asian exchanges and in Europe fell. The U.S. market fell the morning of the news but recovered later in the day. If the Japanese market crashes, however, the repercussions will be felt in this country. The Japanese own a large percentage of our real estate and our Treasuries.

The fallout from these scandals resulted in a severely depressed Japanese stock market.

Yet another blow to the Japanese market was revealed on August 23, 1991. It centered around a sixty-one-year-old woman, Nue Onoue (pronounced "oh-no-way"), who ran a restaurant on a tiny alley in Osaka's topless bar district. It was frequented by Osaka's rich and famous, who felt the place was a gold mine of financial information and key contacts. Bankers and brokers came night after night to get ideas and insider information.

That was their mistake. It appears that Ms. Onoue, a major stock market investor, was running the biggest bank fraud in the history of Japan. Together with a former manager of an Osaka credit union, she created bogus deposit receipts that were then used as collateral to get loans from various Japanese banks who fell for the scam. Some of Japan's biggest financial institutions, including the huge Industrial Bank of Japan Ltd. and Tokyo Shinkin Bank Ltd., were bilked to the tune of $2.5 billion.

Ms. Onoue, a disciple of a mystic Buddhist sect, dressed in flowing robes and maintained she received stock tips from the gods. She required her stockbrokers to attend weekend prayer sessions that she conducted. Ms. Onoue does not have a M.B.A. or a degree in economics, nor even an undergraduate degree. She is, instead, a classic rags-to-riches woman: raised in a small farming village, she transformed herself from barmaid to billionaire and became the single largest individual stockholder in some of the country's best-known corporations, including Nippon Telegraph and Telephone.

The scandal served to confirm the worldwide perception that Japan, where the brokerage business is informal and very personalized, is ripe for abuse by institutions and individuals. Wide selling of Japanese stocks has resulted.

MARKET MOVER TIPS

■ The market eventually recovers from scandals, which is why long-term investing and diversification are the best line of defense against the unexpected.

■ If the Japanese market crashes, move out of Asian mutual funds and into dollar-denominated securities. Also, sell any Japanese stocks in your portfolio. Keep in mind, too, that Japanese bankers lent sizable amounts to U.S. corporations.

A collapse in the Japanese market would hurt U.S. real estate and, to some extent, corporate mergers, acquisitions, and expansions.

DID YOU KNOW THAT?

Not all scandals wind up being illegal. Take the case of Jay Gould and Black Friday—September 24, 1869. On that day thousands of gold speculators were ruined in a financial panic, all due to the outrageous manipulations of the market by one of its greatest speculators, thirty-three-year-old Jay Gould. Gould almost succeeded in cornering the entire gold market.

During the Civil War the United States had issued millions of dollars in paper money, called "greenbacks." Since they were not redeemable in gold, people hoarded the precious metal, which soon became scarce. Gold sold at a huge premium, while the greenbacks fell in value.

At this time, the government had about $80 million in gold in the Treasury. People thought President Grant would sell the government's gold in the public market to end the hoarding and bring its price down to normal levels. Gould, who already owned $15 million of gold, wanted to convince Grant that an even higher price would be in the best interest of the country. Behind the president's back, Gould purchased more gold at prices as high as $130 an ounce. He put some of the gold in his friend A. Corbin's name. Corbin was also President Grant's brother-in-law. It was understood that Corbin wouldn't have to pay for the gold until it was sold. Gould thought that with Corbin in on the scheme, the president couldn't sell the Treasury's gold. He was wrong. When prices shot up, pressure from others convinced Grant that selling was best for the country.

Corbin told Gould of the president's decision to sell, and the two conspired to keep the information from the public. Realizing that the end was near, Gould convinced his business associate, Jim Fisk, to buy gold to keep the price up so he (Gould) could sell his near the top of the market. Loyal to the end, Fisk bought gold, pushing the price from $145 to $160 while Gould privately sold his holdings.

On September 24, when the news hit Wall Street that the government was going to sell, brokers went wild trying to dump their holdings. It was too late. The price plummeted and closed that day at $135. Gould had already sold his at the top of the market at $160.

A congressional hearing followed. Endless lawsuits were brought against Gould, but he was never convicted of illegal activity.

CHAPTER 52

Quirky Indicators

■ ■ ■

Tried and true indicators such as INFLATION, INTEREST RATES, and the GDP are the most obvious market movers. There are also some rather astounding ways for divining the future direction of the Dow, such as hemlines, the Super Bowl, and the Triple Crown. Although analysts may joke about these theories, some of them secretly keep track of these seemingly silly trends. Please note, however, that these indicators, presented in alphabetical order, may merely reflect the market and are not necessarily market movers.

If you decide to use these unorthodox indicators, you probably won't suffer, but remember what Mark Twain said about investments: "October. This is one of the peculiarly dangerous months to speculate in stocks. The others are July, January, September, April, November, May, March, June, December, August and February."

The day-before-the-holiday theory. Get out your calendar to chart this one. The holiday theory says that stock prices tend to rise on the last trading day before most holidays or holiday weekends.

The reason most often given for this theory is that investors are prone to holiday euphoria and won't sell until they get back.

The hemline theory. This is one of the most popular coincidence theories—note we said "popular," not necessarily accurate. There has been some correlation between hemline trends and stock prices, with short skirts indicating an up market and long hemlines a sign that the market is headed for a big decline. This theory goes back to the fact that skirts rose to almost miniskirt levels with the era of short "flapper" skirts in the twenties, a decade when the market made one of its biggest gains in history. In the thirties ankle-length skirts became the rage, and along with it came the Depression. The hemline theory worked again during the bull market of the sixties, when the mini made its first appearance, and during the eighties, when the mini came back. It could be said, then, that short skirts and high stock prices reflect a general optimism among Americans.

The January barometer. This one maintains that as goes January, so goes the remainder of the year.

The January effect. This one contradicts the January barometer. It claims there is a tendency for stocks to perform better in January than during other months of the year. The theory behind this is that the market tends to be oversold in December, when investors sell shares to raise cash to pay for the holidays and/or to establish losses for tax purposes. Then, after the New Year, they come back into the market, and the pressure to sell declines. If this theory intrigues you, read *The Incredible January Effect* by Josef Lakonishok and Robert Haugen, published by Dow Jones–Irwin. The authors maintain that in January, portfolio managers are doing "window dressing," which means they buy better-known stocks in December and then in January go back to smaller, less-well-known stocks in an all-out effort to outperform the market.

The necktie theory. Some say this theory was invented by analysts at the old Smith Barney, Harris Upham and Company. It goes something like this: When ties widen, as they did in the late sixties and again in 1974, the market widens, too. Then, of course, during a bear market they become thinner. A variation on this theme for tie aficionados says that when the market is cool, wild neckties are big sellers, but when the market heads up, bland ties gain favor among American men. This theory probably goes back to the sixties, when the market was booming and muted club ties were in style. Then with stagflation in the seventies, men started buying flashier neckwear. In the decade of greed (the eighties), the Sherman Mc-Coys of Wall Street wore muted paisley numbers. An interesting sidenote: during the 1990 recession, the U.S. retail tie industry grew by 15%, while sales of suits were down. Were men wearing ties without suits? Things probably weren't that bad.

The presidential election theory. The stock market often rises during a presidential election year, when politicians fight for residence in the White House. Behind this idea is the theory that the president, in the last two years of his administration, focuses on economic expansion to boost his chances for reelection, and investors are optimistic. Indeed, stocks have risen by as much as 48% in fifteen of the last twenty-two election years between 1910 and 1998. Ned Davis, one of the country's leading technical analysts, points out that the FEDERAL RESERVE usually keeps INTEREST RATES tight during the early part of a president's term, but then toward the end of the second year or the beginning of the third, it's somewhat influenced by the administration's desire to rev up the economy before the election, and so it lowers rates. Lower rates, of course, tend to boost the stock market.

The Santa Claus theory. A cheerful theory is that the stock market moves up during the days between Christmas and New Year's Day. The rationale behind such moves is that the money managers are busy selling stocks that were losers and quickly buying new ones before their clients undertake an end-of-the-year review of their portfolios.

The Super Bowl theory. Football fans love this one: If a team in the National Football Conference wins, then the New York Stock Exchange composite index will gain for the year. If the American Football Conference team wins, then the index will sink.

The Triple Crown theory. This theory, the brainchild of William M. LeFevre, a Wall Street investment analyst, says that if one horse wins all three big races—the Kentucky Derby, the Preakness, and the Belmont Stakes—the market closes the year with a net loss.

PART VIII

...

MARKET MOVER INVESTMENT BASICS

As you read through this book, you found a wide range of market mover tips given at the end of most chapters. These tips provided specific advice regarding your personal finances and investments, including bonds, stocks, and real estate in response to market movers. In order to intelligently act upon these tips, it's necessary to know some investment basics. If you already have more than a nodding acquaintance with stocks, bonds, and mutual funds, you may skip over chapter 53 and go straight to chapter 54, "Watching the Market Movers," which reviews some specific investment tips based on market movers.

Stocks, Bonds,
and Mutual Funds

■ ■ ■

Stocks, bonds, and mutual funds are the three instruments that every investor needs to understand in order to position his or her money wisely. Different moves in the market may dictate the movement of money from one instrument to another, so investors must be familiar with the workings of each of these investment options.

STOCKS

Stocks can be divided into two basic types, common and preferred. A *common stock* is a security that represents fractional ownership in a corporation. You lose money on a stock when you sell it after it has fallen below your original purchase price—or has stayed the same (in a period of inflation your money is now worth less). There are two ways to *make* money with a stock: by selling it when it appreciates in price or by accumulating dividends.

A stock rises in price when investors sense that the growth outlook for the company is positive and/or when profits are up and earnings are increasing. The key factor to keep in mind regarding stock prices is the law of supply and demand: a stock increases in price when more people want to buy it than wish to sell it.

Dividends are a periodic payment made to stockholders and drawn from a company's earnings. The company's board of directors decides whether or not dividends will be declared. Before a company pays dividends on *common* stock, it first must pay its bondholders and preferred stockholders (explained below). Typically paid four times a year, dividends can increase, decrease, or be canceled, depending upon the company's profits. Generally, the profits that aren't paid out in dividends are invested back into the company.

Preferred stock has favored status over common stock. There are two differences between preferred and common stock. First, preferred stockholders receive their dividends before any dividends are paid on common shares. Second, a preferred stock's dividend is a *fixed* annual payment; it never changes. Because the dollar amount of the dividend cannot increase or decrease, the yield changes in relationship to the stock's price just like a bond. The fact that this dividend is fixed can be a disadvantage: when inflation and interest rates rise, stockholders are locked in at the old, lower rate. For example, a preferred stock that sells at $100 a share and pays a $10 annual dividend has a yield of 10%. (Yield is the value of the dividend as a percentage of the purchase price of the stock.) If the value of that share were to increase to $200, the $10 annual dividend would have a yield of 5%. Of course, if the value of the share falls to $50, the $10 annual dividend increases to a 20% yield. But then you've also lost $50 if you have to sell the share.

Preferred stocks can be cumulative or noncumulative. If a dividend payment for a cumulative preferred stock is skipped because of corporate losses, it will be paid later when earnings improve. In the case of a noncumulative preferred, the missed dividend is not recovered.

There are several varieties of stocks that generally perform better or worse than others during specific phases of the business cycle. There are also stocks that provide better dividend income or higher yields than others, which tend to appreciate more in price.

Income stocks consistently pay above-average dividends. These include electric utility and telephone companies, oil corporations, closed-end bond funds that trade as stocks, REITs (real-estate investment trusts), and some blue-chip stocks. Investors buy them because they value the steady cash payments. The price of the stock itself is less likely to appreciate considerably. For an up-to-date list of top-yielding stocks, check *Value Line Investment Survey*, available at most public libraries and brokerage firms.

Growth stocks pay little or no dividends because the corporation reinvests most of their profits in the business in order to help it expand. Investors buy these because they expect the company to grow faster than the overall economy, which makes the price of the stock rise. These are somewhat riskier than average stocks because you're betting on the fact that the corporation will meet its high growth potential. Growth stocks are particularly good investments when purchased immediately prior to a recovery. *Value Line* runs a list of growth stocks every week.

Recession-resistant (or defensive) stocks are issues of large, financially solid companies that have maintained a dominant place in their industry for many years and consistently perform well, no matter what the phase of the economic cycle. These stable stocks, usually in the food, health-care, or pharmaceutical industries, have long histories of earnings growth and dividend payouts, although their dividends are usually not as high as those of income stocks. They're listed as "Conservative Stocks" in *Value Line*. PepsiCo, Campbell Soup, Hershey Foods, and Colgate-Palmolive are examples of recession-resistant stocks.

Blue-chip stocks are the best-known stocks. These are high-quality stocks with a long history of sustained earnings and dividends, and therefore they are considered low risk. The phrase comes from poker, in which the blue chip is the most expensive and valuable token in the game. General Electric, Exxon, and IBM are all blue-chip stocks. (*Note*: a blue-chip stock can also be a recession-resistant stock, a growth stock, and an income stock.)

Speculative stocks carry a higher degree of risk than other stocks because they are issues of unknown or new companies. (Sometimes established companies that have fallen on hard times but are poised for a turnaround are also tossed into this category.) Speculative stocks may achieve more-rapid growth than larger companies, but they also tend to react sharply to changes in the economy and lag behind a bull market as investors flock to more-popular issues.

Cyclical stocks are issues of companies in industries that are affected by both the business cycle and consumer demand, such as housing, autos, steel, and paper. When the overall economy is booming and demand for goods and services is up, these stocks tend to quickly rise in price. During recessionary cycles these stocks usually perform poorly. In order to invest wisely in this area, study economic forecasts and market movers such as UNEMPLOYMENT, CONSUMER PRICE INDEX, OIL PRICES, and CAPACITY UTILIZATION.

BONDS

Unlike a stock, a bond is an IOU. When you purchase a bond you are, in effect, lending your money to the issuing company, also known as the borrower. Bonds are issued by corporations, the U.S. government and its agencies, and states and municipalities. The principal reason for buying bonds is to receive a high, secure rate of return (called interest) on your loan.

The issuer of a bond is obligated to pay back the bond's full purchase price at a particular time, and not before. This is called the maturity date. In general, bonds fall into two maturity categories: intermediate notes, which mature in two to ten years, and long-term bonds, which come due in ten years or longer.

Until a bond matures, you receive a fixed rate of interest called the *coupon rate*. It is usually paid out twice a year. For example, a $1,000 bond that pays a fixed rate of 10%, will pay $50 interest every six months until maturity. This is only one way that you can make money on bonds. You can also sell your bond at market value before maturity through a stockbroker. You may receive less or more than you paid for it. The increase and decrease in purchase price depends upon supply and demand and upon the availability of new bonds. If, for example, after your purchase INTEREST RATES have gone up, then newer bonds will be paying higher rates, and the purchase price of your bond will fall since the new, higher-yielding bonds are more attractive to investors. The rule of thumb is: when interest rates fall, bond prices rise and vice versa.

A great many bonds can be "called"—that is, the issuer reserves the right to call in or redeem the bond before the official maturity date. Bonds are not usually called if current interest rates are the same or higher than the bond's coupon rate. But if interest rates have fallen below the bond's coupon rate, the issuer may call the bond because it can now borrow money at a lower rate. When a bond is called, the investor receives the principal back and loses that steady stream of interest. Investors can protect themselves by purchasing bonds with "call protection," which guarantees that the bonds will not be called for a specific number of years.

Corporate bonds are issued by such companies as General Motors, IBM, Exxon, DuPont, and others, as well as by many electric utility companies. Corporate bonds are not guaranteed. Your only protection is the financial strength of the corporation, and generally the greater the corporation's financial strength, the lower the coupon rate. That's why corporate junk bonds, which are high risk, have the highest yields.

In order to determine a bond's safety, consult one of the independent professional rating services—Standard & Poor's or Moody's. Their rating books are available at most libraries and brokerage firms. The highest rating is triple A. Medium-grade bonds fall into the triple-B category, while those rated C or lower are speculative and very risky. Inexperienced or conservative investors should stick with bonds rated A or higher.

Government bonds, or Treasuries, as they are commonly known, have much to recommend them. They are high in safety because the U.S. government guarantees them, they are extremely liquid and can be easily sold, and the interest earned is exempt from state and local (but not federal) taxes. Treasuries fall into one of three maturity categories: *Treasury bills* (T-bills) mature in one year or less and require a minimum investment of $10,000. *Treasury notes* mature in two to ten years and require $5,000 for those maturing in less than four years and $1,000 for those maturing in more than four years. *Treasury bonds* mature in ten years or more and cost $1,000 each. (For details call the U.S. Treasury help line at 202-287-4113.) Another type of government bond, *EE Savings Bonds*, is available in denominations starting as low as $50. Because savings bonds sell at a discount, a $50 bond actually costs only $25, a $100 bond, just $50. For details, check your local bank or call 800-US-BONDS.

Municipal bonds are issued by cities, counties, states, and special agencies to finance various projects such as new highways or bridges. In most cases the interest they pay is exempt from federal income tax and from state and local taxes in the state where the bond is issued. Municipal bonds range in maturity from one to thirty years. Some municipal bonds are insured; the insurer guarantees to pay both principal and interest to bondholders if the issuer defaults. Because the interest earned is all or partially tax exempt, municipals pay lower interest rates than most taxable bonds. Therefore they are not appropriate for people in low-income tax brackets and make no sense in IRAs or other tax-deferred retirement accounts.

MUTUAL FUNDS

A mutual fund is an investment company that pools money from thousands of individuals to buy shares in various investment vehicles and securities. The money is professionally invested by a fund manager, who continually studies the market, interest rate fluctuations, and the overall economic climate. He or she buys and sells investments that meet the mutual fund's stated objectives. Some mutual funds buy stocks, while others focus on bonds; many buy a mixture. Some funds specialize in certain industries, such as real estate, medical technology, health, or public utilities. A fund's investment philosophy may be conservative, speculative, or somewhere in between.

The advantage to this pooled investment approach is that it lets you buy fractional shares of many more stocks or bonds than you could own on your own, dramatically reducing your risk level. For example, if several shares in the fund drop sharply in price, the total impact on the fund, which owns many different issues, is minimal.

As a fund shareholder you may make money in one of four ways: from dividend income, from interest income, from profits from the sale of the fund's securities (also known as capital gains), and if the value of the securities held by the fund rises, from an increase in the value of your mutual fund shares. Depending upon the fund and your wishes, you may have your profits reinvested in additional fund shares or paid out to you on a regular basis. If you cash in your shares, you receive back the fund's net assets divided by the total number of outstanding shares.

You should understand two key terms when investing in mutual funds: *yield* is the amount of dividend and interest income paid to shareholders per share; *total return* measures the per-share change in the fund's total value during a given time period, say, one month, six months, or one year. It includes interest income, dividends, and capital gains or losses.

Some funds are sold directly to investors, in which case they have no sales fees (referred to as "no-load") or very low fees ("low-load"). These funds send investors the necessary purchase forms by mail; investors simply call the funds' 800 number. Other funds are sold through stockbrokers and financial planners and are accompanied by a sales fee, or load.

Money market mutual funds invest in a assortment of short-term, relatively safe money market instruments, such as Treasury bills, high-quality commercial paper (short term obligations issued by banks and corporations), banker's acceptances, (similar to a letter of credit) and jumbo ($100,000+) certificates of deposit. Their interest rates change daily depending upon the mixture in the fund's portfolio and overall market conditions. Dividends are paid monthly to shareholders, or they can be reinvested in additional shares. The price per share in a money fund, unlike other types of mutual funds, is held even at one dollar; this means that when you cash in, you will receive back a dollar per share. Most money funds also have check-writing privileges. Money market mutual funds can be purchased directly from the fund itself or from stockbrokers. The safest of the money funds are those that invest only in U.S. Treasuries. There are also tax-exempt funds for those in high tax brackets.

Banks offer a similar investment called *money market bank deposit accounts*. These pay lower rates than mutual funds but have the slight advantage of being federally insured.

CHAPTER 54

Watching the Market Movers

■ ■ ■

By now you know that you can use market movers to anticipate the performance of individual investments. And collectively they can be used to "predict" the next phase of the business cycle. Likewise, the rise and fall of interest rates and inflation can be anticipated through market movers. Preparing for a recession or recovery, inflation, and rising or falling interest rates *before* they occur is invaluable to anyone with a bank account, credit cards, a mortgage, or investments. The following overview helps you put your understanding of market movers into action.

RECESSION AND RECOVERY

You know you're in a recession when the gross domestic product declines for two consecutive quarters. But if you don't have some advance knowledge that the recession is coming, you're likely to get caught with investments that aren't right for the changes about to occur. Likewise, correctly anticipating a recovery will help you keep your investments in the right place.

How to Forecast a Recession

Some or all of these events may precede a recession:

- The industrial production index begins to drop and the GDP hits its peak—5%.
- Inflation is high (the consumer product index is above 5%) and the consumer confidence index is below 80.
- Capacity utilization rises above 85%.
- Durable goods orders even off or begin to decline.
- Unemployment goes above 6%.
- Auto sales drop two months in a row.
- Housing starts begin to fall, which usually happens about six months before the rest of the economy begins to slide.
- The leading economic indicators flatten out and start to turn down. (A recession is likely to arrive in three to six months.)
- The S&P 500 (and other market indexes) will start to fall three to six months ahead of a recession.
- Oil prices approach thirty dollars a barrel and hover in the high twenties.

CAUSE FOR CONCERN

Any of the following developments indicate a recession may be at hand:

- The GDP comes in weaker than anticipated.
- There is a growing number of business failures.
- Personal income is down.
- Retail sales drop.

- An inverted yield curve exists.
- Money supply growth is lower than the Fed's annual target.
- Consumer credit is dropping.
- Henry Kaufman or other people market movers predict a recession, although they may not actually say the *r* word.

You've "predicted" a recession. You know how it can affect your life. Business will face a difficult time; unemployment will rise, and you might worry about whether or not your job will be affected. More specifically, you'll need to review your financial portfolio.

AT THE PEAK—INVESTMENTS TO PREPARE FOR A RECESSION

These moves will help protect against recession losses:

- Sell *cyclical stocks*—paper, chemicals, auto, steel producers, and machinery—as these will suffer in a recession.
- Move into *recession-resistant stocks*—food, beverage, drug, and health-care companies and utilities.
- Hold on to *blue-chip stocks* that are long-term investments.
- Lock in current high yields on *Treasuries, A-rated corporate bonds, long-term CDs*, and *preferred stocks*.
- If high oil prices exist, *stocks in oil and oil-service companies* are good investments.
- If interest rates are low, *multimarket mutual funds* are good investments.
- Buy stocks of *companies with little or no debt*.

How to Forecast a Recovery/Expansion

Some or all of these events may precede a recovery:

- Industrial production rises three months in a row.
- The GDP climbs above 2%.
- Durable goods orders begin to increase.
- Capacity utilization hits the low 70% region.
- Unit labor cost begins to rise slowly.
- Short-term interest rates fall 1% to 2%.
- Auto sales rise.
- Standard & Poor's 500 or other financial market indexes rise, which generally occurs three to six months ahead of a recovery.

CAUSE FOR OPTIMISM

Any of the following developments indicate a recovery may be near:

- There's a high number of business starts.
- Personal income is up.
- Retail sales and auto sales rise.
- The inverted yield curve is flattening out.
- The consumer confidence index rises.
- Consumer credit rises.
- Inflation is low (the CPI is down).
- Henry Kaufman or other people market movers predict it.

AT THE TROUGH—INVESTMENTS
FOR A RECOVERY

These moves will help you take advantage of a recovery:

- Buy blue-chip growth stocks, blue-chip growth mutual funds, or cyclical stocks.

- Park cash in a money market fund to purchase fixed-term securities as rates climb.
- Secure needed loans before a recovery.
- Buy real estate or refinance existing mortgages before a recovery.
- Switch into short-term CDs and Treasuries so you can get higher yields as rates rise.
- Seek stocks in companies with the lowest unit labor costs (which rise in expansion) or those most able to raise prices (inflation also rises).
- Buy collectibles before prices rise.

INTEREST RATES AND INFLATION

Remember that inflation and high interest rates curb our spending power. Low rates encourage the use of credit and the purchase of big items like homes and automobiles. A low-rate environment is also a boon for the stock market, as investors move money from low-yielding bank and money market funds into stocks, where returns are greater.

How to Forecast High Inflation

Some or all of these conditions may precede high inflation:

- The value of the dollar is low.
- The producer price index rises, followed by a rise in the CPI; or the PPI moves up to 8%.
- Capacity utilization rises above 85%.
- Industrial production increases by 10% in five to seven months.
- Auto sales surge and go through the 8 million mark.
- Housing starts look like they will reach 2 million.
- Henry Kaufman or other people market movers predict it.

- Money supply growth is higher than the Fed's annual target.
- Oil prices rise.
- Unemployment is low.
- Interest rates are low.

ANTICIPATING HIGH INFLATION?

If high inflation looms ahead; keep the following in mind:

- Real estate is a traditional inflation fighter.
- Oil stocks are also considered a hedge against inflation.
- Big-ticket items should be purchased when inflation is low.
- Consider the impact of inflation on the dividends of preferred stocks.
- Inflation dampens consumer spending and hurts the auto industry and cyclical stocks.

How to Forecast Higher Interest Rates

Some or all of these conditions may precede a rise in interest rates:

- Inflation is growing.
- The producer price index moves up by several percentage points.
- There's a surge in the consumer price index.
- The yield curve is normal and then starts to flatten out.
- The Fed raises the discount rate.
- Money supply growth is higher than the Fed's annual target, and the Fed is tightening the money supply.
- The Fed actively intervenes to stop the fall of the U.S. dollar.
- War creates a fear of high prices—*i.e.*, a disruption to oil or other global staples.

ANTICIPATING HIGHER RATES?

If higher interest rates appear to be in the offing, keep the following in mind:

- Higher interest rates means your existing lower-rate bonds will fall in purchase price.
- The stock market doesn't perform as well in a high-rate environment. It's particularly damaging to cyclical and speculative stocks. Buy preferred stocks when rates are high.
- Take out loans before rates rise.

How to Forecast Lower Interest Rates

Some or all of these conditions may precede a drop in interest rates:

- A flat or lower GDP growth rate exists.
- Unemployment goes above 6%.
- There's a sharp, prolonged decline in personal income.
- Retail sales are not growing on an annual basis.
- The yield curve has been inverted and starts to flatten out.
- The Fed actively intervenes to halt the rise in the value of the dollar.
- The Fed lowers the discount rate.
- Money supply growth falls short of annual target, and the Fed is loosening the money supply. (*Note*: This is not as easy for the Fed to do successfully as to tighten it.)
- The ISI Group's forecasts predict lower rates.
- Inflation is high and looks like it's about to turn.
- Auto sales are rising.

ANTICIPATING LOWER RATES?

If lower interest rates appear on the horizon, keep the following in mind:

- Falling rates mean your older bonds will not only pay higher rates than new ones but appreciate in purchase price, making them good investments as long as they aren't called.

- Lower rates are a boon to the stock market: companies' profits rise, and stock prices should rise overall. Utilities do particularly well in a low-rate environment, as do the housing market and cyclical stocks. Look in current high rates on preferred stocks.

- Lower rates are good for the housing market, making it easier to buy and sell.

- Put off taking out loans until rates have fallen.

GLOBAL INVESTMENT TIPS

The following market movers are key to global investments and to some U.S. investments, particularly multinationals. Don't forget to keep an eye on them.

Unit Labor Cost. Look for nations with the lowest unit labor costs. These will attract new business and can be your guide to purchasing single-country mutual funds or single-country closed-end stock funds.

Single-Country Closed- end Stock Funds	*Stock Symbol*
Asia Pacific	APB
Austria	OST
Chile	CH
First Australia	IAF
First Iberian	IBF
First Philippine	FPF
Germany	GER
India Growth	IGF
Italy	ITA
Korea	KF

Malaysia	MF
Mexico	MXF
ROC Taiwan	ROC
Scudder New Asia	SAF
Singapore Fund	SNG
Spain	SNF
Swiss Helvetia	SWZ
Taiwan	TWN
Templeton Emerging Markets	EMF
Thai	TTF
Turkish Investment Fund	TKF

Oil prices. When world oil prices are eighteen to twenty-two dollars, Europe, Japan, and the United States can prosper. When prices approach thirty dollars and look like they will stay in the high twenties there's a good chance there will be recessions in most parts of the world. Divest yourself of stocks, except blue chips and oil or oil-service companies.

Interest rates. When U.S. interest rates are lower than foreign rates, invest in multimarket mutual funds or government bonds of foreign countries with stable governments.

Mutual Funds That Invest in Foreign Bonds

Fidelity Global Bond	800-544-8888
GT Global Government Income	800-824-1580
PaineWebber Master Global	800-457-0849
Scudder International Bond	800-225-2470
T. Rowe Price International Bond	800-638-5660
Templeton Income	800-237-0738

North American Free Trade Agreement. Follow developments on NAFTA in order to gauge your purchase and investments in Mexican and Canadian stocks. (Also follow the president of the United States, who is key to negotiating the agreement.)

European Community. Follow developments on the EC in order to purchase U.S. multinational stocks and well-run foreign stocks that sell on U.S. stock exchanges.

These leading foreign stocks trade as American Depository Receipts on U.S. stock exchanges (an ADR is owned by an U.S. bank and represents shares of a foreign stock held at a foreign bank):

Barclays plc
British Airways
British Gas
British Petroleum
Glaxo Holding plc
Honda Motor
Imperial Chemical Industries

National Westminster
New Corporation Ltd.
Novo-Nordisk
Saatchi/Saatchi
Shell Transport
Unilever

Global markets. Read about and be aware of the effects of global dancing on foreign and American stock markets.

Value of the dollar. Investments here and abroad are impacted by the value of the U.S. dollar. Invest in U.S. multinational stocks (companies with substantial earnings and profits derived from foreign business) when the dollar is low. When the dollar is strong, purchase individual foreign stocks. Other market movers that help track and forecast the value of the dollar are the Group of Seven, the chairman of the Federal Reserve, the president of the United States, the balance of trade, the Federal Reserve, interest rates, European Community, North American Free Trade Agreement, and war.

U.S. Multinational Stocks
Abbott Laboratories
American Home Products
Bristol-Myers Squibb
Caterpillar Tractor
Coca-Cola

Colgate-Palmolive
Crown Cork & Seal
Dow Chemical
DuPont
Exxon

Gillette

Heinz (H. J.)

IBM

Ingersoll-Rand

Johnson & Johnson

McDonald's

Merck

MMM

Pfizer

Polaroid Corp.

Procter & Gamble

Ralston Purina

Wrigley (Wm.)

CLOSER TO HOME—THE VALUE OF REAL ESTATE

Real estate, in the form of a house, co-op apartment, or condominium, is typically one of the largest investments most of us make. Not only does our home provide shelter, but it's a traditional way to beat inflation because real estate tends to appreciate faster than the cost of living rises. During the 1991 recession, however, this was not the case. Real estate values dropped in many parts of the country or simply held still.

A key market mover to watch to determine future real-estate values is housing starts, since housing starts and existing home sales tend to move together. Both, of course, are extremely sensitive to interest rates, since builders as well as buyers borrow money in order to complete their real estate transactions.

Follow the various interest-rate market movers, such as the Fed funds rate, the discount rate, and the prime rate; mortgages are directly affected by these rates. You should also keep up to date on what's happening with the Japanese stock market. The Japanese have purchased a great deal of real estate in the United States and often at high prices. A collapse of the Japanese market could force them to liquidate, in which case, real estate prices throughout this country could conceivably drop—and seriously so.

DID YOU KNOW THAT?

You too are an important market mover. Personal income, the government's tally of all our incomes, is also a critical economic indicator. When PI is down, the consumer spending indicators tend to fall.

The government and the Fed consider personal income, coupled with consumer installment credit, an important source of data on consumer spending, because it is your ability and desire to spend money and purchase goods and services that fuel the economy. Since over two-thirds of the GDP is made up of consumer spending, when personal income falls, the GDP will fall. Gross domestic product, the broadest statistical indicator of the business cycle, is used by the government to determine fiscal policy, federal spending, and taxes. It's used by the Federal Reserve to formulate monetary policies—chiefly money supply and interest rates. And the GDP affects our perception of the economy, and consumer confidence. Ultimately, the GDP moves the stock and bond markets.

In a very real sense we are all market movers. If you invest in the stock or bond market, purchase goods with a credit card, buy or sell a house, take out a loan, buy a car, get a raise . . . you move the market. Now that you've finished reading *Market Movers*, you have the tools to assess all those other market movers and transform your knowledge into action.

Index

■ ■ ■